Maryat Lee
The Appalachian Plays

Compiled and Edited by
David T. Miller

Introduction by
Dr. William W. French

Bacchante Books

Front Cover: Maryat in the mid-1970's, in the barn of her farm in rural West Virginia. Photo by Fran Belin. Courtesy West Virginia and Regional History Center. Back cover: Center color photo courtesy West Virginia and Regional History Center. Right color photo courtesy Chris McClary. Black and white photo by Martha Asbury for EcoTheater.

ISBN 978-0-578-81767-5
Except as noted, all material and compilation copyright
David T. Miller 2021. Original plays copyright Maryat Lee. Newspaper reprints and additional material used for educational purposes only and are copyright to their respective rights holders.
Bacchante Books, Lexington, KY

First printing March 2021 – Rev 08102021

No part of this book may be reproduced in any form or by any electronic or mechanical means, including information storage and retrieval systems, without permission in writing from the publisher. The only exception is by a reviewer, who may quote short excerpts in a published review. All rights reserved.

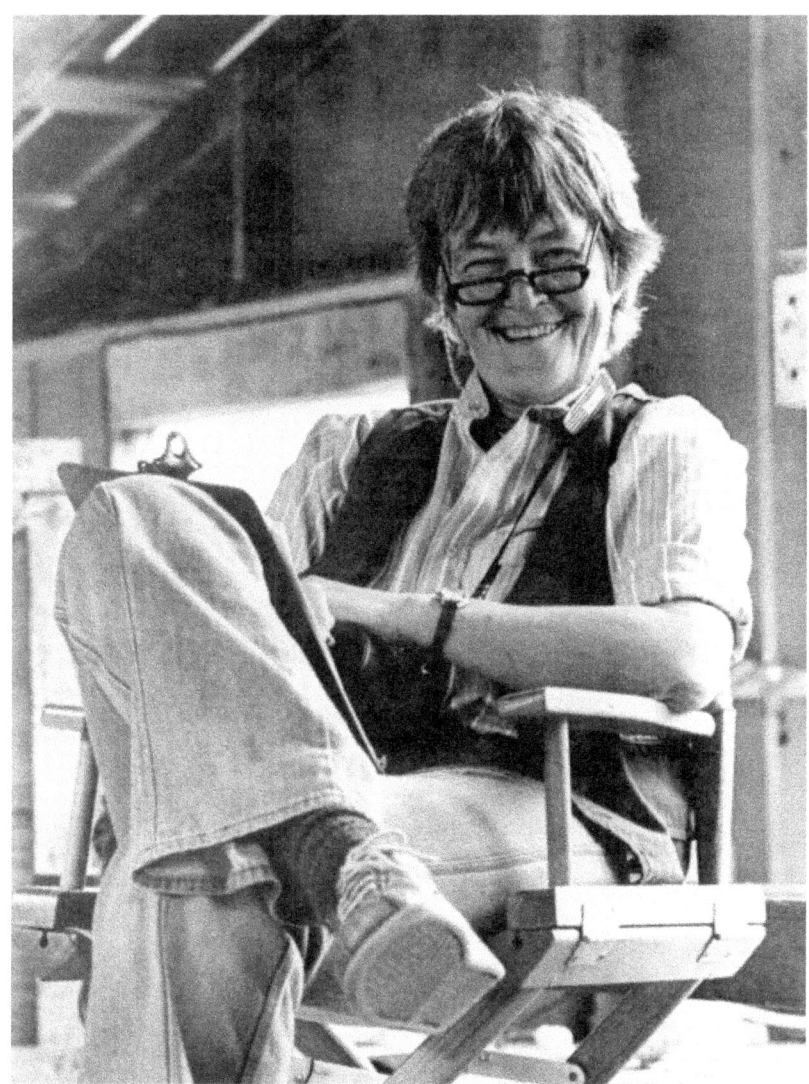

Photograph of Maryat Lee by Darlene Cappitelli in *Appalachian Journal: A Regional Studies Review* (Summer 1984), copyright *Appalachian Journal* and Appalachian State University. Used with permission.

Table of Contents

Dedication vii
Foreword viii
Preface xii
Introduction to *The Appalachian Plays* 1
FOUR MEN AND A MONSTER 42
Author's Note on *Four Men and a Monster* 80
JOHN HENRY 84
Introduction 84
Author's Note on *John Henry* 159
OLE MIZ DACEY 166
Author's Note on *Ole Miz Dacey* 192
A DOUBLE-THREADED LIFE (The Hinton Play) 197
Introduction 197
Scenes from *A Double-Threaded Life* 202
Audience Response and Discussions 248
Acknowledgments 260
A Note on the Sources 262
About the Authors 264
Appendix 266
   Toward a definition of EcoTheater 266
   EcoTheater Standards and Patterns 270
   Notes for an EcoTheater Mission Statement 274
   Unifying Principles of a New Theater 275
   Starting a Seed Company 278
Copyright Notes 280

Dedication
Mary Dean Lee

To Maryat

Outrageous, abundant woman,
spirit of fire, spirit of thunder.
You sang fugues to me as a child,

rocked me to sleep with your stories,
made grand entrances and exits
in a black Russian coat,

befriended the egg lady, painted
a black Christ crucifixion for her country church.
Your presents at Christmas were books

or piano music, giftwrapped in old newspaper.
We played for each other on the Steinway
among ballroom ghosts from another era,

sinking and soaring to find that sweet sound.
After your visits, lone beer cans in brown paper bags
lingered deep in the fridge.

With you, I knew I could do anything.
I read your plays about people trying to escape
what they'd built around themselves

and watched you rage at injustice,
transforming the stories of Harlem's down and out
into powerful street theatre.

But then I visited you in New York,
saw your life, your loneliness,
your struggles to stay healthy.

You told me about your anger
at your mother, your father,
your brothers, how all had failed you,

and among your famous friends--writers,
singers and artists--I had second thoughts.
I retreated to the journal you gave me

while you, whooping like an Amazon,
left New York for West Virginia,
rebuilt a house with your own hands,

started a writing retreat for women,
brought grass-roots theatre into the hollers.
Porch-swing gossiper, fence-post digger,

the summer rain fell softly on your tin roof.
I did not become what you dreamed I would.
I became a professor and a mother

and married a writer. I did not master the piano,
I learned instead how to love.
Now I am grown, I can see

everything is no longer possible.
I see the betrayals you spoke of
and I see yours, too.

We spoke before you died
after keeping our distance for years,
and smiled on each other's good fortune,

saving talk of disappointment for a night that never
came. Ungentle woman, good neighbor, citizen.
Spirit of earth and hard rain.

Reprinted with permission of The Write Launch, *September 2020*

Foreword
Rev. Dr. Georgia Newman-Powell

In this insightful work, writer/editor David T. Miller celebrates the achievements and influence of playwright/director Maryat Lee at the climax of her professional career. Editing, updating, and amplifying the earlier work of Professor William (Bill) French,[1] Miller makes clear why the legacy of Maryat Lee will prove significant to readers of widely differing interests, ranging from Lee's literary association and friendship with writer Flannery O'Connor; to Lee's expression of a religious sensibility in her dramatic art--a sensibility already evidenced in her undergraduate studies in biblical literature and her master's thesis on the religious origins of drama; and certainly to Lee's creative genius as playwright/director and innovator.

To O'Connor scholars, Lee is widely known through letters, extraordinary in number, content, and style, which followed soon after Lee's introduction to O'Connor in Milledgeville, Georgia, at Christmas 1956, and continued until the time of O'Connor's death in 1964. Not until *The Habit of Being: Letters of Flannery O'Connor*[2] was published in 1979, however, did most O'Connor scholars know of Maryat Lee. I had the privilege of glimpsing the selected, but as yet unredacted, O'Connor letters to Lee prior to the publication of *Habit*. These letters, with planned edits revealed only by thin pencil lines through typed text, allowed me a more complete picture. In them I began to sense a rare candor between two friends willing to disregard conventional rules of written discourse to converse sometimes seriously, sometimes playfully on a wide range of topics. Not until nearly two decades later, however, did I become aware of the full scope of this voluminous communication--more than 250 letters between the two writers. Thanks to the extraordinary generosity of Maryat Lee's brother Robert ("Buzz") Lee, I was given access to the entire body of this correspondence (including photocopies of O'Connor's letters to Lee

---

[1] *Maryat Lee's EcoTheater--A Theater for the Twenty-first Century* (1998, West. Va. Univ.; 2d ed. 2020, Bacchante Books)

[2] New York: Farrar, Straus, Giroux, 1979.

and carbon copies of Lee's to O'Connor) and to the entire collection of Lee's private journals before they were gifted by the Lee estate to West Virginia University. Through these original sources, I soon came to see Lee and O'Connor as "contrary kin." Although Lee's life in West Virginia and work on her Appalachian plays came a full decade after O'Connor's death, I believe the insights this book offers will further scholars' understanding of the O'Connor-Lee friendship.

Prominent mention of Lee in contemporary O'Connor scholarship focuses especially on the topic of race, as O'Connor-Lee letters of the early 1960's make especially apparent. Born in the south but rejecting much of conventionally southern culture (including her birth name Mary Attaway Lee), Maryat Lee has often been cited as a powerful touchstone to O'Connor on matters of race, Lee even finding her way into numerous O'Connor characters, sometimes humorously parodied as "the liberal." Nonetheless, in this compilation of Lee's Appalachian plays, Miller invites readers to discover why the label "social activist" belies the intent of this playwright who rejected a specifically social and/or political emphasis in her plays even as she willingly and often of necessity cast an actor differing in age, race, or gender from that of the character.

Readers of this work by Miller may be startled to discover that the friend who challenged O'Connor in any number of ways (and whom I once regarded more narrowly as a religious apostate) shared with O'Connor a spiritual fervor not so readily recognized in their epistolary conversations. While O'Connor insisted that her fiction was always about the "old Adam [who] just talks Southern because I do,"[3] readers of Lee's plays can see how Lee's dramatic art attempts to evoke the authentic, human everyman/everywoman from indigenous actors who may speak in "old Adam" tongues and even present themselves and the characters they uncover in "old Adam" contexts, but who, in Lee's carefully guided process, discover a terrible beauty in themselves, indeed a glimpse of the

---

[3] Quoted in Gerard E. Sherry, "An Interview with Flannery O'Connor," The Critic XXI (June\July 1963) at 29.

divine. Perhaps that is why, at every point in her career as playwright/director, Lee insisted that truly "legitimate" theater was not about pretending nor imitating but rather about revealing. We see that process, purpose, and result in Lee's work of the early 1950's with heroin-addicted youth in East Harlem, where Lee staged her daring street theater productions; we see it in her work with other of New York's marginalized youth in the transformative experience of Soul and Latin Theater (SALT); and in this book we see it in her bringing to life what she called EcoTheater, with Appalachian folk, black and white, young and old, in rural West Virginia.

My interest in theater (a college minor in speech and drama and later a professional partnership in Poetic Theater under the stage name "The Double Entendre") has given me more than scant interest in Lee as an innovative playwright/director. However, I was never able to meet Maryat Lee personally. Nevertheless, in meeting Lee's former partner and numerous close friends during the time of my research on the O'Connor-Lee correspondence, I began to recognize how rich and fertile were Lee's contributions to indigenous theater and how very much contemporary scholars, playwrights, and directors alike could benefit by reading and studying her contributions to a new, yet in many ways ancient, form of theater.

Numerous drafts of Lee's plays--more accurately, numerous versions of a single play performed at different times, often within the same short time span--enable readers to understand Lee's method as intentionally fluid, her process that of true playwright--i.e., builder of plays. In this compilation of Lee's Appalachian plays, David T. Miller makes clear that Lee's plays, even as presented here, are not fixed texts. Although the plays themselves were composed mid-twentieth century, Lee's process of building, forming, evoking is equally suited to a theater for the twenty-first century.

Lee's early trademark of the term EcoTheater expired in 1998, and the umbrella term "eco theater" has subsequently become identified largely with plays that emphasize ecological preservation, particularly in a time of dramatic climate change. Miller has thus aptly chosen to identify the plays in this compilation simply as Lee's Appalachian plays. Yet persons interested in exploring different forms of indigenous theater should certainly explore the what and the why of the term EcoTheater (eco from the Greek for "home") under which Lee developed and directed her plays in rural West Virginia. Indeed, these plays adhere to the philosophy and fundamentals from which Lee never wavered even in her earliest urban-centered plays and for which she also trained other students of theater to evoke the truly indigenous.

Editor/commentator Miller may be the only person still living who worked directly with Lee in theater, even if only for a summer, and who also knew Lee as friend over several years. As such, he is not only well-positioned to understand the need for this collection, but to have the heart to create it. From the time of Lee's first published work to the present, some seventy years after she pioneered street theater in New York City and nearly fifty years after the birth of EcoTheater, Maryat Lee has still not received the professional recognition she deserves. To discover Lee--or perhaps to rediscover her through the lens of her friend, colleague, and now editor David Miller--I invite you to join me in a new look into Lee's dramatic art. I can guarantee that whatever your particular interest in Maryat Lee, you will make a discovery that will not disappoint.

Preface
David T. Miller

I first met Maryat Lee in the summer of 1981. A few years earlier, I had graduated from college in my home state of West Virginia and, with some hope, had been roaming around the country, looking for my future. However, after working a variety of dead-end gigs for too long, I returned home broke, disillusioned and aimless at the dawn of the Reagan era. I needed a job!

A friend told me about a newspaper ad I had not seen, about a paid internship at a small theater that I had never heard of. The ad mentioned need of a music director who could help with a group of teenagers employed under the Governor's Summer Youth Program. I wasn't a formally trained musician but did come from a musical family and could play guitar and knew how harmony worked from my father's gospel group. I had also been a counselor for several summers at a nearby youth camp, so thought I could handle it. But a theater on Powley's Creek, way out in the country? I hesitated. Yes, I had acted in school plays and liked my college literature professor, Bill French, but I had little regard for or interest in *theater*, which seemed stuffy and artificial. Still, whatever that unusual role required, the position advertised seemed better than whatever other menial jobs I might find in that area.

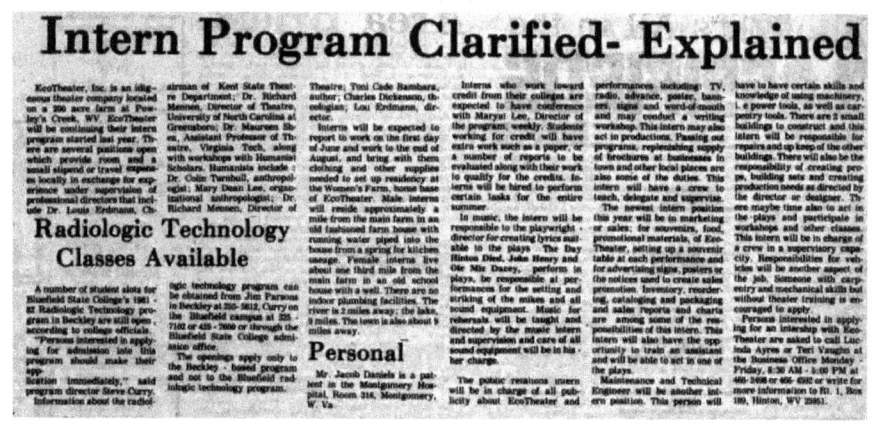
The ad, courtesy *Hinton Daily News*, May 19, 1981.

I called the number in the ad and spoke briefly with Maryat Lee, EcoTheater Director, who said that she had employed a diverse bunch of teens under a summer jobs program and that she was working with them on an outdoor play about local legend John Henry, the "steel-drivin' man." In addition to a music director she needed someone to keep the teens in line.

So it was that I picked up my guitar, reviewed in my mind the traditional, gospel, and pop tunes I knew, and, guitar case in tow, drove my battered Corolla through winding side roads to meet Maryat Lee. The route to Lee's Farm--which I learned later was called The Women's Farm--wound along the Greenbrier River and through an impossibly narrow tunnel leading up Powley's Creek, then up a steep hill to the farm. Navigating the tunnel that day, I had no idea that I would later be challenged to drive a wide flatbed truck bearing a rudimentary stage created by and for our EcoTheater troupe, sometimes with teenagers riding in back, through that same tunnel with mere inches to spare on either side. The residents of Powley's Creek on the upside of the road beyond the tunnel often cheered from their porches as we drove by, celebrating the sheer feat of our negotiating the tunnel.

Meeting Maryat was memorable. We talked, and together we sang a few songs, including "I'll Fly Away" and a few verses of "John Henry." I played guitar and sang the melody as Maryat harmonized with a very fine voice. (I would later hear her play piano, beautifully.) She told me the job was mine if I wanted it, but to think it over and call her back. She gave me a copy of her play *Four Men and a Monster* and wrote a nice inscription on it about our working together. (Oddly I thought, that copy was filled with Maryat's handwritten notes and marginalia, a working draft for yet another edit of her long-published play.) Of course I was going to take the job! I called her later that day.

It soon became clear to me that Maryat Lee was an odd duck for southern West Virginia, apparently (though not provocatively) a lesbian, an intellectual. I learned from local friends that, as is typical for rural, southern West Virginia, she was viewed with suspicion and disdain when she first moved to the area. But she and I hit it off immediately, as soon as I stopped trying to impress her with pretended knowledge of things I could not possibly know.

Since I was to be part of the EcoTheater production team, Maryat invited me to move into the old two-room schoolhouse she owned, just up the road from her farm. (Two other interns, Rita and Betsy, shared a somewhat better place on the farm proper.) I had cold-running water and an outhouse and could hear snakes in the ceiling and bobcats on the porch at night. I did not mind anything except the snakes.

Maryat lent me a small desk and swivel chair, casually mentioning that Daniel Keyes had written *The Minds of Billy Milligan*[4] while sitting in that chair. I soon learned that Lee was not just name-dropping,[5] she simply had an enormous circle of friends and acquaintances, from well-known stage and screen actors to baseball great Jackie Robinson, to teacher-friends Margaret Mead and Paul Tillich, among many others.

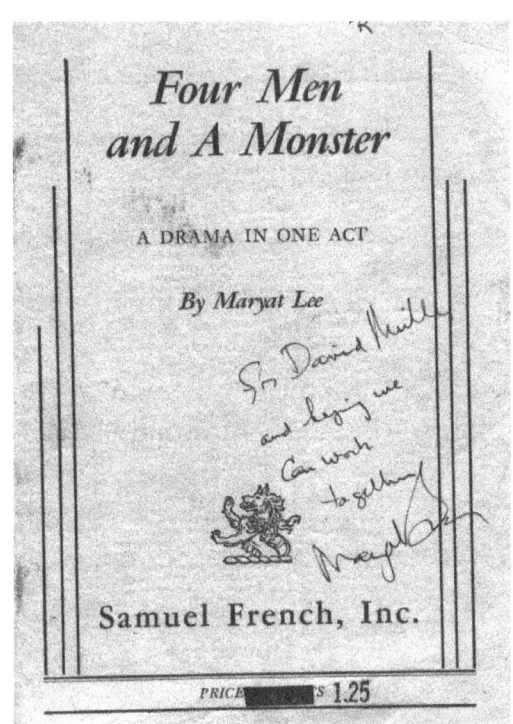

Maryat's intense three-hander (despite the title). *Collection of the author.*

On Monday of my first week working with EcoTheater, I met with Maryat and twenty teenagers, of mixed races, girls and boys, in whom I saw a lot of myself and the coal-miner's-kid friends I grew up with. A few had returned from the previous summer, but most had no idea what they were getting into or would be called on to act. But it had to be better than

---

[4] The book (by her friend Keyes) about the re-integration of a man's multiple personalities made a big impression on her. "The core personality seems capable of doing all the things that the dazzling 'almost real' personalities did, but with a genuineness and honesty and even awkwardness without which, as Billie began to perceive, there is only a hollow empty simulacrum of the real thing." Lee writing in "...To Will One Thing," Drama Review Vol. 27 No. 4 (Winter 1983).

[5] She could have dropped plenty and did so when it was strategically valuable, such as in grant applications. Guest artists in the first years of Maryat's time in West Virginia included actors Ossie Davis and Ruby Dee and Estelle Parsons in addition to actress/poet/Macarthur fellow Billie Jean Young. Anthropologist Colin Turnbull would come by a few years later, along with many university professors. The Today Show did a brief video feature on the theater.

picking up roadside trash.

In fact, they would not be acting, not right away anyway, for Maryat initially put them to work building and repairing sets and costumes and the like. Only gradually did Lee introduce her unlikely actors to daily improvisation exercises and rehearsals. Maryat also coaxed them into talking to their families about local folklore (and gossip) that she might turn into scenes. Maryat worked the kids hard that summer. We played dozens of shows anywhere the flatbed truck could find an audience, as well as in public squares, a federal prison, state parks, wherever someone would have us. I drove the truck, handled the music and sound, made sure the kids got to where they needed to be. Some of the teens took to the work right away; others took longer. I watched some of the teens find entirely new people inside themselves that summer. A few never did, just talked back and sulked and picked up their small stipend every other Friday. In my "help with the teens" role, I was called on to break up a few fistfights, none over skin color and only one between girls.

Local teenagers who would otherwise have been picking up roadside trash through a state summer jobs program instead found themselves at EcoTheater. For some it was life-transforming. *West Virginia and Regional History Center.*

My summer got even more interesting when Maryat gave me a major role in the other play she was producing that summer, without the teens, *Ole Miz Dacey*.

I had other, more personal assignments from Maryat too, as she gave me several books to read in my meager spare time. I learned less from them, however, than from my unique mini-seminar that summer: conversations with Maryat about theater, theology, men and women, and more. I learned much just observing her way of dealing with people-

-being her charming, irritating, stubborn, flexible, kind, charismatic, demanding *self*.

One book from those reading assignments proved exceptional, however: *The Habit of Being*--writer Flannery O'Connor's then-recently published volume of letters, which I read in the evenings. Many were to Maryat,[6] all warm and chatty, O'Connor in some teasing Lee about Lee's wild adventures in New York City (at the time I had never been there so this sounded impossibly exotic) where, as Dr. French describes in his Introduction, Lee created and staged a unique form of street theater in Harlem.[7]

During that summer of 1981 Maryat and I talked some about O'Connor. I was already familiar with a few of her stories and was aware that her protagonists could have been people I knew personally from West Virginia. After all, O'Connor's "Christ-haunted" Georgia is not that different from the Bible Belt Appalachia I grew up in. I learned that Flannery had lived near Lee's brother Robert in Milledgeville, GA; that she and Maryat had become acquainted in 1956; and that, in addition to several visits by Lee to O'Connor, the two had exchanged hundreds of letters over nearly a decade. It came as no surprise to me to discover that Lee, supportive of the civil rights movement and

Teens built and repaired sets and costumes before they started improvising and working on scenes. Photo by Fran Belin from *Appalachian Journal: A Regional Studies Review* (Summer 1984), copyright Appalachian Journal. Used with permission.

---

[6] After reading the letters from O'Connor I wondered what Maryat had written back to her. O'Connor biographer Jean W. Cash has had access to some--there were almost 300 between them--and they show even more clearly how close Maryat and Flannery were, see "Maryat and 'Flanneryat': An Antithetical Friendship," *The Flannery O'Connor Bulletin* Vol. 19 (1990), pp. 54-73. Georgia Ann Newman had access to even more letters, not to mention Maryat's journals and other writings. In addition to her Foreword, see "A 'contrary kinship': The correspondence of Flannery O'Connor and Maryat Lee, Early Years, 1957-1959" (Doctoral dissertation, University of South Florida 1999).

[7] O'Connor wrote to Lee that she was fascinated by Maryat's "little play" *Dope!*--"a real morality play if I ever saw one and altogether powerful in spite of it. I was able to fancy myself hanging from one of those fire-escapes and watching it with complete absorption." O'Connor letter to Lee, Jan. 31, 1957, quoted in *The Habit of Being* at 200-01. The play would go on to be one of the most produced one-act plays of the 1960's.

at the time living in a mixed neighborhood in Harlem, became a Northern liberal foil to O'Connor's Southern traditionalist, especially on matters of race, and that Lee was the model for at least one of O'Connor's short story characters. ("You can have half interest in Mary Grace," O'Connor wrote to Lee, referring to the story *Revelation* and its Wellesley College student visiting her Georgia family over the holidays.)

The Lee-O'Connor connection continues to interest me. But it's unfortunate that the genius of the Maryat Lee I came to know in indigenous Appalachian theater sixteen years after O'Connor's death has received such little attention, far less than has the Lee-O'Connor friendship itself. And while I'm glad that O'Connor scholars have explored their conversations, especially about writing in general and unavoidably about race and writers of color,[8] I think there is still a lot to be learned about what now might be called Lee's transgressive experience in New York City, exploring the until-then hidden world of junkies, urban gay life before Stonewall, and the daily struggles of the inner-city poor, as well as her work in West Virginia.

The reader of Lee's Appalachian plays collected here, plays developed in the 1970's and 80's after Lee's move to West Virginia, will discover that in EcoTheater Lee's praxis itself develops even more fully those conversations she broached with O'Connor a decade earlier. Maryat was bringing to Appalachia two principles she had worked out by living in Harlem. Both were, I think, a continuation of her good-natured but sincere sparring with O'Connor: first, living in New York reinforced Maryat's conviction that people can't be reduced to the shorthand of their skin color, gender or sexuality. People are not symbols. Every life is unique. Real lives beat fiction any day.

Maryat's second principle was more startling: When people are helped to honestly be themselves they again become universal, and Maryat believed that's what real theater,

---

[8] Carole Harris' "James Baldwin, Flannery O'Connor, and the Ethics of Anguish" is an interesting starting point, *https://hungermtn.org/james-baldwin-flannery-oconnor-and-the-ethics-of-anguish/*; as more of Flannery's letters are made public the debate over her racial views has intensified, see "How Racist Was Flannery O'Connor?," *https://www.newyorker.com/magazine/2020/06/22/how-racist-was-flannery-oconnor.*

her kind at least, a "rough" theater drawn from everyday lives, can do--paradoxically, help people take off the mask they wear every day. A case in point: In line with Lee's view that indigenous theater must involve ordinary people mostly out of the "hollers" (or in New York City, literally off the streets)[9] Lee gave the title role of John Henry to a skinny young Black woman, and she was completely believable. By working with Maryat she completely "got" John Henry's outside-ness, his importance to the hardscrabble community around the tunnel, his hope. His doom. She became a Presence. I've never heard an audience as quiet and moved as when the broken and dying "John Henry," defeated by the steam drill, was lifted onto the other players' shoulders and carried slowly offstage in silence. I saw this at every performance and was moved every time.

Consider too how the character of Miz Dacey, which started as a man playing a prank on Maryat by calling her in the voice of an old woman eventually became a flexible vessel for several actors' own stories, especially Lucinda Ayres,[10] thus expanding Maryat's comedy to contain hard-won, or at least hard-admitted, truths about what it was really like to be an older woman in Appalachia.[11]

The dense, remote hills where Lee set to work with teenagers in West Virginia were in many cases as racist and segregated as rural Georgia in O'Connor's time. For Lee to throw all these teens together into such an odd summer project, to have them ride together in the back of a flatbed truck, to have all their families make their way up the narrow side

---

[9] Maryat lived in a fifth-floor walk-up at 192 Sixth Avenue and to her "off the street" meant literally: "Maryat found the people [who would appear in *Dope!*] by standing on the street with a large sketch pad and drawing," attracting curious passers-by including kids; then she "picked a house--the third house, the third floor, the third door--and went up and knocked. Finally the inhabitants let her in, and they became friends. Later they acted in Maryat's play…" Mary Clare Powell, "Creativity and liberation: a study of women writers and artists" (Doctoral dissertation, Univ. of Mass at Amherst 1992), at 68.

[10] "[A] housewife--rather, a single parent of four kids--who has played the role of mother and father for 20 years suddenly unleashed on a stage to be who she really is: a dreamer, maker of webs and delights, a cross-patch of connivances and gullibilities, a steadfast rock, an old country woman, a haughty town's lady, jilted wife, flashing sensuality, and incredible richness at the core." Lee writing in "…To Will One Thing," supra.

[11] Consider, in one of the excerpts included from *A Double-Threaded Life* here ("Miz Dacey has a weak moment"), the expression of the "cravin'" a woman feels for physical connection after the loss of her husband, a concept rarely spoken aloud by Appalachian woman of that era.

road to Powley's Creek to drop them off and pick them up, was radical in its day.[12]

What Maryat recognized and enabled these non-actor performers to embody is a principle she worked out in her New York experience: that people's stories include their skin color and income level, and society may define them by those attributes, but their stories are always both their own and universal.[13] Through her unique way of creating her plays, Lee strives to enable each player to hear their own voices in what they're saying, edited and shaped but unmediated by either sympathy or condemnation.

> [H]er thesis on theater and religion speaks to the core of her own religious insights into a culture she knew well and rebelled against, yet whose people--especially the marginalized--she loved deeply.

As with her friend Flannery O'Connor, it is impossible to talk about Lee without considering the role of faith in their work. Associated with no church as such, Maryat was nevertheless deeply immersed in religion. Her undergraduate degree in Biblical history, her master's studies in comparative religion from Columbia University and Union Theological Seminary, her studies under prominent theologian Paul Tillich, her thesis on theater and religion, her sparring with O'Connor about religion, all speak to the core of her own religious insights into a culture she knew well and rebelled against, yet whose people--especially the marginalized--she loved deeply. *John Henry* can be seen as a Christian allegory with a foot in labor history; and the players in *A Double-Threaded Life* demonstrate that they know that their world is troubled, perhaps by bad husbands or sexism or--

---

[12] Poet/playwright and MacArthur award fellow Billie Jean Young remarked, after the first of her several visits to Maryat as a guest humanist, of seeing her first production of *John Henry* that it didn't occur to her until halfway through it that the cast was racially mixed. And this was probably before John Henry "himself" was played by a thin young black woman.

[13] Maryat's move to the country seemed to be an extension of the dare she accepted in writing *Dope!* and her need to prove that what she saw as transcendence within the ordinary life didn't require the rigors of city living. Both she and O'Connor were trying to get at bigger things than New York or Milledgeville or Hinton could contain. "[O]f course when you're a Southerner and in pursuit of reality, the reality you're going to come up with is going to have a Southern Accent, but that's just an accent; it's not the essence of what you're trying to do." FOC quoted in *Conversations with Flannery O'Connor* (University Press of Mississippi 1987) at 8.

especially true in Appalachia--by an economic system that will discard them when whatever skills they possess become dated. The damaged trio in *Four Men and a Monster*, for example, destitute Southern Appalachian hillbillies, find themselves at the end of their resources, adrift in a cheap big-city hotel. (Lee was born in northern Kentucky to a well-to-do family and considered herself a Southerner and was familiar with the post-war influx of rural men looking for work.) But because Lee's characters emerge from within the players themselves, after much work with Lee to break through their everyday selves, they steadfastly refuse to become symbols.

> [T]he hills that give birth to the darkly comic Hal, Tot, and Upjohn presented a deep, unfamiliar well of history from which Lee drew, a history every bit as complex as New York City's.

They also live in a world, as in much of O'Connor's fiction, where the full range of humanity is simply there, all mixed up together. In the brutality of John Henry's tunnel and the grotesquery of Maryat's "monster," there is also love, expressed in John Henry's tenderness toward an orphan boy, and in the community created by the hard life around the tunnel; and the bond between Hal and Tot in *Four Men* is nothing if not a kind of love story. Maryat Lee's Appalachian plays seem to reach precisely for what her friend Flannery O'Connor called the "ultimate concern," a "moral force" that reveals the hidden workings of God's grace through "what God gives you."[14]

As Dr. French explores, Lee's familiarity with medieval "mystery plays," in which common people--farmers, merchants, tradesmen, most of them illiterate--re-enacted Christian stories in public squares and haywagon pageants, was certainly a model for all her plays. All of Maryat's characters, and her players, are nobodies passing by in a grand pageant, none important except for that moment when they inhabit a role, in flesh no one else possesses, with a presence that refuses to be metaphor. In specifically Christian terms, Lee can be seen throughout her career thinking about those illiterate peasants who, in that

---

[14] Quoted in *The Habit of Being*, pp. 221, 275.

moment, are transfigured; they become--they *are*--Cain, Lazarus, Mary Magdalene.[15] On Lee's stage a skinny young Black woman *is* John Henry.

Paradoxically, for Maryat the moment her non-actor actors fully inhabit a character is when they finally become themselves. And through these plays--always being revised--Lee can be seen searching for a theater that "suggests the ultimate and the present in the same instant that we sometimes call Presence…[T]he word becomes flesh, the invisible is made visible, a door opens to another world, and the actor and audience find a communion based on truth, not a trick or lie. The theater takes on the meaning of a sacrament."[16] In her theater, matters of gender, age, race, and other outward identifiers are just costume and makeup, not who they actually will become in the great procession toward that communion. As Maryat put it, "[O]nce they believe they can be who they are in the safety of the stage, a wonderful thing begins to happen. These performers are not talking about, or acting out, or imitating the meaning of life. They are experiencing it in front of our eyes, and they are incandescent."[17]

I hope that in making this collection of Maryat's plays available we can imagine some of what Maryat might have continued to bring to contemporary religious and social discourse through the voices of her characters--insights into city and country, men and women, skin color, faith, and the possibility of transcendence immanent in every life.

I worked for Maryat for only one summer--the sixth and last she brought together a troupe of mostly teenagers. Her imprint on me was indelible, however, and we stayed friends and I would later serve on her theater's board of directors.

I hope this book will revive interest in Maryat Lee's visionary ideas about

---

[15] Lee's players in *A Double-Threaded Life* are all certainly familiar with those stories and the archetypes they contain, and some believe them down to the King James comma. Maryat traced her inspiration to a modernized version of a mystery play about Noah, where at age twelve she played the title role. "'I was Noah, but I was also myself…On stage, I could be emotional because Noah emotional. It was all right to be that part of myself." Quoted in French, "Drama for Appalachians," at 308.

[16] Lee writing in "…To Will One Thing," Drama Review, supra.

[17] Quoted in Powell at 119.

indigenous theater, which in her view was hardly theater at all--just people transcending their daily lives by being given the permission and tools needed to see "what God gave them"--to simply *be themselves*. I have often wondered what all those kids (and later, elders) who worked with Maryat Lee thought about their experience, how it may have helped change them into whomever they became. Perhaps this book will find its way to them and they will remember.

Introduction to *The Appalachian Plays*
Dr. William French

The plays in this volume constitute an extraordinary corpus. They represent an attempt to bring to life a primitive theater. As such they differ from most other forms of modern theater. These plays might be called "indigenous" drama for they are rooted in their creator's deliberate effort to make a genuinely populist theater. In several senses they might be called "Holy Theater," Peter Brook's phrase in *The Empty Space* for a theater where the Invisible is made visible, where the traditions of a people among who tradition still lives are made into ritual, and where the ceremony of theater is given new meaning.

> These plays might be called "indigenous" drama for they are rooted in their creator's deliberate effort to make a genuinely populist theater.

This is a rather large claim. But the claim only matches the audacity of a playwright who says simply to herself, "Let's put on a play. Let's put on a play without the usual trappings," and proceeds to do it, and has been doing it for thirty years now. The play texts that result from such a bold program are bound to be "different." They resemble what Brook calls the "rough theatre":

> Salt sweat, noise, smell: the theatre that's not in a theatre, the theatre on carts, on wagons, on trestles, audiences standing, drinking, sitting round tables, audiences joining in, answering back; theatre in back rooms, upstairs rooms, barns; the one-night stands, the torn sheet pinned up across the all, the battered screen to conceal the quick changes.[18]

Maryat Lee's EcoTheater is all these things. But it is more and would surprise and, I believe, please even Peter Brook. How did these plays come to be, and what do they suggest about theater today?

---

[18] Peter Brook, *The Empty Space* (New York: Penguin Books, 1972), p. 73.

Maryat Lee

Their author, Maryat Lee, moved in 1971 from New York City to Powley's Creek, near Hinton, deep in the most rural part of West Virginia's Alleghenies, close by the Greenbrier, New and Bluestone Rivers. She bought and tended a 300-acre upland farm. She revised her New York plays and gathered material for new ones, and worked to establish herself as a good neighbor in her remote farm community. In 1975 she organized EcoTheater as an indigenous Appalachian theater, continuing the work she had begun in the early 1950s, giving life to a theory of grassroots drama evolved through a lifetime spent in the theater.[19]

Born Mary Attaway Lee in 1923 in Covington, Kentucky, Maryat Lee grew up in a family devoted to music and the arts. Her mother sang professionally. Her father, a lawyer and amateur musician, delighted in quoting from memory long passages of Shakespeare and Marlowe. The family spent evenings together playing music and reading plays aloud. After an unhappy year at Northwestern University, Lee went to Wellesley College, graduating in 1945 in Biblical History.

She completed her formal education in 1955 with an MA degree in Comparative Religion at Columbia University and Union Theological Seminary. Her thesis explores the problems in forging creative links between drama and religion in the post-war world and articulates many of the themes that recur throughout her plays.

---

[19] See French, "Drama for Appalachians," *Appalachian Journal* (Summer 1984) at 306 for an extensive study, based on interviews with Lee and others, of her experiences in theater before moving to Summers county and how she adapted and extended those with the rural EcoTheater troupe.

> **Robinson Is Leader In Harlem Crusade Against Dope Racket**
>
> New York, April 20—(UP)—Baseball's Jackie Robinson will touch off a fight Monday to wipe out the use of drugs by teen-agers in East Harlem, described as the "most heavily doped" section of any city in the nation.
>
> The Brooklyn Dodgers' star second baseman will introduce a play entitled "Dope," which will be staged in vacant lots next week in the Harlem district.
>
> The play, written by Miss Maryat Lee, 24, Columbia University, and sponsored by the East Harlem Protestant Parish, shows a 14-year-old addict torn between his hunger for dope and a peddler's efforts to "use" the teen-ager's younger sister.
>
> "I am shocked and alarmed by the increasing number of teen-agers and younger kids caught by this vicious dope racket," Robinson said today.
>
> "They are egged on by dope peddlers who promise them a thrill. Soon they find themselves hopeless addicts and headed for criminal careers. The tragedy is they start taking dope to escape from their environment."

Courtesy Cincinnati Enquirer, April 21, 1951.

In the course of writing this thesis she risked walking into the "wild streets" of Harlem to research a way of conducting theater that would be more like the

> "After spending an evening with them, you know what they mean…[The audience] milled around the stage, jumped up on it, yelled at the actors, never stopped moving or talking."

drama of ancient Greece or medieval Europe, before religion and theater had split apart. *Dope!*, the play that evolved from this experience, created an overnight sensation, launched her onto a career in what would later be called alternative theater, and originated the practice of modern urban street theater. Reviewers described the play as "unprecedented," "hard-hitting," "shocking."[20] Significantly, *Dope!* was not produced inside a "legitimate" New York playhouse. Maryat Lee had not written it for that. She persuaded the East Harlem Protestant Parish to produce it using a vacant lot in Harlem.[21] The stage was a wooden platform, built to resemble the pageant wagons of the medieval English theater, with a single canvas backdrop. Playing to a raucous, milling street crowd of 2,000, *Dope!* was acted almost entirely by street people (in at least two cases

---

[20] *Variety*, 25 April 1951, p. 1.

[21] For an account of how the play came together, see Oliver, *Street Theater Epiphanies: Maryat Lee and the Making of Dope!*, Journal of American Drama and Theatre 10 (Spring 1998) at 26. The *New Yorker* also published a long piece mostly about a young man living out Harlem's drug problem but describing a performance of the play (complete with a barker calling up to the "Man on the stoop! Woman in the windows! Come on down! See the play!"), see Eugene Kinkead, "A Reporter at Large," *New Yorker*, November 10, 1951 at 44.

Maryat Lee

by actual heroin addicts) recruited through the parish. Directing the play herself, Lee hired one professional actor to play the lead, but she later decided that his presence was disruptive. The play was published in 1953 in *Best Short Plays of 1952-53*, and in 1957 by Samuel French (and a revised edition in 1965). Revived in the mid-1960s as a New York street play, *Dope!* became during the 1970's one of the most widely acted plays in the United States; more than fifty companies produced it in 1974 alone, and it was re-issued in 1979 in *A Century of Plays by American Women. Dope!* has thus performed one of the tasks Maryat Lee sets for her indigenous theater: to feed the roots of American theater.

Discouragement followed, however. She worked in a number of capacities in the New York theater, the experimental off-Broadway groups like the Open Theatre of Claude von Itallie, and wrote several plays for the "indoor" theaters. One play, *The Tightrope Walker*, was produced in 1963 at Centre College in Kentucky, which many in her family had attended, and again at the Judson Poets' Theatre in 1966.

Maryat's SALT theater. Simple sets and an up-close audience hearing stories from their own community. *West Virginia and Regional History Center.*

She witnessed the birth of several street theaters in the early 1960s, some of them producing *Dope!* In spite of some interesting successes, in her opinion the street groups were all annexes to the indoor theater. She tried to get other groups started, but street theater was not a live issue until the late 1960s.

In 1968 Lee moved decisively into indigenous outdoor theater, founding the Soul and Latin Theater (SALT) in East Harlem. *Day to Day* (Samuel French, 1970) and three

The Appalachian Plays

The Tightrope Walker, written and directed by Maryat Lee, starred Tom Coyle, Barbara Babbage, and Glenn Rogers.

From a 1963 production at Centre College in Danville, Kentucky. *Courtesy Centre College Special Collections and Archives*

unpublished plays: *After the Fashion Show, The Classroom,* and *Luba,* all written for SALT. Urban street theater in its purest form, SALT used a pageant--a haywagon--to carry its drama into the ghetto streets. Most of the actors were "indigenous," like those for *Dope!* While the audiences milled, hooted, and clambered up on the wooden platform stage, they were appreciative, and they came back for more.

By contrast, Lee found the audiences at the "legitimate" downtown theaters cool and unresponsive. Relations among the professionals--actors, directors, managers, writers--were also cool, businesslike, "edgy," Lee puts it.[22] In the streets a passionate commitment to the act of theater occurred, and the transactions among playwright and actors and audience bristled with vitality. As Dan Sullivan put it in the New York Times:

> The young people of East Harlem's Soul and Latin Theater (SALT) say that after their first summer performing in the streets, they are going to find indoor audiences "sort of pale." After spending an evening with them, you know what they mean...[The audience] milled around the stage, jumped up on it, yelled at the actors, never stopped moving or talking. Some of the people on the fire escapes even dropped water-filled balloons that crashed through the plastic roof of the stage. But none of it damped SALT...[T]hey could tell that the audience, except the balloon throwers, was not rejecting the show but reveling in it. Once you opened your ears and shed your downtown

---

[22] Unless otherwise indicated all quoted or ascribed material comes from interviews with Maryat Lee in August and September, 1981, and June and July, 1982; from letters to the author; or from her private papers.

prejudices about how a proper audience should behave, you knew they were right... But they pitched in joyously anyway, taking sides, shouting encouragement to the good guys, pitilessly booing the bad.. You felt yourself very much in the presence of the fabled ritual power of drama, its ability to speak not just to an audience but for it, and with it.[23]

Eulogy for Black Actor: He Lived Role Too Well

By FRED FERRETTI

Yesterday, Richard Mason's family and friends came to the Unity Funeral Home in Harlem to say good-bye to him.

The 24-year-old actor, whose first role five years ago was as a heroin addict in a Mobilization for Youth street theater play called "Dope," died last Thursday in his Upper West Side apartment from what the Medical Examiner's office called an acute reaction to heroin.

Five days before, Manuel Vasquez, 19, died from the same cause in Metropolitan Hospital. He, too, had played the addict hero in the Soul and Latin Theater production of "Dope."

Drugs, their use and abuse,

er of the Negro Ensemble Company, for whose "Open Theater" the actor once performed; Gil Noble, of WABC-TV's "Like It Is," for which Mr. Mason had been associate producer; the playwright, Lonne Elder 3d, who wrote "Ceremonies in Dark Old Men"; Carl Lee, son of Canada Lee; Denise Nicholas, the school teacher on television's "Room 222"; Arnold Johnson, who played "Putney Swope," and Billy Dee Williams and Douglas Turner Ward with other members of the Negro Ensemble Company.

At first they stood on the street outside of the whitewashed brick funeral home on Eight Avenue and 125th

Richard Mason, the most successful actor to emerge from the *Dope!* productions, died just five days after Manuel "Tony" Vasquez's overdose. Maryat wrote the litany for Mason's service. "[He] flowered out of a tight crack in the pavement, at the center of a storm....A gentle warlord, bemused curator of crime." *Courtesy New York Times, May 7, 1970.* Losing such young men may have helped Maryat make up her mind that she was done with city life.

In the streets it was possible to create theater as Lee thought it should be: the experience of self-discovery in a communal atmosphere, the finding of meaning in a moment of common consciousness. Her experience with *Dope!* and later with SALT and a stint of teaching street theater at the New School for Social Research pointed her toward a new resolution: to discover if the primitive street theater she had developed in New York City would translate into a rural idiom. The New York State Council of Arts awarded her a Creative Arts Program Stipend to begin the work. Equipped with professional as well as indigenous theater experience and a handful of street plays, and also wanting to find her Appalachian roots--long before it had become a popular pastime to trace one's roots--Maryat Lee came to rural Summers County.

In 1975 she established EcoTheater, a theater uncontaminated by what Lee felt were the corruptions of the professional New York stage, a theater in which she was free to write

---

[23] August 30, 1968.

and produce plays that touched the sacred in life without dogma and that spoke directly and unpretentiously to their audience.

Lee readily acknowledges that in our society she will not realize a totally indigenous theater. But she strives to come as close as possible; therefore she lived on her Powley's Creek farm for five years before opening EcoTheater, knowing that she needed time to let her neighbors get acquainted with her and to gain their trust.

The first two summer seasons, 1975 and 1976, the EcoTheater plays were performed in the most primitive possible conditions. To frame a playing area--in a field, a meadow, or a town park--a few unevenly-cut banners, sewn together from scraps of household fabric, were hung from poles. Sometimes a few flats were painted and roped together and braced from behind to form a scene. The small audiences--usually fifteen or twenty, fifty at most-- would stand or sit on the ground in a semi-circle. The actors performed on the ground. Costuming and props were minimal and for the most part consisted of jeans and other items of everyday country dress. A few costumes were designed and sewn. Neither artificial lighting nor amplified sound embellished the EcoTheater plays. This rudimentary theater

Maryat at work in her office on Powley's Creek, at the "Women's Farm." *West Virginia and Regional History Center.*

represented to Lee the essence of drama: *three planks, two actors, and a passion*, a saying from Lope de Vega she is fond of quoting.

Maryat Lee

As the idea caught on locally and support developed, EcoTheater grew. For the 1978 season, Lee acquired a farm wagon which could be converted for playing in about twenty minutes. Drawn by an aging van, the pageant could be drawn into almost any location for performance: a pasture, a town square, the parking lots and lawns of restaurants, parks, institutions. The wagon was outfitted with rudimentary lighting and sound systems and had canvas backdrops of two frames set into brackets. Costuming and props remained minimal and reflected the primitive condition of EcoTheater.

Between 1978 and 1981 EcoTheater drew support from several public and private sources. Through the Governor's Summer Youth Program, a federal work program for youth, Lee augmented the EcoTheater troupe each summer with fifteen or twenty local high school youths. Rather than cut weeds and pick up trash along the highway, these children of indigent families learned the basics of a wide range of theater skills--stage carpentry, painting, electrical work, and acting. Each youth contributed the skill he or she possessed and wanted to develop, both practical and artistic. For the 1982 season, the EcoTheater troupe was cut to a handful of actors. But the company now included a few senior citizens, a group Lee long wished to nurture. Rehearsals are conducted in a barn built in 1978 for the purpose. A room in the farmhouse serves as the business office. Lee encourages the indigenous troupe with visiting artists, musicians,

The first teenagers who signed up for a summer job had no idea they would appear on stage. Later Maryat would ask them to go home and collect oral histories from friends and family for use as play material. *West Virginia and Regional History Center.*

directors, actors, technicians and visiting scholars. The audiences consist for the most part of local people though EcoTheater also plays in penitentiaries, hospitals, and state parks. Noisy and restless when outside, full of milling adolescents and farm children with energy to run off, the EcoTheater audiences and actors thoroughly enjoy themselves. Performances take on a communal and festive atmosphere, just as Lee wishes them to do. A core of attentive--even awed--children and adults attends respectfully to the play. All EcoTheater plays are written by

> She tried to imagine the "simpler state" in which the medieval Mystery plays were created. She developed everyday "Harlem situations"--a purse-snatching, a confrontation with a tough cop, a family quarrel over money.

Lee herself. She has no scruple against producing the work of another playwright, but she will not violate her principle that all EcoTheater material must arise from its native audience. The EcoTheater plays are: *Four Men and Monster, Ole Miz Dacey, John Henry,* and *A Double-Threaded Life* (aka *The Hinton Play*). The latter was added in 1981 first as *The Day Hinton Died*, retitled and expanded for the 1982 season. These four plays were offered in repertory between in various combinations of about thirty performances annually. All these plays draw upon local material. The dialogue attempts to capture the language and speech rhythms of the local people.

The situations and themes express underlying beliefs and values that power individual and community actions. Lee is probably correct in saying that EcoTheater comes as close to a truly indigenous Appalachian theater as it is possible to come in our time. Her conception of EcoTheater has long roots. As an adolescent she thought that in the theater a person could expose specific and universal truths hidden by appearances. "As a southerner I grew up feeling that we were all hiding behind appearances and the roles assigned to us very early. Theater offered the chance to step out, under the protection of whatever character we played, to reveal vital, if hidden, aspects of ourselves. This sharing act of truth would help bridge divisions and create a cleansed and loving community."[24]

She found these ideas confirmed through her experience of music. She speaks fervently of attending musical performances in which the musician seems mystically to become more themselves, more real, in the act of playing, as if in the playing they remove a mask and exposes an inner, real self. Lee's participation through the music in this act of self-exposure resembles to her the experience of rebirth that accompanies a religious conversion.

SALT's gay-themed *After the Fashion Show,* with Jose Colon. *West Virginia and Regional History Center.*

Corning to theater with this sort of expectation, Lee was disappointed with her first college year, spent in the Northwestern University department of Speech and Drama. To her, drama school was not concerned with providing moments of self-discovery. The methods of acting taught seemed to intensify the conflict between playing roles in life and playing them on-stage. Her disillusionment deepened during the 1950s: she found the plays for professional New York theater, with few exceptions, trivial and meaningless, the audiences jaded, and the actors and managers working only for money and self-aggrandizement; these were not the motives she felt should propel the theater. Her distress encouraged her in the idea that American theater had been "strangled in its crude infancy" by the arrival from England of brilliant

---

[24] "Legitimate Theater is Illegitimate," in *Toward the Second Decade: The Impact of the Women's Movement on American Institutions*, ed. Betty Justice and Renata Pore (New York: Greenwood Press, 1981), p. 12.

acting companies playing sophisticated dramas. These put our native American players and playwrights to shame and captured the audiences that should have been theirs. This importation, she believes, has resulted in the isolation of theater from the poor and even the non-theater-going intellectual classes of the United States, an effect she has sought to redress through her indigenous theater.

> "Instead of the drowsy nods and inattention of the congregation, the audiences for *Dope!* snapped with life."

The success of *Dope!* in 1951 prove to her that a living theater might be re-born. She was researching her MA thesis on the religious origin of drama under Paul Tillich at Union Theological Seminary. Lee was appalled that her fellow seminarians, in preaching to Harlem congregations, used seminary terms which their mostly illiterate parishioners could not understand. Her study of ancient and medieval drama had convinced her that drama in a vernacular language effectively conveyed religious messages. She was especially impressed by the English medieval Mystery plays, with their apparently primitive form, their direct messages and simple language, and their crude, home-spun playing conditions. She admired the way the Wakefield and York plays mirrored the daily lives of the people for whom--and by whom--they were written. At lunch one day over a refectory table a fellow seminarian engaged her in an intense debate and dared her to try reaching a congregation through such a play.

The Soul and Latin Theater, with Maryat second-row left. *West Virginia and Regional History Center.*

That was the last

encouragement she needed; that dare sent her into the "wild streets' of East Harlem where she "stumbled into an audience/play chemistry" that she has developed and refined since.

April 25, 1951. *Courtesy Variety.*

Her play, like the old Mystery plays, spoke to its audience in the vernacular. simple and unpretentious, the play concerned the people for and about whom it was written. Instead of the drowsy nods and inattention of the congregation, the audiences for *Dope!* snapped with life. The spectacle of an addict injecting heroin into his arm evoked catcalls and groans of delight and despair. Impassioned spectators shouted to the actors; they became part of the play. In Lee's mind the ancient congruence of religion and drama had been revivified. In the playing of this simple drama she believed her audience--and actors--recreated an act that became a transcendent moment in which the human and the divine converged. Thus the proper and true purpose of theater--as it was practiced among the ancient Greeks and the medieval Europeans--was re-created. *Dope!* changed her life. In a letter she writes:

> *Dope!*--the whole event, writing, rehearsals, production--was on the order of a conversion for me--one at which I worked very hard laying the groundwork, one which placed my single inexperienced intuition against all advice. It meant going against comfort, safety, reason, against my family and friends' expectations. I even hid this big ego of mine like a wild, brooding bird, from the piercing gaze of my analyst--to his evident disgust when I offhandedly placed *Variety* in his hands with its banner

headline of April 25, 1951 proclaiming the arrival of *Dope!*

In the city streets she had found the seeds of EcoTheater and the means of linking creatively the abiding interests of her life.

She refined her discoveries about working with indigenous actors in *Dope!* and while the use of untrained, lay actors presents a host of difficulties, it not only bears rewards enough for her, she is uncompromising in her belief that an indigenous theater must use predominantly indigenous talents. In her first experiments with home actors she would compose scripts based on Biblical experimented with or mythic stories. Finding the acting impossibly stiff, she turned to improvisation. She tried to imagine the "simpler state" in which the medieval Mystery plays were created. She developed everyday "Harlem situations"--a purse-snatching, a confrontation with a tough cop, a family quarrel over money. In one that later developed into a play (*Day to Day*), a young man is caught trying to sell his family's belongings to buy drugs. He must then confess his addiction to his parents. Giving her actors a basic situation, she would encourage them to improvise upon it. She would have them switch roles. This kind of activity displayed the resourcefulness, imagination, and good humor of the street people and confirmed her idea of the "soundness of an unimposed organic drama."

A young Maryat in 1951, deep into the *Dope!* experience. *Courtesy Cincinnati Enquirer.*

She found she could not generate a script from this procedure, however. At some point--the earlier the better--she found she must present a script to the actors and allow the play to evolve during rehearsal, when an actor would adapt and refine his or her role. For example, in a Christmas play she wrote in 1950, the young woman playing Mary was intensely shy, almost inarticulate. So Lee expanded the role of Gabriel and re-wrote the role of Mary to take advantage of the actress's bashfulness. Because many in the audience knew how painfully shy the Mary was, the play touched them in a special way. It made them perceive both the young woman and Mary in a new way, and the experience gave the young woman a shot of needed self-confidence. Thus the characters evolved through a script fluid for a time and then set once each actor realized his character.

Lee later discovered psychodrama, a psychotherapeutic technique pioneered by Professor J. C. Moreno, a pupil of Freud.[25] The technique was developed in Vienna during the early 1920s and brought by Moreno to the United States in 1925. It involves a drama in which the participants--actors and spectators alike--are patients.

> "[T]he line between drama and reality is frighteningly thin and can even be abolished. The impulse to act out one's life, she found, is not foreign to anyone."

---

[25] J. L. Moreno, *The Theatre of Spontaneity* (Beacon, New York: Beacon House, 1947; repr. 1973). See also Lewis Yablonsky, *Psychodrama* (New York: Basic Books, 1976), pp. 274-286.

> **Actor, 19, Who Played Addict Dies of a Narcotics Overdose**
>
> Manuel Vasquez, a 19-year-old East Harlem youth who played the lead role in the Soul and Latin Theater's presentation of "Dope," died in Metropolitan Hospital Saturday night in circumstances strangely like those in the play.
>
> On the stage Tony Vasquez, as he was known to friends, played a junkie who struggles against addiction and narrowly wins out. He dies at the final curtain after a vindictive pusher stabs him.
>
> The young actor, who apparently died of a narcotics overdose, had been engaged in a similar struggle offstage for over a year. He had seemed to be winning it, but friends said he got "shot up" on Saturday and, with that, he lost the
>
> "His life was as typical of an experience in ghetto living as you could find anywhere on God's earth," John Weckesser, the general manager of the troupe said last night. "But this young guy was exceptionally talented, gifted, intellectually, artistically, emotionally. He's a statistic now, I guess, but he was no statistic in the minds of anyone he ever performed in front of, or with whom he in any way came in contact."
>
> Young Tony was a dropout from Benjamin Franklin High School, but as he had emerged from addiction he had showed renewed interest in education.
>
> Last week he took a seven-hour series of tests as a preliminary to entering a makeup program to qualify him for college.
>
> He had joined the troupe a year ago and had controlled the sound equipment for street performances that a critic said were "full of the rage and gaiety and despair of the ghetto."
>
> The Soul and Latin Theater, 174 East 104th Street, produces "street plays" based on ghetto themes using untrained slum teen-agers, blacks and Puerto Ricans, as actors. "Dope" has been playing about summer months.
>
> He was admitted to the cast when he agreed to take no more narcotics and he went into Beth Israel Hospital for detoxification treatment. He had been out for almost a month and was going to Exodus House, 10d Street near Second Avenue. He lived with his mother, Candida Soto, on East 102d Street.
>
> "All the junkies in the whole neighborhood were trying to get him to get back," said Maryat Lee, the author of "Dope."
>
> "They lurk around like vultures. The other junkies are jealous, very deep down, that somebody else is out, so they want to prove that he's not making it so they won't have to make the effort themselves. Well they proved it."

April 27, 1970. Vasquez' death may have helped Maryat decide to leave New York City for the mountains. *Courtesy New York Times.*

They generate the source material and the production of the drama; the playing of the drama is a totally cooperative, communal act, no part of which originates from an outsider. It usually develops around a conflict and may be spontaneous or planned or even rehearsed, depending on the circumstances. The director-analyst carefully supervises the drama to develop specific emotional syndromes in detailed dialogue. Actors and audience alike, by living through their syndrome in mimetic form, may be purged and liberated. Over the years, Lee has adapted many of Moreno's ideas. Through her work with psychodrama it became manifest to her that and very powerful in some people. Repressed and shy people particularly make some of the best actors for indigenous drama

Lee's method of working with EcoTheater actors is, then, derived from her New York experience with *Dope!* and SALT and psychodrama. She specifically rejects any sort of Stanislavski-derived method acting. She admires Stanislavski's dissatisfaction with acting as he found it in nineteenth-century Russia and lauds his effort to work toward more genuineness and realism. She, however, has worked in the reverse direction. Where

Maryat Lee

Stanislavski tried to help the actor identify with and become his role,[26] Lee's aim is to enable the actor to grow to his or her fullest, to realize what is most hidden within.

Therefore, instead of adjusting the actor to his role, she adjusts the role to the actor. In the acting, a truth about the actor will thereby emerge. Lee's concern with her actors may be her ultimate concern; it is certainly a major force.

SALT up-close in the 60's. *Courtesy West Virginia and Regional History Center.*

She believes that most professional actors' training disables them, prevents them from seeking or discovering truth in themselves. They are taught to put on a mask rather than take one off, Lee's goal with her lay actors in EcoTheater. She is fond of quoting Peter Brook on this point:

> Time after time I have worked with actors who after the usual preamble that they'd put themselves in my hands are tragically incapable however hard they try of laying down for one brief instant even in rehearsal the image of themselves that has hardened around an inner emptiness. On the occasions that it is possible to penetrate this shell, it is like smashing the picture on a television set.[27]

She tells her actors about her piano teacher Sam Harwill, a sometime pupil of the virtuoso Busoni. Harwill taught Lee intensively three or four hours a day. "Don't do

---

[26] Constantin Stanislavski, *An Actor Prepares* (New York: Theatre Arts Books, 1969).
[27] Brook, p. 29.

> Lee's working method, then, is a holistic art that legitimate theaters cannot cultivate because the economics of their operation do not allow it, nor do their aims include it.

anything with the notes," he would say to her. "Give no emphasis, no interpretation. Do not retard the tempo or speed it up. Just play the notes." The practice sessions agonized her, she recalls, until one day, after months of effort, she played the slow movement of Beethoven's C Major Sonata as monotonously--she thought--as she could. "And then it happened," she says. "I stopped imposing my 'self' on the music, that is, my role of pianist, and the music became itself--huge, utterly immense. As I played 'monotonously' the music was allowed to be, and I was allowed to be. It works with acting the same way." When she gives them a script she tells her actors, "Just say the words. Don't act; don't do things to it. Hide the art." After patient hours finally something breaks through that stuns her with freshness and genuineness. She--and the actors--know what they have been looking for.

Soul and Latin Theater (SALT) continued the rough theater model in the late 60's. *Courtesy New York Times*

One young man, for example, had come to EcoTheater after several years of work with a community theater group in a medium-sized city. Lee found his acting impossibly artificial, trumped-up, hammy. She worked for days with him, as Tot in *Four Men and a Monster*, trying to get him to be his natural self. Finally, one day he became frustrated and very angry--it had been building--and read through one of Tot's speeches in as monotonous a voice as he could muster. His performance stopped the rehearsal and brought tears to several cast members' eyes.

The payoff comes, however, not just as a stunning performance, as important as that is. Even more important to Lee is to help her actors discover new perspectives on their everyday reality, thus making their lives a little more meaningful or joyful. Sometimes the effect is dramatic and long-lasting. One young man, a high school student from a very remote farm area, found through his EcoTheater acting experience that he wanted to go to college, a goal he had never before imagined for himself. He has since graduated as a chemistry major. A young woman nicknamed Kiwi confessed to Lee that her EcoTheater experience gave her a chance to share with others a dimension of herself that she had hidden even from herself--"a poetic thing," she called it.

The concern of the legitimate theater rests strictly in a finished product packaged to be sold and consumed. Lee's chief concern lies more with the process of self-discovery: Lee will not set the lines in a script until an actor has made his breakthrough, signaling that the lines work. Free of the necessities that restrict most theaters she can change a script right up to the last night of a season, a closing which she refers to sometimes as opening night. Rehearsals, therefore--and performances--under Lee can be agonizing for her EcoTheater actors. Many break down in tears and self-pity and frustration; many quit in disgust; some become defiant and angry. It is hard for anyone to lay aside the protective armor of his or her delicate psyche. But those special few who bear it out obviously are elated with their own performances. For them EcoTheater takes on a distinct and special meaning that clearly enhances their lives.

Lee's "rough" theater would fit on a flatbed truck and could be set up virtually anywhere. *West Virginia and Regional History Center.*

Lee pushes her actors to plunge ever deeper into themselves, revising her script until an actor becomes comfortable with the risk it involves. Like many directors, Lee may ask the actor to improvise about a neutral subject until, caught unaware, he will reveal. the honest response she seeks. Then she returns to the script to add the revelation. Lee has written about this process:

> I'm continuing to explore theater as a place where people are permitted to take off the roles we all wear in this life, risking the exposure of some part of the psyche, and when it happens it is quite a sacred or luminous moment, when artist and priest are very close to being the same thing. This is why until this year (the 1979 season) I would not allow trained theater people in the company. I will screen them carefully, and they know they must not impose their styles, or disturb the careful ecological or ecotheatrical balance.

Lee's object in this kind of acting is not psychotherapy or clinical experimentation. The object is to reveal unaffected responses to everyday situations. Once the actor gets to that truth in himself, he conveys it to his audience, and the release--an event in which psychic energy moves between audience and performers--provides this "luminous" moment of insight. Lee speaks glowingly of a 1980 production of *Four Men and a Monster* for which she used local mountain men, two of them from Powley's Creek. The production became a "burning bush, testifying presence," a metaphor Lee uses to indicate intense moments when, for actors and spectators alike, theater yields to religion and a transcendence is experienced.

The intimacy achieved between EcoTheater and its audience makes Lee's drama unique in American theater today. Lee speaks sadly of the over 90% of the American public that never attends theater. It is a small part of this vast body of Americans, especially the underprivileged classes, that Lee hopes to bring into the theater through EcoTheater. Her audience is not conversant about professional theater. Their major experience of theatrical entertainment consists of television drama, movies, an occasional high school play. Some of the EcoTheater audience is indigenous, coming from the upland valleys, isolated farms and hamlets of Summers and surrounding counties. Prisoners, hospital inmates, townspeople of Hinton and other small towns some times come. Often outsiders attend, tourists at a nearby state park, many of whom return year after year to experience EcoTheater's latest offering.

> Lee pushes her actors to plunge ever deeper into themselves, revising her script until an actor becomes comfortable with the risk it involves.

The strength of EcoTheater rests upon the close relationship it establishes among the major constituents of drama: theater--place--actor--play--audience.

Actor and audience live together in the same place--indeed the actors emerge from the audience, are part of it, and are not, as in most cases, imported professionals. The play emerges directly from the day-to-day experience of the audience. The drama is presented where the audience live. Therefore the audience feel a special relationship to the theater for it is at home, to the actors (they are friends, relatives, neighbors) and to the play, for it reflects their everyday life in their own language. As Lee says, "We sense our roots in the earth in this setting, and now and then glimpse the awesome power of the ancient theater."

Such an aesthetic program imposes a severe discipline on Lee's art. She has for years eschewed the use of art for any sort of propaganda, religious or political. In her MA thesis she wrestled with the issue of the uses of drama, especially the use of drama for social amelioration. Before she finished she renounced altogether the idea of direct social utility for the arts. She wrote recently of her early experience in using drama to inculcate certain specific beliefs: "I began to see that to use a play for my own schemes would be as calculating as to use a person for my intentions, however good they may be. I was not comfortable until the play was its own master, not my slave." She eschews not only propaganda, therefore, but also most dramatic forms that characterize serious theater today.

> In the EcoTheater plays the audience acts itself out, and in this acting out the deepest human needs are fulfilled--the need to imitate, to mime, and to "play," and to see oneself clearly and without the pretensions and psychic armor that daily life require.

For this reason, Lee's drama is distinctive. It is certainly not what we usually call "avant-garde." As A. D. Coleman put it some years ago, Lee's plays are "irrelevant and useless to the audience for avant-garde theater," but also "avant-garde theater is irrelevant to the audience for her plays."[28] Coleman was writing about Lee's New York audience, but his words remain true today for the rural audience of EcoTheater. For similar reasons, Lee avoids most popular commercial forms. Anything outré, highly convoluted, expressionistic, or consciously "arty," anything with radical political or psychological messages or mockery of values and beliefs deeply-held is anathema to Lee's art. Similarly she avoids sentimentality, condescension, extravagant theatrical effects, easy moralizing. She wishes neither to alienate her audience nor to lull them with false simplifications.

The task she has set herself, coupled with the need to build an indigenous audience, makes the most difficult item on the EcoTheater agenda. Rural Appalachian people are not theater people; no tradition of theater exists in this part of the world. It is hard to get them out. Moreover, the usually small audiences are what a professional would consider impossible: rude, noisy, inattentive. Children shout, throw Frisbees, run among the spectators. Adolescents wander in and out, make obscene sounds and gestures, chatter

---

[28] A. D. Coleman, "Theatre: Soul and Latin Theatre," *The Village Voice*, 29 August 1968, p. 8.

with friends. Even the adults walk out for soft drinks, talk with friends, doze off. A less tough person than Maryat Lee long since would have been driven into some other work by the frustrations and discouragements. Yet the relationship that sometimes sparks between Lee's audience and the play compensates for all these trials. Lee was struck by the response of some audience members during her first experiences with street theater. The street audiences came to the theater because they were curious. But they also came because they are culturally starved and need the kind of spiritual nourishment that only theater can give. Writing of *Dope!* Lee says: "Following the play each night, a substantial hunk of children and teenagers got to know the play by heart and were heard saying the lines along with and sometimes before the actors during a performance." Extraordinarily, these children would present their own versions of the play at school and on the streets.

An essential part of an EcoTheater performance is a discussion with the audience following the play. Sometimes Lee leads the discussion, sometimes a guest does. For several years, Lee had a series of "guest humanists"--directors, scholars, actors--who lead discussions with the audience following the play: how it affected them, what features they especially noticed, what they did or did not like, what the play meant to them. Anything, in short, they want to air. The audience become the critic. Usually Lee invites the actors and technical crew to join her with the audience. They celebrate community--with each other, with the land, and with outside guests and tourists.

Lee's audiences sense correctly that underneath Lee's plays, built into their structure and their language, lies a desire to share with them a common humanity. This sharing--obviously not money or fame or comfort--is what motivates Lee. To her, theater is a place to celebrate and explore human relationships. In giving advice to others who might wish to develop an indigenous theater, she writes, "Pick an audience that never attends the theater and for whom you feel affection. Like families, an audience unmistakably influences and shapes you. You affect and change each other as you grow."[29] Not smashing success at the box office; not advanced ideas or forms; not shock value or stardom for a few actors are Lee's aims; but rather an open relationship with a small audience who care about their theater-at-home and in whose plays they may view their own lives in their own language is what Lee seeks. If most of Lee's community ignores EcoTheater, those who come attend regularly; a few become passionately committed. These commitments are slow to generate, slow to grow, but they are what matter to an artist of the indigenous like Lee:

Maryat drew on many of her New York friends, including Parsons, to become "guest humanists." Later would come university professors, anthropologists, novelists, and so on. *Courtesy Daily Telegraph.*

---

[29] "Legitimate Theater is Illegitimate," p. 22.

> Once you choose your people simply go to them; be with them; listen to them; let them happen to you; record them; be sensitive to their voices, cadences, and concerns and to the stories and messages between the lines. Improvise with them, cast your play with them--these experts who have experienced the action. Rehearse, set up performance dates, announce the opening, invite friends, and--do it.[30]

Clearly, EcoTheater is like no other theater in the United States. Its characteristics compel us to classify it among the "Sixth Theater" in a scheme worked out by Philip Arnoult, Director of Baltimore's Theatre Project.[31] Arnoult distinguishes the first five American theaters as commercial, regional, the "New York-based research theater," university, and community. Obviously EcoTheater is not commercial, not university, and not New York-based research theater. Neither is it community theater, which relies on a small, traditional, class-bound audience with fixed tastes and a repertory drawing heavily on the commercial "hits" of recent New York seasons. EcoTheater shares some important features with regional theater, but the very term " regional theater" today evokes organizations like the Guthrie, big-money operations with extensive physical plant, a large core of professionals, and a blended repertory of drama classics, commercial hits, and a narrow experimental edge or avant-garde. EcoTheater, then, clearly belongs among Arnoult's "Sixth theater," along with several dozen more or less isolated theater groups currently operating around the United States.

> An indigenous or grassroots theater worthy of the name must produce plays that evolve from the people who constitute its audience. Such a theater takes a faith that the people have a rich oral tradition worth rendering into dramatic form.

But even compared with this group Lee's EcoTheater looks unique. Most of these groups represent an artistic outgrowth of personal commitments to late 1960s liberal ideals.

---

[30] Ibid.
[31] "The Sixth Theatre in the United States, 1968-1979," a paper delivered to the International Theatre Institute's 18th Biennial Congress, Sophia, Bulgaria, June, 1979.

Lee's commitment to the ideas of EcoTheater reaches back to the early 1950s, and even her New York street plays of the late 1960s reflect not political radicalism but dedication to humane values. If a political message is carried away from her plays it is strictly by inference.

> Lee's Appalachian plays are as indigenous to Appalachia as any play in the Twentieth Century is likely to be indigenous to its region.

In other respects, of course, her work resembles that of other alternate groups. But Lee insists that most of the other alternate theater groups, especially in the South, are not indigenous in the same sense; too often they impose alien ideas (especially political) and forms upon their audiences, implying to their audience that they should think or act a certain way. Clearly Lee chose the name for her rural mountain theater carefully: a viewing place for the house.

One of EcoTheater's most exciting and promising features is that it holds out the possibility of a respite from the serious artist's alienation from American society without total compromise of aesthetic values. Lee would be the last person to claim that the people of Summers County have fully accepted her, or she them. They live together uneasily. But they live together and grow and learn together.

Living with an audience often proves trying, and it takes extraordinary courage and dedication for any but the most solidly planted native. But it's the only way Lee feels indigenous theater can work. It must grow from the ground up. It must reveal something authentic about its culture and strengthen its audience's sense of self. Most of the actors must be local people, coached by local people. The plays produced must evolve from local, indigenous materials. The language must sound like the vernacular.

Settings should be built by local craftsmen using local materials and reflecting local sensibility. The completed drama, in a careful ecotheatrical balance, must represent life as it is lived there. But she exercises careful aesthetic control over the evolving text. She works in the confidence that only an artist can penetrate illusion and reveal the underlying structure of human experience, the real beliefs and values that animate any society. A superficial or compromised art will miss this dimension of the Invisible.

They spring from gossip and tale-telling, from folklore and oral history. Each is drawn from a different kind of material, and taken as a group they exploit and demonstrate the full range of possibilities available to an indigenous dramatist. They demand little to produce, not requiring elaborate staging or costuming. None requires professional acting or musical talent, or extravagant modes of production. Even the most elaborate, *John Henry*, requires a minimum of simple, inexpensive scenery. Lee stresses that the simpler, more primitive their staging, the closer they will hew to her intention, even if this means altering the script to fit a director's specific requirements (as, for example, cutting the dance number from *John Henry* in the absence of the proper talent).

A play constructed from oral history calls for rudimentary staging just as a painting in the primitive or folk mode wants simple lines, bold colors, an easily recognizable subject, and an appeal on a mythic or subconscious level. The requirements are set forth in Peter Brook's concept of the Rough/Holy Theatre.[32] Both the visible and "the Invisible" must be made manifest to make sure the spirit of the production coincide with the way stories are told in Appalachia. The craft may be hidden from an unobservant eye, but it is certainly there. Thus each EcoTheater play derives from the unwritten words--stories, tales, gossip, memorized information, songs, jokes, poems--of the people of Summers County.

---

[32] Brook, pp. 73-109.

The Appalachian Plays

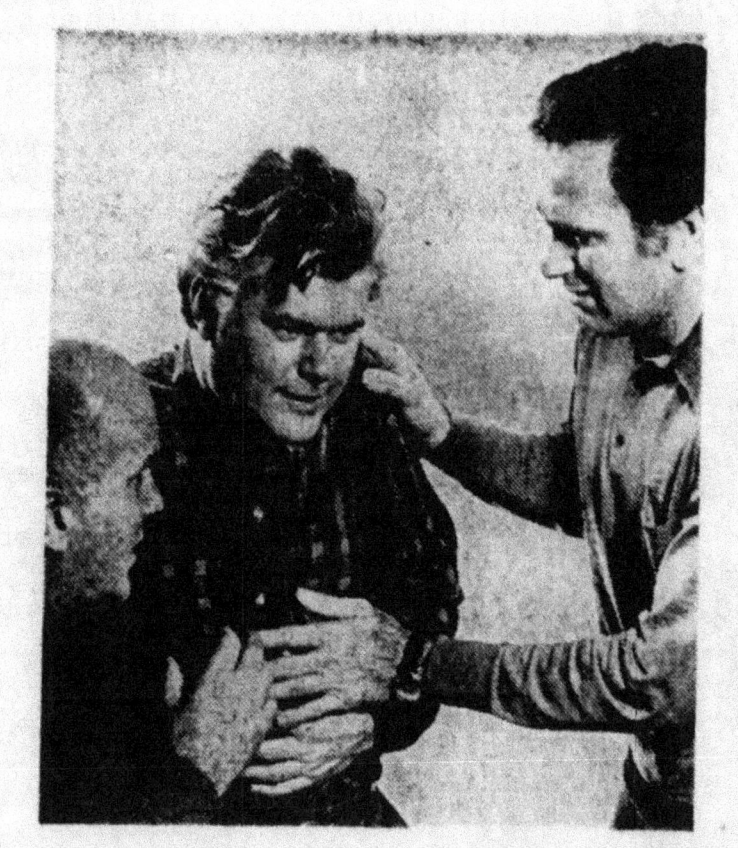

Playhouse Premiere Wednesday

Ronald Bishop, Paul Millikin and Dick Latessa in a scene from "Four Men And A Monster," which premieres at Playhouse In The Park Wednesday through Sunday. The play is a hillbilly parable by native Kentucky playwright Maryat Lee. Three buddies, Upjohn, Tot and Hal are down and out in a big city flophouse. One of them, Upjohn, is about to marry a girl who is to inherit a fortune. "Monster" will play in the Shelterhouse Theater for only seven performances. For ticket information, call 421-3888.

From the first production of *Four Men*, 1968. *Courtesy Cincinnati Enquirer.*

The only exception is *Four Men and a Monster*, which draws in large measure upon Lee's memories of childhood in Kenton County, Kentucky. During her adolescence in the 1930s she witnessed drifters and unemployed men and social misfits. These hoboes of the 1930s became in the 1950's a class of migrants drifting to Midwestern cities in search of work and the American dream.

They often left behind a family on a hard-scrabble farm in hollow or upland, an unplumbed shack in a mine patch. By the early 1950s cities in Ohio, Michigan, and Illinois had Appalachian ghettos, slums where the displaced mountain people eked out a bare and alienated existence. In the cities they held on to mountain ways and beliefs and dreamed of return. Those who succeeded often come home to retire. Others return to a life of welfare hopelessness and squalor. This pattern persists today, and stories about these people abound in any Appalachian community. Whatever one's social or economic class, he or she will have known some of them and will have heard stories about others. Hal, Tot, and Upjohn of *Four Men and a Monster* typify this class. Lee has given dramatic life to a human sort as familiar through oral tradition to Appalachians as Flannery O'Conner's "good country people" are to deep Southerners.

A chief form of oral tradition is gossip, and local gossip furnished part of the basis for *Ole Miz Dacey* (as *Dacey* did as material for the other plays). In the case of Miz Dacey, a telephone joke augmented the gossip and, as Lee tells us in her notes to the play, the character took form from her knowledge of other local women. An indigenous playwright uses everything at hand.

The entrance to the Great Bend tunnel, under construction. A whole mixed-race community would grow around a large construction project like this. "And all the family we got is this here little camp." *West Virginia and Regional History Center.*

Well-established local folklore and song furnish the basis for *John Henry*.

Appalachians know the hero of the Big Bend tunnel on the Chesapeake and Ohio Railroad mainline near Talcott, West Virginia, from a large body of materials oral and written. Also, Lee has interviewed Summers County people who claim to know people who knew John Henry.

Local folks can tell many stories about the old times, though many also deny that John Henry ever existed and are somewhat scornful of the legend. One of the characters in the play, Slick, represents this local ambivalence: Slick does not want to be caught believing in John Henry, but he certainly takes delight in telling the story, and his belief soon becomes evident. His attitude embodies the idea that while the legend itself is well-established, the actual existence of John Henry, like that of many legendary heroes, remains questionable. More important than whether John Henry actually existed, however, is the imaginative reconstruction of a time and place that really did exist and of a human spirit that lived through that time and in that place. Lee drew initially upon characters sketched in song and legend and set them into a researched historical framework. Then she began adjusting her text to suit her actors, fitting the roles to their talents and contemporary perceptions of characters dead for two generations. The ethos represented, therefore, may not be historically accurate (though it is arguable) but it certainly reflects living Appalachian values, and one supposes it misses its nineteenth century mark by not much.

All the EcoTheater plays share certain characteristics: they exist in multiple versions, one for each year of production; they are simple in structure and language; their themes boldly project the values of their society and yet explore philosophic and religious understandings; and, being inspired by the Medieval Mystery plays, the EcoTheater plays resemble in certain ways those civic dramas of the Middle Ages. Thus, *John Henry* underwent a series of revisions, one for each production year, each adjusted to fit different actors' strengths and sensibilities. The present text--a conflation of several production years--tries to make the play producible in any kind of theater--grassroots, community, academic, or professional--and as accessible as can be to a general American audience.

Maryat Lee

Lee's method of composition involves a series of revisions making editorial choices difficult. Lee sometimes starts a scene with tape recordings or improvisations; at other times she begins from notes following an improvisation session. The script is then adjusted to make the actor feel that his words justly represent the character inside. Lucinda Ayres, one of EcoTheater's most active performers, was often heard to remark, "Maryat, I can't say that; it just isn't Miz Dacey." Of course, all actors say similar things. But coming from the part of Lucinda that was Miz Dacey, her protest conveyed authority. *Miz Dacey* was originally written to take advantage of the many talents of Jimmy Costa, musician, folklorist, and oral historian in his own right. Costa's joke inspired her to write the play; but Lee says, only half-joking, "It was part of his Karma to be an old mountain woman. I saw her in him." In that case her job as writer was simply to manifest that important but hidden part of Jim Costa and then to help him give birth to Miz Dacey. So, with the role of John Henry, Lee hopes that the actor will find a part of himself (or herself--the role was played three times by young women) like John Henry and will grow toward it, as the role grows toward the actor.

> The EcoTheater plays are made, like the medieval plays, to adapt to any environment they are set down in.

To facilitate the breakthrough that Lee seeks for both actors and audience--in which a mask comes off and a truth underneath is revealed--she keeps the structure of the EcoTheater plays simple. They deliver their messages clearly, the purpose being to change people's lives by making them see themselves clearly. The plots are straightforward, like the medieval Mystery plays that Lee so admires, the actions recognizable to an audience accustomed to looking at life in a literal, practical way. The one structural innovation of the EcoTheater plays may be Lee's so-called "tuck scenes." A tuck scene may be removed from the play or shifted within without impairing plot or theme. A director lacking the necessary talent may simply remove the dance scenes from *John Henry*. If time is a factor in presenting *Miz Dacey*, the scene with Albee Hood may be cut. Any condition of playing-- limited time, physical conditions, audience sensibility, and especially available acting and musical talent--may dictate a director's decision to cut or rearrange scenes. The EcoTheater plays are made, like the medieval plays, to adapt to any environment they are set down in.

Language, too, is kept simple and direct, like the language of its audience. Indeed, in Lee's mind the idea of indigenous drama consists largely of speaking in the people's own voice. That voice thrills her. She speaks eagerly of sharing her joy with her actors and audience, "at seeing themselves rise up with mysteriously mountain sounds that are sweet and powerful. " She strives, she says, paraphrasing Adrienne Rich, for the "release into one's own language--not the jargon of an elite."

Lee does not simply transcribe dialogue taped or written down. She holds that a playwright must transform the raw material of experience by a principle that universalizes the local into a work with sufficient human comprehension to justify the name of art. "Indigenous" certainly does not mean artless to Lee. Her dialogue is surprisingly subtle and betrays the casual observer. She strives to capture an audience's attention with simple plots, uncomplicated characters, and vernacular language that turns poetic without warning. Thus "monster" in *Four Men and a Monster* is an accurately-chosen word to put into the mouths of characters like Hal and Tot. An Appalachian speaker is comfortable with the idea that such men would call a grotesquely fat woman a "monster." But the word also signals the audience that their use of the word is a warning on the monstrous dimension in their own thought. That thought is focused through Hal, whose perception, misshapen by his maleficent ambition, is more grotesque than the enormous body of the woman he plans to exploit and murder. Furthermore, it is the monstrous quality of Hal's mind that leads to Tot's death and his own remorse. The contrapuntal keening at the end of the play, with the three voices weaving in an harmonic and rhythmic continuity, suggests very strongly the way in which the lives of the three men have been similarly woven and intertwined and have formed a complex, integrated rhythm of their own. The cadenced words, full of grief and remorse as well as joy, express the love the three men have felt all along for one another, but did not realize until this catastrophic event ends one of their lives. Lee has a keen ear for the idioms and rhythms of Appalachian speech. Also, her musical training is evident in her plays, and the climactic moments are marked by highly cadenced, poetic prose, pictorial imagery, and vernacular diction that surprises with its poetic suggestiveness. When she has the Messenger in *John Henry* proclaim with dramatic irony that "man's trapped," he certainly says more than he intends, as he does when he tells about the powderman "wrastlin' around with the fuse, like it was a great snake."

Much could be said about the themes of the EcoTheater plays. With compelling directness, the plays mean what they say. Their occasional gentle satire of follies like greed draw fire. After seeing a Lee play, one woman said, "You always know you're going to get taken over the coals, zapped by some little message. I don't know why I go back." But more often Lee's plays depict the ever-immanent power of love to transform lives and straighten out the distortions of everyday selfishness and thoughtlessness. The experience of love--often sorrowful but always enriching--is accompanied by a grotesque mode or act: the "monster" of *Four Men and a Monster*, the green men of Miz Dacey's imagination, the tunnel life in *John Henry*; violent, brutal, bred of greed and ephemeral power. Sinful acts occur often, but they anticipate a salvation, like the conclusion of *Four Men* in which Hal's greed turns into a realization of his love for Tot. As a character, John Henry bears a simple human grace and integrity and Thoreauvian self-reliance that lift him out of the horrors of the tunnel existence and redeem his life. His modesty--he "ain't nothin' but a man"--and his reluctance to participate in the race become grace under pressure.

> These characters confront the harsh conditions of their life with a stoic acceptance of suffering, almost as if they were meant to be crucified.

John Henry, Tot, Miz Dacey, all manifest specifically southern Appalachian virtues and mores. John Henry is inwardly strong but gentle with children and women. A deep male bond links Hal and Tot and Upjohn. These characters confront the harsh conditions of their life with a stoic acceptance of suffering, almost as if they were meant to be crucified. Indeed, a kind of crucifixion takes place in each play in which an old self dies and is resurrected as a new being, a theme reaching back to *Dope!* and her early exposure to thinkers like Paul Tillich, Reinhold Niebuhr, Karl Barth, and Paul Lehmann at Union Theological Seminary.[33] But in part her religious themes reflect the values of the Southern Appalachian society she seeks to dramatize.

The overriding religious aim of Lee's Appalachian plays may be understood only by inference, of course, for she has not been overtly didactic on any level since *Dope!* But these plays were also in part inspired, we remember, by the medieval English mystery plays and are thus linked to them in several ways. In one respect this link applies to actors and audience as well as play. Lee's actors are not professionals; like the members of the craft guilds that performed the mystery plays, Lee's actors perform for the joy of the activity or other personal reasons. Lee has trouble finding Summers County people willing to go through the agony of learning to play a role. Similarly, we may imagine reluctant guild members having arms twisted by masters needing a role filled. But those who have acted know the rewards, especially if they have done improvisations under Lee's direction.

She does not deliberately aim at a therapeutic result; she simply believes that the process of acting out in a controlled situation the realities of one's life can trigger astonishing self-discoveries and release of psychic energy. This belief has long since become empirical with her. The effects on personality, she points out, can be described either in religious terms, or simply as a means of knowing and accepting life and loving it, or in psychotherapeutic terms, as a way of resolving emotional problems, or as a "personality integration," or as a form of catharsis (that may apply to audience and actors alike) occurring to the individual in the spontaneous "category of the moment" (a truly non-mechanical, dynamic, active experience) during the acting-out of an inter-personal relation.[34] The experience may be understood at any level; the general aim is to become whole, or as Summers County folks would say, "hale," meaning full of health. Certainly

---

[33] Paul Tillich, *The New Being* (New York: Scribner's, 1955), could serve as an introduction to this dimension of Lee's work.
[34] Yablonsky, pp. 3-6 and 125; cf. Moreno, pp. 3-13.

mental health or spiritual wholeness is the general goal of psychotherapy, and specifically of the psychodrama to which Lee was attracted in the 1950s. This parallel is clear and pervasive in the EcoTheater plays. The actors are exposed throughout rehearsal and performance to the integrating powers of a drama that subtly, slowly tears away the masks and defenses of the personality and gradually opens up the possibility of a stronger, more integrated person. We may find a parallel in Everyman, one of the English medieval morality plays that inspired Lee years ago. In preparing to meet the summons of Death, Everyman must learn the hard lesson that only his good deeds will accompany him. He realizes that he must divest all his other attributes and possessions and that his friends must take their leave. The revelation at first disheartens him; but gradually he finds courage and resolution to face his fate. Clearly, religious doctrine or propaganda does not infiltrate Lee's plays. But the plays do participate in a broad sense in a search for what is true about the people around her, for the ground of being human, for the unbroken bond between man and God.

> If EcoTheater is to be thought of as a "group theater," which in some senses it is, it is so only as the Greek or English medieval theater was--a theater that arises from a homogeneous society and identifies with its society and manifests its ideals.

It is this broadly religious dimension of Lee's Appalachian plays that separates her work from other recent alternative theater in he Appalachian South. Many of these groups are wholly or in large part professional and non-local, whereas Lee steadfastly eschews professionals except for occasional use. Lee's adamant stand on this issue causes her severe emotional stress and compromises in certain ways the quality of her productions from a critical perspective. But EcoTheater thereby retains a claim to being "indigenous."

What the future holds for alternative theater in the South remains to be seen. Some may feel that EcoTheater and any theatrical group that approximates it is long overdue as an alternative to the blandness and lack of courage and cultural vacancy of most commercial theater and the intellectual and moral excesses of the avant-garde theater. Also the EcoTheater audience is one that other theaters in the United States totally ignore. Lee's real problem is to broaden her audience beyond a narrow group of the intensely committed who support the theater in a number of ways and a larger, slack group of very occasional attenders.

One grave problem in developing an audience and a following that indigenous theaters in the South like EcoTheater face is that they are tagged as politically radical. This charge no doubt carries some truth. Many of the groups belonging to the Regional Organization of Theaters South, a network of some three-dozen performing groups in the South, do have radical political agendas. In some cases the epithet "radical," however, is applied merely to denote an unpopular political position. And in some cases, as with Lee's work, the charge is totally unfounded. The EcoTheater plays have no overt, specific political agenda. She seeks rather to share an understanding with her audience. If that motive sometimes offends her audience, that is a risk any artist takes. If her audience refuses to engage in dialogue with her, the loss is theirs.

The lack of dialogue between audience and theater that Lee felt in American theater in the 1950's in some measure inspired her founding EcoTheater in 1975. That bleak situation of the theater has been substantially alleviated during the 1970s and early '80s by the significant growth of regional theater.[35] But Lee believes that American theater remains the preserve of a tiny elite that rigidly controls its play selection, and that playwrights need not expose their cherished work to this system when they could, she says, "take control of their own lives by building their own theaters" as she has done. Plays now--as then--must still be either box office hits for the commercial sector or outrageously outré in some way for the avant-garde sector. Lee points out further that most of the "group theaters" that developed during the 1970's consisted of troupes of professionals almost totally isolated from their communities, a situation equally as unhealthy as the commercial theater. If

---

[35] Gerald M. Berkowitz, *New Broadways: Theatre Across America*, 1950-1980 (Totowa, New Jersey: Rowman and Littlefield, 1982).

Maryat Lee

EcoTheater is to be thought of as a "group theater," which in some senses it is, it is so only as the Greek or English medieval theater was--a theater that arises from a homogeneous society and identifies with its society and manifests its ideals. At least those are Lee's aims. If her effort falls short she joins a large and distinguished company. US theater has long been castigated for its commercial corruption and lack of values. Alternatives have attracted actors, playwrights, and audiences alike. Between the world wars the Neighborhood Playhouse in New York City, the Washington Square Players, the Theatre Guild, the later Group Theatre, and, of course, the Provincetown Players were all efforts to establish a native American theater.[36]

> Appalachian people are relatively untouched by the abstractness and evasiveness and euphemism that blights much American daily language.

Another alternative thrust has been inspired by Bertolt Brecht's "Epic Theatre" and its popularized cousins, the outdoor stage spectacles, "sound and Light" shows, and historical pageants. These latter grow well in the Appalachian South, where they started in 1937 with Paul Green's *The Lost Colony*, and continue with Kermit Hunter's *Unto These Hills*, the Cherokee Indian chronicle.[37] Peter Schumann, like her, has moved theater out of the theater and onto the street as a protest against the deadening effects of a conventional theater upon an audience. As James Roose-Evans puts it, "He regards the audience that doesn't go to the theatre as the best one."[38] The Carolina Playmakers of Frederick Koch was a regional response to the widespread feeling that commercial American theater should address a wider audience on its own terms.

This sense had been expressed by W. B. Yeats years earlier, and his disappointment

---

[36] John Gassner, "Pioneers of the New Theater Movement," pp. 15-24 in *The American Theater Today*, ed. Alan S. Downer (New York: Basic Books, 1967).

[37] John Gassner, "Varieties of Epic Drama," pp. 281-308 in *Directions in Modern Theatre and Drama*, ed. John Gassner (New York: Holt, Rinehart and Winson, 1967).

[38] James Roose-Evans, *Experimental Theatre from Stanislavski to Today* (New York: Universe Books, 1970), p. 138. See also James Schevill, *Break-out! In Search of New Theatrical Environments* (Chicago: Swallow Press, 1973), pp. 21-27.

with the Abbey Theatre suggests how this feeling pervades modern culture.[39] Lee has inherited this tradition of rebellion in American theater against the American theater itself. She shares. an impulse to animate her community, to bring her friends and neighbors to see--as in a mirror--the richness of their lives and traditions, endowments that often lie beneath the conscious surface of their lives or are hidden in shame. She wants people--her indigenous audience, Summers County people--to see the value of what and who they are rather than mimicking the values of the mainstream society. She wants to make a theater meaningful to a people not part of a theater audience. In this respect EcoTheater does not differ from dozens of attempts in our century to make theater a truly democratic art form dedicated not to the sentimental or the quaint but to keeping alive the useful values of the past and to cultivating living values for the present. Lee has written that we Americans need to develop a drama of our own, a drama not handed down from Europe, even if--or especially if--that means a primitive theater in which one may hear unpolished American voices.

Maryat Lee's work with EcoTheater--her place in the unfolding of American theater--is not to be defined, however, as a breaking of conventions. Her effort aims more at re-discovering the roots of theater in the American experience and feeding those roots to bring about the exfoliation of a new theater. Lee would like to see indigenous theater flourish throughout the United States. To that end she plans to turn her attention in the future to teaching others how to do her kind of theater anywhere, particularly in unlikely places. She believes that the necessary skills can be learned by any well-motivated person with some artistic judgment. As with the medieval Mystery plays, some, like those of the Wakefield master, will be better than others. But the creation of drama indigenous to any place is not necessarily a competition. What counts is for the artist to share his or her community with itself and to end the isolation of theater from the American masses.

---

[39] W.B. Yeats, "A People's Theatre, " pp. 327-338 in *The Theory of the Modern Stage: An Introduction to Modern Theatre and Drama*, ed. Eric Bentley (Baltimore: Penguin Books, 1968).

Maryat Lee

Lee reasons further that Appalachia may be the most fertile ground in the United States for the seed of theater to take root. If Appalachia has no tradition of theater, it has a rich tradition of story-telling. This tradition is strong in invention and variety and humor, and it exercises and keeps alive a deep historical consciousness. The past lives in Appalachia and ties people to one another, to their ancestors, and to their land. Traditional beliefs and values are strong. Fittingly, the only drama of any national consequence to emerge from Appalachia so far is historical, costume plays. In a sense, *John Henry* belongs to this tradition. But *John Henry* contributes a new dimension to that tiny tradition, and the play begs the attention of other Appalachian playwrights to the strengthening of the tradition. Appalachia is strong also in the riches of language: Appalachian people are relatively untouched by the abstractness and evasiveness and euphemism that blights much American daily language. The language of the Appalachian story-teller is muscular, close to its experiential source, poetic in its rhythms and images. Strongest of all, perhaps, is the fact that Appalachians in general have a definable communal ethos accompanied by strong religious beliefs. Appalachian people form strong bonds reinforced by a powerful group ethic. This is expressed, for example, in the bond among Hal, Tot, and Upjohn. Hal's secret remorse that he is yielding to the corruption of the city manifests the strong Appalachian sense of sin. Closely allied to this is a sort of Christian stoicism, an acceptance of the harshness of the physical conditions of human life and the suffering that a human must undergo. One might even believe that to an

Jose Colon in a storefront performance of *After the Fashion Show*. West Virginia and Regional History Center.

Appalachian the final reality of life is to suffer and be deprived, to endure, to cherish and assist friends to the point of self-sacrifice and to fight enemies to the death. It is, in short, as close to an heroic ethos as the modern world is likely to come. *John Henry* participates in this ethos.

The richness of Appalachia for the growth of an indigenous drama has been only dimly realized, and we may cherish the EcoTheater work of Maryat Lee as a beginning. Indeed, part of the "meaning" of these plays is the direction they point for others to begin developing a truly "regional" theater: not a steady diet of plays imported from New York, with New York ideas and done by New York talent for New York audiences. These things are fine--for New York. Appalachia--like every other region of the United States--needs its own drama, a drama that expresses it, explores it, shows it to itself, mocks it and makes fun of it, and finally loves it and takes pride in it unsentimentally. Lee's EcoTheater plays do some of these things and that, too, is part of their meaning. She has long wrestled with her own beliefs and values as an artist and worries about the extent to which she should impose them upon her material. EcoTheater cannot really be understood apart from Maryat Lee's humanitarian concern and old-fashioned charity (though she would hasten to deny this). Her use of welfare youngsters for EcoTheater productions, for example, led for several years to excruciating problems. The youngsters at first would resist. An outside observer must keep reminding himself that he may not judge EcoTheater on the grounds used for professional theater or even more conventional "amateur" theater. Lee's theater is a theater of social concern in the truest sense, for actor and audiences alike. Lee will not compromise on this point. Yet she is aware of the danger of imposing her own values and of trying to "do good." She is fond of quoting Emerson that the "results of doing for others can be seen in colossal ugliness over the world." Because her community is so close, intimate and relatively static, she distances her art from it, sometimes in strange ways. The uncanny, eerie atmosphere of *Four Men*, not to mention the "monster," the gentle eccentricities of Miz Dacey; the remoteness in time and the exciting strangeness of the tunnel life of *John Henry* all work to distance her audience from her art. For such distancing, she believes, removes us from our normal outlook and allows for the in-breaking of revelation that is the true and ultimate function of art. In her mind drama and religion are inseparable, the acts of drama being religion's definitive characteristic. The EcoTheater plays therefore seek to rescue in the acts of Appalachian people a few distinctive ones that re-establish for their viewers special meaning and relevance in their lives. Her position is a lonely one: outside both church and theater, she eschews the restrictions of institutional formalities and dogma on the one hand and those of commercialism and (to her) debased values on the other. She must avoid, therefore, on the one hand, a missionary spirit or outright didacticism, and, on the other, the slick, the ostentatious, the easy gag, the overly intellectual, and the avant-garde. An indigenous play must speak for itself, for its source in its audience, and for its own success, its message inherent in its form and structure. People usually do not like to see themselves mirrored: The popular, outdoor epics avoid doing this.

> They always started the summer with hostility toward acting and theater and even toward Maryat Lee herself. Some resisted to the last day; yet some of the angriest yielded the most moving performances.

But a truly indigenous theater like EcoTheater has no choice but to define and face its own limits and yet to range freely and confidently within those limits. If EcoTheater does not draw large audiences in Summers County; if the local people make reluctant actors; if Lee herself is still viewed by some parts of her community as an outsider and a meddler or even as an FBI agent; and if EcoTheater does not receive the sort of community support it deserves, yet it does continue to draw enthusiastic if small audiences (and sometimes enthusiastic and large audiences from other parts of Appalachia).

A few people--especially some of the actors--truly love EcoTheater and are passionate in its defense and in the conviction that it has changed their lives for the better. Support gathers slowly. Who knows at what point a critical mass is achieved and a social change is suddenly initiated and a day comes when someone says, "Now we need a

The Appalachian Plays

theater," or "Let's do a play about that new highway," or whatever. Such a day may never come. But in the meantime these EcoTheater plays set themselves against the nihilism of so much modern art, infused as they are with the social and religious values that provide their very substance and structure. And in these values we find the most important aspect of their meaning.

Maryat leading a breathing exercise, or perhaps demonstrating how to be a tree. *West Virginia and Regional History Center.*

FOUR MEN AND A MONSTER

FOUR MEN AND A MONSTER was first presented at Playhouse in the Park, Cincinnati; directed by Brooks Jones; settings and lighting by Joe Paucity; costumes by Happy Yancey; stage manager, Bob Stevenson; incidental music by Johann Sebastian Bach and Brooks Jones.

CAST

HAL	Dick Latessa
UPJOHN	Ronald Bishop
TOT	Paul Miliken

A second, revised version was produced in 1980, directed by John Gulley and Maryat Lee, settings and costumes by Eileen Cramer; Stage Managers Carolyn Cobb, Katrina Davis; incidental music by Vicki McPherson.

CAST

HAL	Charlie Haywood
UPJOHN	John Gulley/Robert Anderson
TOT	Mike Buckland/Bill Kimmons

STORY OF THE PLAY

A run-down hotel room in a large city is the setting of this drama about Hal, Tot, and Upjohn, three displaced men from the Appalachian hills who have lost their bearings in the city. Their native ethos calls upon them to act as if they were a family. But in the effort to end their impoverished, scavenging existence, they are making last-minute preparations to commit a violent crime. However, from their loose-sewn seams a tough sweetness leaks forth to clash with greed and revolt against the violence. But it is a little late, "and the room becomes a microcosm of the world gripped in spiritual disaster" in the words of the *Kentucky Post*. The Cincinnati *Times-Star* called it "deeply moving." A long short play, performed in double bill or as a whole evening.

The text approximates speech actually used by southern Appalachian people. Actors need not feel that they should attempt to approximate this speech but are encouraged to use their own local speech from childhood. Imitated southern accents, especially with soft instead of hard "r's," are to be avoided. However, actors should feel free to use native Appalachian dialect if they wish. If so, diphthongs in many instances become monophthongs, and in Appalachian speech emphasis often falls on the initial syllable of a word (such as *co*rrupt). Some other dialect usages include *et* for *eat*, *warsh* for *wash*, *mought* for *might*, *twoss* for *twice*, *hail* for *hell*, *wunt* for *wouldn't*, *thu* for *through*, *biness* for *business*, and so on.

FOUR MEN AND A MONSTER

SCENE: A bare hotel room with a couple of frayed chairs, a swaybacked bed, sofa bed, desk, lamp, threadbare carpet, wastebasket. A religious calendar featuring Jesus hangs on rear wall, Stage Right. The door to hallway is Center Rear, and it has a transom.

TIME: Present.

AT RISE: Three men enter from hallway and close door after, giving a cautious look down the hall. They bring a suitcase, an old tool kit, a newspaper, a suit and shirt in the plastic cover of a dry cleaner. Tot looks around and finds a hook to hang it on. These men in faded shirts and patched trousers almost seem to be on the alert, as if they were being hunted. Each of them approaches an imaginary window downstage and looks out and down as from six stories high, draws back at the height from the street below. They make no reference to the window. One of the three, Upjohn, is treated with affection by both men as if he were a child or pet puppy. Tot enjoys showing him various features of the room, bed, wastebasket. Tot examines the calendar, takes a pencil from Upjohn and draws a circle around one day. As Upjohn brings out his bag of "collections" from his pocket, Tot sees something new in Upjohn's bag, a twig with a couple of wilting leaves. He pulls it out and puts it in an empty vase. The rear wall of the room, stage left, is of particular interest to Hal who approaches it stealthily and puts his ear against the wall. He is almost afraid to touch the wall, and whenever he is close to it, speaks with lowered voice, throughout the action of the play. He puts out a cigarette in ashtray on desk.

Hal

Psst.
   (Motions Tot to come listen at the wall. Neither of them can hear anything. Hal goes to door, opens it a crack, glances up and down the hall. Shuts it and then goes to Upjohn, tousles his hair.)
What are you going to say to the woman?
   (Silence.)
What are you going to say?
   (Upjohn smiles.)
What are you going to say to the woman? Come on, Upjohn! We got to practice this here thing. We got to go thu these formalities. Don't you understand, we got to go thu without a hitch. Now, come on, what are you going to say to her?

Upjohn

(With some difficulty.)
That's my biness.

Hal

And it's your biness to tell us.

Upjohn

My biness is my own biness.

Hal

We learned you to say that to other folks. Other folks. Not us.
   (Pause.)
Gimme a cigarette, Tot.
   (He has none.)
Upjohn? Gimme a cigar.
   (He has none.)
Go out and get some, Tot.

(Has no money.)

Neither have I. Upjohn, you got any money?

 (Shakes head.)

 (Hal swears under his breath. Tot picks at carpet. Upjohn screws foot on carpet, looks at it.)

All we been thu: the backroads, the high and mostly low ways, the way we worked our way up thu the hills, inch by inch. Cold, starified nights under every kinda bridge there ever was, 'til we got up here to these hallways, cellars and cells of this here Sodom!

 (Having picked a butt from the ashtray while he talked and lighted it, he now looks at it.)

No. No. We ain't boys. See that butt? That is the last butt I'm gonna smoke. Hear me, Upjohn. Tot. One thing I ain't gonna be if it's the last thing I do--and you know what that is--I don't have to say its name--I don't care what I have to do, is--!

 (He stubs out the butt.)

Now, Tot. Tot! Quit pullin' that carpet to pieces. Now--

 (He opens the door and looks down hall and swears under his breath, then closes door.)

Tot

I don't feel so good.

Hal

You don't feel so good. What about me? What about me, tryin' to get up enough get-up to get all three of us somewhere in this godforsaken evil and corrupt wilderness. Don't you understand nothin'?

 (Goes to Tot, seizes him by the hair,. turns his face up with a snap. Hal raises his fist to strike him and then careens away.)

This ain't the way. This ain't the way. You must want to stay at the bottom of this here barrel. Well, I'm tired scrapin' it. 'Cause pretty soon there won't be no bot tom left to it. And then where would you say we'd be? Mother!

 (Takes out his knife, carves the air.)

Here I am, trying to make something for us, Jesus! Squeeze a little, bitty place for us up there in that rich wickedness. (Tot: Come on, Hal.) And you two don't gimme no help at all.

Tot

Come on, Hal, let's pass time like we used to--when we wasn't waitin' on no man. We're under the bridge. There's the river squirmin' thu the dark. It just turned night. Remember, Upjohn? Come on, Hal, we used to pass time pretty good. Upjohn lit up his little fire. (Upjohn: Yeh.) We just et. Umm, we et pretty good, too, in them days, and then we lay back on the rocks (Both: Yeh) after a hard day's work, cold as a witch's tit.

 (All smile now.)

Hal

That's more like it. Tell it, Tot, tell a good one. Not one of them sad ones, neither.

Maryat Lee

Tot
(Hal and Upjohn punctuate Tot's story quietly as he builds it.)
The day we was gonna eat some pigeon in a pie? The time I went to the hospital? (Upjohn: Yeh.) It wasn't no ordinary pigeon, neither. Caught her with a wire hanger, just like a chicken. Cop seen me do it. So there I was in a high wind down the street, runnin'. Run into a door, glass flyin', between two tall buildings, whooom, right into 'mergency. I had the pie, but where was it? The pigeon? Couldn't find her. I couldn't even find my belt buckle. I couldn't find the little buttons on my shirt. I guess they was buttoned, I don't know. But in a minute I didn't have no time to figure it all out because I was signing up in the big book, printing my name. It said "Print it." And somebody was sayin' you done lost your trousers, as well. As well as what? I said. And looked down and, Law, they was gone, somewhere along the was they just dropped. Oh me, I said, the pigeon is gone, the pie is gone, the belt buckle and the buttons, they're all gone and now my legs is just gone--running off without me. I liked to died.

(He is finished with story, but suddenly tacks a new one on the end of it.)
The woman said, you poor thing. And I said to her, we got to marry this woman, that's why. There's this here girl--a monster, just comin' into some money, and twice as mighty monstrous, and the bridegroom is in worse trouble,

(Smacks Upjohn on the back. Hal tries to interrupt.)
getting pushed into her stable, and she, six-headed, and twelve-busted, twenty-cheeked, five-hundred miles, seven-thousand scales on her hide, and here is this here little voice crying in the wilderness, the voice of the crying bridegroom, Shall all *these* valleys be exalted, and all *these* mountains and hills made low? Shall the crooked be made straight and the rough places plain? Who can measure *these* rivers in the hollow of his hand? Who can put this much of the earth in a sack and weigh these mountains on a scale? Not us, I'm grass, or I'm weed, and they both wither and fade when the breath of the monster bloweth upon it. Even Him, Him that can push the little island s back under the sea would faint and fall in front of this one. Yet, I said to this lady--it is all set up. They got her a vast veil--and us, they got us a pile of money for the trouble to split around four ways. We're gonna be rich. Only I ain't got no legs no more. They has gone running a million, trillion miles away. Doomed, I said

(Hal throws him on bed.)
and downcasted.

Hal
Shut that mouth. Trouble with you is--you don't think, you ooze. How do you think you're going to get ahead if you spill over thataway. When you set up to tell a story, you don't spill out everything. You got to leave the facts out.

Tot
It's the only way to tell a story. I ain't that keen to get ahead.

Hal

That's a crack.

                              Tot

   (Mumbles.)

Can't tell stories any other way. Ain't about to change.

                              Hall

Well--here we was going to nave a nice time passing time and you had to go ruin it.

                              Tot

I didn't ruin it. You never used to complain.

                              Hal

Don't pick on me. Here I am--trying to look out for all our futures. single-handed, And got all these worries--and here you set up to complain I ain't good-natured, and empty-headed like I used to be. And you can't even harp up a little music to relax Upjohn and me. No, you set up and drum up what we're in and rub our noses in it, just rubbin' it all deeper. And we without even cigarettes, dagnab it.

                              Tot

   (Pause.)

Hal?

                              Hal

That carpet don't belong to you!

   (Goes over and snips off the thread Tot is pulling on. Then goes to the door, looks
   out again, and then listens at wall, mumbles, and sits, head in hands.)

                              Tot

   (Aware now of a familiar and dangerous situation.)

Upjohn?

                              Upjohn

Um?

                              Tot

How's things? How's my baby doin'?
 (Goes to Upjohn and examines his hair, his neck, etc., pats him.)

That's pretty good. You missed right here. Listen, Upjohn, where'd Hal go to? You got any idea where he might have went? What you reckon you and me would do without Hal? What's happened to Hal?

   (Egging on a dog.)

Where's Hal? Find him. Where is he? (Etc.) Hey, look at him, Hal!

   (Upjohn looks vacant at first, then joins in the game and pretends to look around for
   Hal. He is liberated while he searches. Looks finally under the wastebasket and,
   pretending to find him, points there delightedly.)

                              Hal

Hey. HEY. What kind-a thing is that? What I go through for freaks. Both of you.

   (Takes tool case from under bed.)

Maryat Lee

Tot

Hal--you know, I think I'm having a hunch. Now, don't look at me that way, Hal.

Hal

I don't want to hear nothing about signs.
>(A deep subdued sound of MOVEMENT from the next room. They are awed.)
>(Whispering.)

Okay. What is it?

Tot

Well, first, it's this way. It's like this. It's in the wrong sign, Hal. It's in the head or arms, and see, on this calendar, it's in the light moon? Why don't we wait till--let's see--
>(Studies moon sign on calendar.)

Hal

Puh, you still believe in all that old stuff?

Tot

Yeah, I believe it. I seen it happen too many times. Listen, Hal, I got dots creeping along my back, goin' straight up into my scalp, drillin' little holes into my brain.

Hal

Hungh. You always holdin' back--everything we ever done.

Tot

But you done always had your way, and we always went blunderin' straight on, didn't we, and mostly land up in the same place we started off, or worse. Don't look at me that way, Hal. This time you better listen to me.

Hal

For an instance?

Tot

Well--firstly: folks change. Look at yourself. You done changed, Hal. Look how you tryin' to better yourself, not content any longer to lick-- (Hal: That's a lie. I never was content.) --lick around the bottom of the heap. Now--we all three might be a little different.
>(Stops.)

We are different, Hal.

Hal

You're about to talk about--jobs--Well?

Tot

Listen to me thu. If--if it's bums you don't want to be, and you got your heart set on it, listen, we wouldn't be bums no more if we just tried harder to find--

Hal

>(Bursts out.)

I told you about using them words.

Tot

Wait, I know, I know about that!

Hal
I don't want to hear no more. That word, both them words make me vomit. We done tried, all over!

Tot
Yet the fact remains.

Hal
What fact?

Tot
In the second, no, third, place, you're a planner.

Hal
Yeah?

Tot
And a planner thinks ahead.
  (Very carefully, to let every word sink in.)
Now, if we three might be different, then IT might be different--can't say the word myself, to tell the truth! But before it's too late, we still got a chance--and we got a right to think twice. Nobody can push you around, can they? Buena ain't gonna push you round, right?

Hal
Tot--what's there to think over? You and me and Upjohn swore on the Bible and the flag. You think we needed to swear? That was just dressin' up the facts. We can't work for nobody. You and me, as well as him. You and me more than him. He can't read--but you and me--

Tot
But we ain't the same, Hal, as we was.

Hal
Yeah? Each of us, every last job we took: s'pord ination, assault, assault, assault, arson, uh-- there was one more. And we ain't the same? Nobody changes that quick, least not for the better. We are the same, you hear me? People don't change, Tot.

Tot
But, Hal. Listen--we never done put nobody out of their misery but dogs and cats--never mind rabbits and coons.

Hal
Don't give me none of this timid talk. We gone thu that. (Tot: But such a big LOT of misery and it's human misery, Hal.) This is the only way left. Don't you want some respect and duties from society? Wouldn't you like to pay taxes someday? No, we got to stand fast, Tot. Got to keep our noses on the grindstone, And we'll make a pile of money. We can't be backing down. And if we stick at it--then we can run our own business.
    (Bursts out.)
All I want is a machine shop--or a little factory or a garage. Look, Tot, this is our only

Maryat Lee

chance--maybe last chance, and you know it. We're gettin' on! Now, grit your teeth. We have got to girdle up our chops, there ain't no two ways about it. Upjohn!

Upjohn

Yeh?

Hal

Gimme some change.
   (Upjohn reaches in one pocket, then another, and hands it over happily.)
That's a nail.
   (Studies him.)
Upjohn, you *have* changed, ain't you? You seem to talk and think more than you used to. What makes you talk so much now?

Tot

Leave off him, Hal. He don't understand that kinda talk.

Hal

   (Whispers.)
The hell he don't.

Tot

Look--he's cleaning his nails.

Hal

What's he going to do next? See--that's what I mean,
   (They watch Upjohn intently.)

Tot

What?

Hal

That boy is getting complicated.

Tot

How do you mean? He's cleaned his nails before, ain't he?

Hal

He did not. He never had none before.

Tot

He did too.

Hal

   (Looks at watch. Beckons to Tot.)
   (Upjohn, seeing their backs turned as they confer, takes a worn book hidden under the bed, turns from them, and begins to study. It is a primer.)
What's that he's got--some kind of book?

Tot

Funny papers, I expect.

Hal

I don't think so. What's that book?

> (Upjohn pulls funny papers folded in the primer and waves it over his shoulder.)

Funny papers.

Upjohn

I don't mean no harm.

Hal

> (Alert.)

Who said you did?

Tot

Quit pickin', Hal. Look at him--do anything you say!

> (Goes over to Upjohn, discovers the primer with shock; almost tells Hal, then tucks it further in Upjohn's pocket. Puzzled, he looks again at Upjohn's neck and ears.)

That's pretty good. But don't forget this spot.

Hal

Oh, God, I wish we'd get this over with. If there's one thing I can't stand--it's waitin', hangin' around. It's bad as somebody sniffin' over your shoulder. Oh, Lord, how long, how long do we limp thu this vale of tears? How long before the great day when the sun goes out and the stars rip across and tear that lid off so we hear the tick of all time, and the dark glass is gone, and we see! Face to face!

> (Looks at Upjohn.)

Face to face... Face--to face! We got to get him ready. What are we waitin' for, as if we didn't have nothin' to do? Come on, Upjohn. Hear that tick way off yonder waitin' on you.

Upjohn

I--I can d-do it.

Hal

Do what?

Tot

Upjohn's getting cold feet too!

Hal

Cold feet? I ain't got cold feet.

Upjohn

Me neither.

Hal

> (Confirmed by this lightning bolt of intelligence, Hal and Tot stare at Upjohn and each other with open eyes. Hal sidles backwards and they huddle. Upjohn takes off some clothes.)

You heard him. You heard, Tot.

Tot

Well, that's just what I been talking about, Hal--how we're different than we was.

Hal

> (To Upjohn.)

Maryat Lee

What the hell are you doin'?

                          Upjohn

    (Takes towel.)
I'm gonna warsh.

                          Hal

You done warshed already.

                          Upjohn

    (Exits.)
Tot says I missed some spots.

                          Tot

    (Watches him down hall.)
You know where to go?
    (Closes door.)

                          Hal

You heard him. Are you some idiot yourself? Those weren't no moron words, Tot. I'm going to see first if that's a funny paper.
    (Goes to Upjohn's thing.)

                          Tot

    (Suddenly.)
No, you ain't. You listen here to me: he's--uh--just risin' up like the sun finally hit a few of them leaves in there. Now, let him have a few tiny leaves without stompin' them out! If you ain't gonna trust him--

                          Hal

Yeh, but where's it all gonna end?

                          Tot

--Then you ain't gonna trust me next. You hear me?

                          Hal

    (Backs down slowly.)
He's getting awful damn smart.

                          Tot

It wouldn't hurt him none.

                          Hal

Yeh? It would be a fine time now for him to get some sense.
    (Sits and sighs.)

                          Tot

Oh--he could go quite a ways and not hurt much.
    (Lapses into quiet fear.)
Hal, what are you thinkin' about?

                          Hal

    (Biting nails.)

What you think I'm thinkin'? What would you want me to be thinkin'?

Tot

Not to do it--forget her and all of it.

Hal

  (Sings.)
I'll neverrr forget herrr. Neverrr in a thousand yearrrrrs.

Tot

I see it now. Us going out every day early in the morning with our fresh shirts on to work.

Hal

NO. I said NO.

Tot

  (Teasing.)
To marry'er yourself?
  (Pause. Serious.)
To marry'er YOURSELF?

Hal

He's makin' me uneasy. We got to have an alternating plan.

Tot

Now wait a minute. Don't look at ME thataway, Hal. We decided how to do it, and that's the way we'll do it if we're goin' to do it. We don't have to do it. But if we *do* it, we already done thresh it out. Upjohn is the only one who can marry. If you married her, then neither Upjohn nor me could pull the trigger. Like I said, you got to trust Upjohn. Maybe he's tryin' harder now he's gonna marry. I said maybe he's tryin' harder.

Hal

  (Studying small ads in newspaper. Reads syllable by syllable.) What about win-dow cleaning and jani-tor-ial? Listen to that! "Present staff--can remain." That's good.

Tot

How much?

Hal

They do...a hundred--thousand--plus.

Tot

How much?

Hal

  (Disappointment.)
Oh. Got to write a box.
  (Glum, he looks further, reading word by word.)
"Cigar and newsstand"--"Carwarsh: sixty-five down." "Good opty for three am-bit-ious men!" How about that?... But this'n's got a phone number. Tot? You can make the call this time?

Tot

Maryat Lee

But I thought you wanted a factory.

Hal

Don't you understand: There ain't no factories for forty thousand, and this one says for three men.

Tot

It does?

Hal

It surely does.

Tot

But it says for sixty-five thousand, don't it?

Hal

> (Lies back.)

They'll come down.

Tot

How you know?

Hal

I know.

Tot

That much?

Hal

We can figure something--like Mr. Snaky Silkpurse.

Tot

We gonna meddle with Buena?

Hal

Meddle? Him and fifty per cent cut! Why, it's a hog's cut for doin' nothin.

Tot

Yes, but I wun't meddle with Buena. We was glad to get our own fifty per cent cut. Maybe he'll put in a little.

Hal

Buena? Umhum. "Put in a little." Knowin' him, he'll be puttin in a little blackmail on us for the rest of his life, if he can. He thinks we're pretty dumb. Tot, he thinks we don't know nothin'--he thinks we're straight down from the hills. Now, if he's gonna blackmail us, we might as well do it to him, to let him know we ain't dummies.

Tot

I wun't do that.

Hal

Hell, Tot, I got him figured out. When I wake up nights, I study him--him and her--how high up they started on the tree, hangin' dribblin' there in the sun, and how hard they fell down to the germy, oozing, blackveined, warted place underneath--as if they had no choice, Tot.

(Outrage)

As if they had no choice! The band of bums. He couldn't have put his own sister nice and clean in a nut house for waywards--could he?--and low mentalities, long ago, could he?--or she'd lose that money. Oh, no, he has got to sell her up the river everyday for ten years 'til she's legal age, and THEN he's got to scrape up some sucker, some freak--that's all he wants, who can say, "I do" so he can do her away and get his rotted hands on the money. Sell his own kin. Ten years, making her earn nickels and dimes, cheatin' the public, the crook. The cheatin' crook! House of hoodlums. Tree of vultures sucking their pieces out of the broken bodies of babies and honey mamas! And now out of the bodies of grown, hungry men. Comm'nist! Rotten, dirty, water-headed comm'nist. He'll get it. Vengeance is MINE and I'll knock him into a spittoon mat yet, it's the word of God I will.

(Upjohn enters in towel, his hair spikey.)

Where you been at all the time? They gonna be here before you done dressed, And he ain't gone over his lines yet.

Tot

He'll do all right.

Hal

(Handing clothes to Upjohn and helping as he dresses. Hal and Tot make a game of dressing Upjohn as bridegroom, making over him and dressing him from head to foot. He repeats here and there some of their words.)

Look at that, Tot, Upjohn, your skin is so white, Turn around, Upjohn--you got that little body nice and clean? Listen, Upjohn, you remember that if you feel bad, you can't show it, You got to make believe, right? Now she scares some folks--but not you. See?' Cause you're brave. She won't hurt you. We got knowledge she won't hurt nothin'. And if you can do all this real good, then just remember you gonna help us all get a real place we can live, and you can take it easy, and you can have a place for your collections.

(Upjohn listens and nods.)

Tot

Sshh, she's waked.

(They all hear some bigger-than-possible heavy MOVEMENTS next door, the BED SPRINGS under stress as someone sits up. They look at Upjohn, pat him, ad-libbing syllables of comfort as he continues to put on his clothes.)

Upjohn

Can't show it. Make believe. Not me. Brave. Collections. Not me.

(They both help him now, making incomprehensible cradle sounds. Finally Upjohn stands off and they admire his aspect and fix his hair.)

INTERMISSION (if needed)

Upjohn

Well--I'm goin' to see the woman.

Maryat Lee

    (He goes to the bed and from under it takes out a box wrapped in newspaper and a bedraggled ribbon.)

Tot

Yeh--maybe Upjohn should go and see her.

Hal

    (Sees box.)
What's that?

Upjohn

That's my biness.

Hal

Your biness, hell. That there is a present.

Upjohn

No, it ain't.

Hal

Then what is it?

Upjohn

    (Has difficulty with the words.)
It's a birthday--gift. It's her birthday, ain't it?
    (Moves to the door.)

Hal

What do you mean, birthday?
    (He and Tot look at each other.)
How do you know it's her birthday? Soon's he learns to write his name he thinks he can do anything. You think you can give presents just because you can write your name.
    (Tears off card.)
"Upjohn, Ohio River" (Or local river.)

Upjohn

(Has put present in Tot's hands to fix the bow and replace card.)
There.
    (Gently takes it and EXITS.)

Hal

Hey! Hey How come? Tot. How come he heists off like that? Who's he think he is? This here card--it's one of them practice papers we made him write on.

Tot

Sshhh.
    (They go to the wall and try to find a place where they can hear into the other room.)

Sshh. Can you hear?

Hal

The door's still open.

Tot

It's still open. Sshh.

Hal

They don't say nothin'!

Tot

He--he ain't moved.

Hal

He's just standin'? He don't know NOTHIN'.

Tot

He's stand in'. He makes her out settin' there, puffed-out and fillin' the corner to the ceiling, and him, a little cardboard silhouette in the doorway. Ssh! He took a step!

Hal

The door's still open.

>(A couple of steps can be heard. Door shuts. Hal and Tot look at each other, mystified. They listen.)

I can't hear nothin'--

Tot

Sshh. Upjohn reaches out his hand--he's scared now.

Hal

What?

Tot

Sshh. She's smiling a little.

Hal

How in sense's name do you know? You can't see nothin'!

Tot

Sshh! I'm goin' in the hall! I can't see nothin' with you talkin'.

 (Tot EXIT.)

Hal

>(Hal rummages in a tool chest and brings out a brace and bit and puts it together and then places it against the wall to bore a hole through it. He puts it against one place, then another, to find the best place and finally begins to turn it. While he screws, he enters another world.)

There. Sshh. Easy now. Ain't gonna hurt.

 (He hears a MOVEMENT from within.)

Oooh. I did? Oooh. Sshh. Sshh.

>(Hal continues drilling very slowly. His eyes close as he bears down. A slight NOISE makes him jump around. No one saw him. Steadying himself, he resumes listening to the wall and then drills an eighth of a turn, then a quarter, then half a turn, and then rhythmic whole turns, deeply engrossed until the bit suddenly goes through with a bump. Shocked, he almost faints. Falls onto the bed. Seconds later he leaps up

for fear the bit will have entered the other room and be detected. Very stealthily he pulls it out and listens and is relieved that no one noticed. Then he remembers what the hole is for: to be looked through. He goes to look but he cannot bring him- self to look. He rummages and finds a piece of newspaper and gently puts it in the hole. The thing sticks out. In haste he takes the wall calendar, with Jesus as Shepherd on it, from another wall and hangs it over the hole. He wasn' t caught! He throws himself on the bed face down and his body rocks. Interrupted again by a NOISE, he jumps, falling off the bed. It is no one. But so vivid was his dread that he begins to yell at the intruder.)

OW! What's the idea sneakin' in like that! OW!

(Rises up, clutching his chest. Glances around and sees that it is not the person he expected.)

So--it's you, comin' in here without knockin', Mister Silky Sow's ear.

(Takes out knife, fiddles with it.)

Do it again, I'll show you what I mean. If it's one thing I can't stand it's waitin' around, and the other thing is bein' spied on by somebody who can sell his own kin down the river without battin' his snake eyes. Listen, wait a minute now, you told me the other day that a leopard don't change his spots, And I ask you how did them spots get there, huh? And you said, you LET her do what she wanted for ten years, LET her, and you said it was a fee country (which is a lie), and how she loved earnin' money thataway 'cause it makes her feel useful. And you said, "In her dull-witted way, and in her ignorant heart she's bent on it." I mean, she raised her little flag and paraded down the middles of the small streets at night with her banner ripplin', and how she blew a tin bugle or a dime flute with a ribbon on it. How she held competitions and contests, and how she always won. Then you tell me she was sent up and how it broke her, how she came back fat, warty, hairy, stinkin' but worst of all, you said how she wasn't mean or angry, and how inside, her spirit weren't broken, at all, yeah, how she had this kinda happy thing in her still. And what could you do with her now, you say, lookin' thataway--pitiful, hairy, mountains of cheese that no one on this here earth ever wants to climb or cross--yet her life's work to be done in spite of her being a monstrosity. And you tell me how you wept? Mister, how you WEPT. And how, if she can't be seen and nobody's eyes could look at the sight, except to make people's bellies sick, what else, you said to me, what else could you do except let her move into the real night, where there ain't no light except from secret sparks sprayin' from her mountain ranges of feelings rubbin' together. And you WEPT, Mister, you wept. I saw you. And yet you gonna turn 'round, rob her, and KILL her.

(Pause.)

ME? Well, wait a minute, that's easy. You CAN'T trap me. 'Cause I never knew her before, that's why I'm adoin' it. I'm adoin' what you'd go and do in any case, right? If I didn't do it--if me, Tot and Upjohn didn't do it somebody would, right? Just like killin' for the army. So don't try to extricate me in none of your smart traps, mister, 'cause afore I'm thu, I ain't

gonna take none of your cracks about us being what you call drifters. I know you didn't say it, but you think it. 'Cause I can just cut out that little tongue of yours like it was nothin' and that's easy. That's no problem to do 'cause I done it!
    (Another sound from the next room.)
What was that? Upjohn? Upjohn is IN there. Yeh, Upjohn is in his suit and done went in already. He's in there. How could I know what he's doin'?
    (Suddenly wily.)
Listen, it so happens that I found a little place where you can peer thu, yeh, I did. You want to see? Here, it's right here.
    (Pushes calendar aside.)
First you pull out that plug. Go ahead. Won't hurt you. Go on. Pull it out.
    (Finally Hal grabs and pulls it out.)
Now you can put your nose into it like I know you want to do. Go ahead. You can see everything for yourself. Go on.
    (He is very excited. Breathing sharply.)
Look. Look into it.
    (Ad-lib softly.)
Go on. Won' t hurt. You won't look? Well? Do you want to put somethin' else in it? Yeah?
    (Draws over a chair next to the wall under the hole.)
There! Go ahead!
    (Tot comes in. Hal goes limp against the wall--sliding down it, attempting to stop the calendar from wagging. Hal crawls to the bed where he lays out, wipes his face.)
What's the idea sneakin' in like that? Scarin' a soul outa his senses? I was just figurin' where we'll be by next week and so on Tot, listen. This kinda waitin' around has worn me down, raw, ragged electric wires. Feelin' I'm about to electrocute myself if not somebody else.
    (He spreads out his hand like splayed wires and shows to Tot.)
See? Nerves. What's the matter, Tot? Somethin' is wrong with you you can't feel where I'm at.
    (Hal covers his head, Then suddenly he seizes Tot by the throat and shoulders and shakes him, back and forth. Tot is limp.)
What is it? Come out of it, Tot.
    (Yells.)
TOT. Hey, Tot! Look at me.
    (Etc Finally he sees Tot's face and touches the tears and looks at his fingers, then back to Tot, who is a loose-limbed doll.)
Tot--look at them wet fingers, It's like comin' outta pen, ain't it, hittin' in the open air and them little hot gems rollin' down the bank--no walls, no bars, no orders, with a few of the prettiest little clouds in God's own wide open sky. Now.
    (Yells.)
What the hell's wrong?

Maryat Lee

Tot
There's a snake in that sky.

Hal
What?

Tot
Outta nowhere there he comes straight across the sky like a rope. Everyone reachin' up, pointin' as if they could touch it, pluck it, like a string. And, Buddy, that snake is a real gentleman! He's got the power to flick his tail, curl it around us, and pluck us outa here. But he's movin' across the sky in a straight, steady streak, ain't stoppin' for nobody. He's goin' al'way'round and give a little tug and yank tight just once and squeeze us all to death. Everybody's weepin' 'cause they know it'll crush 'em sooner or later. No, they ain't cryin'. They know it, but they can't cry.

Hal
What the hell's wrong with you'!

Tot
I told you!

Hal
Shut that mouth.

Tot
You--settin' here waitin' for us to be cut down again, piled up like brush waitin' for a match.

Hal
I'm gonna slam the livin' daylights outa you.
    (Starts fight.)

Tot
We're gettin' burnt! We'll end up worse than we ever did! Worse! This time there won't be no next times.
    (Fight. Hal pins Tot.)

Hal
Freak. You're a freak! That's all you're good for--your long-winded 1ies!
    (Nose to nose.)

Tot
You lie. You *lie*. Not me. (Pause.) You lie to yourself.
    (He gets through to Hal.)

Hal
    (Pause.)

Hal
You think so?

Tot
    (Softly.)

I know so.

                                Hal
Tot? I got to try to tell you something.
    (Pause.)
I can't do it.

                                Tot
    (Misunderstands.)
You can't do it?
    (Hushed.)
You mean you ain't goin' through with it?

                                Hal
    (Immediately toughens, pushes Tot away, then begins to push him around.)
    (Tot hollers.)
Yeh. I know you. You want to change me, too. You want to back out. You want to back down. You want to turn tail. You want to pull us all back. You want to keep us down. Well--you done held me up enough. I'm sick of you and your holdin' me back. I'm where I'm at on account of you, and that's nowhere. NOWHERE, you hear me?

                                Tot
Hal. Listen! Listen to me: them two!

                                Hal
    (Stops.)
Yeh?--Them two?

                                Tot
Them two!

                                Hal
    (Yells.)
Them two! Them two! What about them two!

                                Tot
Them two are cuddlin'. Them two are cheek to jowl.

                                Hal
    (Snatches Tot's hair.)
Are what?

                                Tot
Let go! Them two are cheek to jowl. Upjohn was kneelin' here, see? and he puts his hands out just a little bit, (He does it.) open like that and there they stayed. She didn't move. Neither did he and there they stayed. Finally Upjohn looks down, maybe his head dropped, I can't see his face. And you can't look at her nohow, but there she is, tucked into every corner of the room, every nook and cranny filled with her, and she lookin' at this little tiny Tom Thumb waitin' there. So when he looks down, a tree limb reaches out slow, and his hands are--still there, open, like he wasn't scared. Well, this ugly, twisted, hairy

limb quivers and shakes and twists in the air for awhile and then comes swoopin' down! But instead of grabbin' Upjohn, it--I don't know how--it don't do nothin but put itself down in front of Upjohn's hands like that.
> (He does it near Hal's hand.)

And then after a minute he, Upjohn, reaches out slow and takes one of them little, crooked, scaly twigs, and crooks his little finger around it.
> (Hal winces. Tot sucks in his breath. They pull their fingers away at the same instant. Silence. They look at each other.)

Hal
> (Glum.)

Well--what are we gonna do?
> (Tot's eyes close.)
>
> (Hal misunderstanding, yanks him.)

You kiddin' me? You made this up so I'll quit. 'Cause that's what you want me to do. Quit?
> (Finally Tot nods.)

So you tell me these lies?
> (Tot shakes his head.)

Answer me.
> (Tot breaks loose.)

Tot

I can prove it. I walked in.

Hal

You walked in that room?

Tot

I walked in that room.

Hal

They didn't know?

Tot

By that time he was over there, rockin' her, a little piece of her rockin' back and forth with her like, well, it was like a little doll was rockin' who it belonged to. Then Upjohn keep rockin' and saw me, And puts his finger up over his mouth and says Sssshh. Then I whisper! What are you doin', rockin' her? You can't rock her.

Hal

Touchin'. They was touchin'. Them two, touchin'?

Tot
> (Slightly exhilarated.)

Hal, there they were. So ugly, both. When I told Upjohn he couldn't rock her, you know what he said? He said to me, he says--you know him, Hal, how he never had no one, and how we saved his skinny life when he was gettin' filled with water and heavy as stone and drowned up and down, and how we pulled him, this little dead rat out of the river, and brought him into this here life, pumped him out for hours, and how he had no brain left when he woke, like it got drowned without him, but not so's he ever hurt anybody, and how we took him over and raise him up, savin' the government a lot of money, and how he was ours and we was his and how he do anything for us, anything we said? Well, he says, "Go 'way, Tot," and he never said that in his whole life! He said, "Go'way, Tot."

Hal
(Stunned momentarily.)

Tot
(Curt.)
Them men are comin' in less than one hour. You and me got to get ourselves together, get on our suits and be ready in less than one hour.

Tot
Hal, them men are comin' in less than one hour. We can get ourselves together and get out of here.

Hal
And when they come, Buena will have the official, the papers, and we all go in there and have the ceremony. *And I will wed her*, you understand?

Tot
Huh!

Hal
I'm gonna do it. You hear me? I'm gonna do it. Upjohn loves her. He LOVES--(Bang.) He loves her. Upjohn is in love. Don't you understand nothin'? Upjohn is going to double-cross us.

Tot
Not if we get away.

Hal
And lose everything? Our hopes for ever being respectable? We ain't young, Tot. We ain't hippies.

Tot
That ain't why! That ain't why you changed your mind.
    (Tot sits in dismay while Hal continues to disrobe and begins to dress. Now and then Tot glances at calendar.)
There was a piece of cheese. In a piece of cloth. The first cheese.
    (Pause.)
Moldy. Hairy. Rotted, and green. Smelled. Had bumps. Smelled rotted all the way thu.
    (Pause.)
Now, who was it--who was it that peeled it off, rubbed off the bumps and scraped off the rot with his fingernail and cut into it and BIT into it? Must have been awful hungry.
    (Pause.)
Then, after a short, very short, while, others got to wanting it, too. You got me? *Others got to*

Maryat Lee

wanting it, too. I know you, Hal--hey, listen to me.

    (Pause, notices calendar.)

Shoot. Listen, one day everybody in the world is gonna stop and rub each other's faces and scrape, and the faces are going to slide off them nasty old faces and even most of them pretty, young, slick faces and underneath--Hal?

Hal

    (Hal strips off shirt, puts on new one.)

What.

Tot

Why's the calendar changed sides? Lookit. There was nothin' on this wall when I went out.

Hal

You forgot what way you done looked.

Tot

I did?

Hal

I'm tellin' you to get your clothes off and get ready. Next shave you get may be in another country. Think about that.

    (Tot takes down calendar and he reads small print of scripture half-aloud as he looks
    for and finds a nail on another wall and hangs it. He doesn't see the hole.)

Hal

You put every scrap in that black suitcase. Don't leave nothin'. Love of Pete! Don't know where he thinks anybody's gonna see it.

    (Tot catches sight of the hole. His eyes return to it several times. He looks at the
    calendar and back to the hole. Hal continues to change.)

Can't say I'm sad to leave this place. It's been one hell all our lives having to fight and scrap to get somewhere and gettin' pushed down, pinned down, put down and puked on. It ain't right for any human to start out at a point where scratch is way up there, and it's about all you can ever hope to get to. Other folks start at scratch. Why can't we all start at scratch? Why do we have to rob, lie, and now kill our ways to it?

Tot

What's that?

Hal

Seems to me if we wasn't left so low there wouldn't be so many bad things goin' on. It's a hole. Can't you see it's a hole! You figured which shoes is mine? Tot! Get changed.

Tot

That's funny I didn't see that calendar over there before. And I didn't see no hole, neither. Here.

    (Hands shoes.)

Hal, I got to have the bigger ones, 'cause I'm gonna have to move quicker.

Tot

It's funny you never mentioned that hole--seein' as how it wasn't there before. Especially since it's on the same wall as the woman's.
    (Exchanging shoes.)

                          Hal

It was already there.

                          Tot

Uh-hum. Listen--I bet you could see thu that hole, right into her room. Couldn't you, Hal?

                          Hal

You better shave.

                          Tot

    (Goes closer.)
Looks like that hole was fresh made.
    (Is about to look through it.)

                          Hal

Wait.

                          Tot

Yeh?

                          Hal

Tot?
    (A different Hal.)
What if I told you I made that hole?

                          Tot

You did!

                          Hal

Yeh, I did.

                          Tot

You made the hole?

                          Hal

I made it. It's my hole,

                          Tot

In the hotel wall?

                          Hal

Yeh.

                          Tot

Then you did look.

                          Hal

No, I didn't look.

                          Tot

You couldn't bore all the way thu?

                          Hal

Maryat Lee

I bored all the way thu.

        Tot

Then you was about to look?

        Hal

> (Pause.)

No.

        Tot

Well, then--if you didn't look, what then DID you do with that hole?

        Hal

> (Shouts.)

Nothin'

> (Silence.)

        Tot

Then you still have somethin left to do to the hole.
> (Softly.)

Hal? You want me to look?

        Hal

No.

        Tot

Why?

        Hal

I can't tell you, Tot.
> (Hal gets the calendar and hangs it over the hole..)

        Tot

You told me I didn't know where that calendar was when I said it didn't start there.

        Hal

I know.

        Tot

When I come in the door and you was there by the calendar, what in Sam Hill were you doin', Hal?

        Hal

I was figurin' out the days. I told you.

        Tot

> (Soft.)

So.
> (They stare. The rift is growing. Hal gets pistol and unwraps it. Tot is matter of fact.)

I was always honest. Loyal. Always thought you'd come clean with me someday, if I stuck by you. But it's just lies, little ones, and big, both, and me always tryin' to believe it each time.
> (Gets closer.)

You weren't figurin' out the days, you was wantin' to take a look and see the *truth* in there, and you couldn't, you never could look at it, even now, through a peephole. Dag!

Hal

(Continues preparing.)

Get dressed, Tot.

Tot

Uh, uh--Hal?

(Whispers.)

Hal, there ain't no *law* say, I gotta do what you say.

(Tot picks up his bag, starts to leave. Hal makes no response. Continues packing. Tot at door has nowhere to go. Drops bag. Now Hal puts pistol in Tot's hand. Then Hal motions to the hole.)

Hal

All you got to do is pull it. Easy. And you'll have a shiny new life. Now, get your things on. It's time.

Tot

Sure is.

Hal

He'll do what I say. Don't worry. I got a plan!

Tot

(Shaking his head.)

I don't--um. I know--

(Looks at Jesus on calendar.)

I can't do it, won't do it.

Hal

(Rage again.)

What's got into you?

Tot

I won't.

(Turns to Hal.)

It's something for you to think about. You and him--Buena.

(Waits until he has Hal's attention.)

Listen, Hal, if I back out you'll have to kill me, too, if you go through with it. So I wouldn't talk.

Hal

You

(Interrupting him.)

Tot

In fact, if you and him get the money, you might kill me later anyway. If I *did* go along. And you'd *have* to kill Upjohn. And--there's no question, one of you'd kill the-other, over

the money. So--it's me, Upjohn, her--and probably one of you. Four killings. Four. Hal? And the survivor for sure'd be caught, and be up for life.
> (Delicately.)

Or even--death.
> (Tot hands the gun back go Hal. They are quiet.)

Tot

All my life I dreamt of seein' someone look at me, like her and Upjohn was looking at each other. Seeing through every ugly thing, seeing 'round the warts and moles, seeing through to what is 'way inside. And good. And now I seen it.
> (Hal is frozen in concentration on Tot, who has never crossed him before, then turns away in deep thought. Takes out his knife absently.)
> (Enter Upjohn)

Tot

Hal. Here's Upjohn.
> (After a moment Hal turns to Upjohn. The three look at each other. Hal is suddenly gentle, human.)

Hal

Upjohn--come here.
> (Upjohn hesitates and then goes and stands in front of Hal, and Hal looks him over and feels something in his pocket and pulls out the primer.)

There! Look at that. What's that, Upjohn, a book? See, Tot! It was a book. He's learnin' to read.
> (Terrible rage beginning,)

Tot

> (Quietly.)

He's got a right.

Hal

Why! Why's he learnin' to read! Tell me why and I'll tell you if he's got a right. Answer me that. You want to know why?
> (Shouts.)

So he can keep her. That's what I been tellin' you.
> (Hal goes to door to leave.)

Tot

Hal. Where you going?

Hal

Remember what I said? Remember? I'm gonna do it. Upjohn, look here, we done have a change in plan, whereas you got to stick with Tot here, and I marry her. That's right. We can go into the whys and wherefores later. Yes sir, I know, it don't suit you--but we got technical reasons beyond controls. Now, you set easy here,
> (Hal starts again to leave.)

Upjohn

(Slowly.)

Now--wait just a minute, Hal. You know you didn't want that fat girl before.

Hal

Ah. That's just the point, Upjohn. I'll explain that later.

Upjohn

(Holding him back.)

But you want her now. Not just because the money.

Hal

Upjohn--I declare you have gotten out of your class.

Upjohn

(Sweet.)

I never had no class noways. And I found somebody who's the same.

Hal

That woman in there? Upjohn, do you know anybody in the world can have her for money? Maybe not even money. A touch here, a tickle there, a slap yonder. Seventy-five cent, fifty, twenty-five cents or even nothin'.

Upjohn

That ain't much.

Hal

That's the point, you moron.

Upjohn

(As if slapped.)

I-I-I don't care what you s--say. She sh-sh-she n-never met anyone as g-good, as sw-sweet as m-m-me.

Hal

Or as dumb.

Upjohn

(With terrific effort.)

And, and I'm g-goin' to ma-ma-ma-marry her.

Hal

You ain't. You understand? You ain't.

Upjohn

Hal? Did you say d-d-dumb?

(Upjohn goes to Hal. Hal puts up his knife.)

Tot

Hal! Put that knife away.

(Upjohn puts his fist around the full open blade. He and Hal are staring at each other.)

Hal

Maryat Lee

Let go the knife, Upjohn, let go. Who's boss? Who saved you and your little life? Who's looked out for You. Who?

    (Hal twists knife a little.)

Upjohn

Don't hurt me, Hal. Don't wiggle it.

Hal

Then let go.

Upjohn

No!

Hal

    (Outraged.)

Why not?

    (Twists knife a little more.)
    (Upjohn sucks his breath.)

And why are you so damned high and mighty smart and brave like you never was in your whole life, nor your mama's and papa's whole lives put together? You ain't got no right neither to speak--when you ain't never said a dozen words altogether in a month of Sundays in your life. You ain't got no right.

Upjohn

I'm agonna marry.

Hal

Let go, Upjohn, by the time I count three. ONE.

    (Tot steps away, murmurs the cheese story in counterpoint as they struggle.)

One--you ain't gonna marry her. A big, ugly, dumb moron! TWO.

Upjohn

Sh-she don't w-want y-y-y-you.

Hal

TWO. I'm gonna marry her.

Upjohn

N-no you ain't, Hal.

Hal

    (Hal pulls out knife and pushes Upjohn to get to the door, but Upjohn hangs onto him, in spite of his bleeding hand.)

I'm goin' in there, Upjohn; let go and I won't hurt you. Get outa the way, Upjohn!

    (Lifts knife to threaten him.).

Tot

    (Finishes story, jumps in.)

No. No, Hal. Don't!

    (Tot throws himself at the two; Hal gets panicked and wild and knife slips and goes into Tot.)

                                  Tot

AIIIIWWOOCH, oh, oh, Hal, you done it.
    (Tot backs off.)
                                  Hal

Oh, my God Jesus.
                                  Tot

    (Doubled with pain.)
 AH, uh. 'Scuse me.
      (Hal gets hold of him.)
                                  Hal

Tot! Tot.
    (Upjohn runs around with towel from basin for Tot. Upjohn mops Tot's brow. Hal
    emits a low tone behind closed lips as he tries to make Tot comfortable.)
                                  Tot

Un--do--
    (Upjohn muttering: Oh my, oh, my, oh my, oh my.)
Give me breath. Don't leave. Upjohn? Upjohn?
                                  Upjohn

Yeh, Tot?
                                  Tot

Hurt. I'm hurt. Hurt?
                                  Hal

    (Yells.)
I know, Tot. I done it.
                                  Tot

Listen--Upjohn? Listen, I'm dying.
                                  Hal

NO. No, you ain't.
                                  Tot

Undo my belt.
    (Hal undoes it. Tot grunts.)
Listen.
    (He breathes deeply.)
That feels better. That belt--squeezin' me to death.
    (In the following "trio" the lines of the characters flow in their own continuity, and
    then also fit in with one another. The main voice is Tot's, with the other voices
    providing an almost harmonic and rhythmic structure. The exact sequence of lines
    will depend on the actors' own rhythms after they have memorized and are able to
    speak the lines at the same time listening and feeling with the other lines--and, of
    course, at the director's discretion. Some will be successive, some simultaneous,

Maryat Lee

some intoned, and some spoken, etc.)

<u>Hal</u>	<u>Tot</u>	<u>Upjohn</u>
	Upjohn?	
Yeah, Tot.	Hal?	I'm here.
	Here we are.	Yeh, I'm here.
Yeah, Tot.		
	Cut down	
Oh no.		Cut
	The tree cut down.	
No!		Cut
	Ah, Hal, you was always	
	so quick.	
No! Now I lay me--	Down	I lay down my arms
	An old, straggly pine	
	tree, cut	
Down		Lay me down
	Sawed up	

Now I lay me down		
	Into firewood.	Lay me down.
Now I lay me		
	Hal?--Upjohn?	
Down.		Umhunnmn.
	Listen--	
I lay down my arms.		
	What for?	What for?
My arms.		
	What for?	
My hands		What for?
	Waitin' to get lit by a	
	little match	
I lay down my soul.		
	And burn into the night.	
		Into the night.
	Into the night.	
		Into the night.
	Into the night.	
		I'm sayin' it.

Maryat Lee

                      Into the night.

Don't take Tot.

                      Say

Don't take Tot.   Into the night.

                      Say!
                      What's that I see?

                      A little green leaf is

                      Apeekin' and pushin'

                      out of your bark.

                      What's the matter with
                      You!

Don't take Tot.   Don't take him.

                      You think you're gonna   Into the night.

                      Be a tree or something?

Oh no.   You ain't even got no

                      roots.

                                                    No roots.

                      To mention nothin'--
                      else.

Please.   Please.

	Then this here log with a	
	green leaf pushin' thu	
Green leaf		Green leaf
	This here green log	
		That log
	Gets full of guilt	
Guilt	Full of guilt, and it shuts	
	up its knotholes	
Holes, guilty holes.		
	It shuts up its knotholes	
	Tight. And it says	Says
	It says	It says
	It says, I can't help it, it	
	says	
		Me neither.
		I can't help it.
Me neither.		
	It says, I done tried	
	My best,	Tried his best
He tried his best		

Maryat Lee

                          (Breathing hard)

He tried his best.   We tried,

We tried our best.   We tried.

                          I done the best I could
                          But the last bit of life
                          Apokin' up outa me left

                          From when I got cut

                          down

Cut   Cut

                          I--Upjohn, Hal! I can't
                          keep it back.
                          (He dies.)

                                                                  I'm here.
                                                                  I'm here.
                                                                  I'm here, Tot.

Now I lay me

Down.

Now I lay me

Down.

Now I lay down
My arms.

                                                                 Cut.

Now I lay me down.

The Appalachian Plays

                                Sawed up.

Now I lay down
My soul.

                                Into the night.

Don't take Tot.   Into the night.

                                Into the night.

Don't take Tot.
One green leaf.

                                A green leaf.

Guilt.

                                Into the
                                Night tried

Holes. My best,   That log.

                                That log.

Guilty holes,
Lord

                                        Shut.

He tried
his

Best.   He tried so hard.
                                He tried his
                                Best

                                He tried so hard.

77

Maryat Lee

He's dead, Upjohn.　　　　　　　　　　　　　He tried his
　　　　　　　　　　　　　　　　　　　　　　Best.

He's dead.

(Hal and Upjohn put Tot's hands together. Upjohn pulls out his primer and puts it in Tot's hands, then the little wilted twig from the vase. He quietly EXITS. Hal watches but does not move. Unable now to look at Tot, Hal nearly follows Upjohn, stops, goes to the calendar and removes it and puts it on original nail, and tries to look once more, and this time slowly he looks. After appraising the scene in the next room, he gets the pistol, puts it to the hole, squints as he is about to shoot. He looks around at Tot, and the hole and wall are forgotten. The pistol drops. He moves now toward Tot, kneels. He tries, but cannot bring himself to touch Tot. His anguish grows until finally with almost superhuman effort he breaks through and seizes Tot, nestling his head and shoulders close. Hal begins to rock him, mouthing or crying aloud:)

　　　　　　　　　　　　　　　　　Hal

Don't take Tot.
　　(Repeats over and over.)
　　(Musical phrase begins with the rocking.)
　　(Hal freezes at the End.)
　　(Woodblock.)
　　　　　　　　　　　　　　　　　END

PROPERTY LIST
Single bed and sofa bed
2 bedspreads and pillows
2 ashtrays with butts
Tool chest with brace and bit and carpenter pencil
Newspaper with "funny papers" and want ads
Wilted twig
Primer book
Box wrapped in newspaper and ribbon
Lined paper signed "Upjohn Ohio River" or local river, attached
Calendar with religious picture
Armchair
Standing lamp
Suitcase (big cardboard type)

Carnation
Dull knife in pocket
Gun wrapped in National Esquire
Underwear (new) and three ties
Envelope of plane tickets
Box of blank shells
Shopping bag with 3 pairs of new cheap shoes tied in pairs
Roll of toilet paper
Shaving cream and razor
Cuff links
Towel, washcloth
Chair to stick knife into
Wastebasket
Wooden folding chair

Personal:
Hal: Suit, shirt on hanger
Upjohn: Suit, shirt, cigar box with collection (nail, buttons, chip, towel). Blood.
Tot: Suit, shirt, Army blanket. Blood.

Maryat Lee

Author's Note on *Four Men and a Monster*
Maryat Lee

Courtesy Dayton Daily News.

This play was written while I was still living in New York, and in response to producer Neil McKenzie who needed a play for four male actors. The first half of it was written that very week. It is the only play I've written in New York that reflected the place I came from--Kentucky. When I first lived in New York, I suffered the same things as these three men--the ordeals of making a phone call or asking directions, or adjusting to the frantic rhythm of the city, or not seeing anything resembling a tree from the window. All these things in the city caused great unease in me. The three characters in the play came pouring out of me as if they had been waiting there in the wings a long time.

The original play was to have four men, the three from the mountains and the decadent Buena they meet in the city. Brooks Jones, who directed the play first in Cincinnati, expressed his doubts about this character's appearance. Was his appearance really necessary? (Besides, Jones had only three actors available.) On reworking, I was very glad for this suggestion; the play improved when Buena was left out. Only in Hal's memory does Buena taunt and madden him. Hal's obsession propels the other two, essentially men with morals, to commit the one crime of their lives. The original title, however, seemed right, and so it stuck.

I have a vivid recollection of cringing each time the actors spoke during the first production of *Four Men and a Monster*, my play about uprooted mountain men trying to make good in a city. Performed by professional actors at the Playhouse in the Park, Cincinnati, and sensitively directed, the performance was a torture to me. Between rehearsals the actors demonstrated that they could speak Cockney and distinguish whether it originated on the east or south side of London; but they had not the slightest glimmer that southern American speech has even more important variations, not to mention that it is worlds removed from southern mountain speech at all. The actors indulged themselves in heavy-mouthed diphthongs, even though there are few of them in mountain speech; they softened their "r's" where in the mountains the "r's" are hard. They had no feeling for the dryness about emotional matters in mountain speech that intensifies emotion. And the story-telling of rot made no sense whatever to them. Tot has quite complex, even Baroque, sentences, and it takes a certain ear used to the cadences of old-time sermons, political speeches, and Shakespeare, to keep the speech thrusting onwards, dropping clean parenthetical phrases without making periods. I told them patiently, and they looked at me blankly and continued smugly to do what to them was the right thing. On observing this production I concluded that either the play was really bad or that someday I'd like to see it done by real mountain people, or at least by amateurs with their own local pronunciations, or with no special pronunciation at all. The play can be done powerfully as people talk locally anywhere. I also concluded that I would not seek a professional production again.

Years later, in 1979, we had a large company at EcoTheater, and one of my neighbors, Charles Haywood, had done so spectacularly in a small part in *John Henry* that I was itching to see him tackle something really challenging.[40] While *Four Men* had not been

---

[40] In the local paper *The Hinton News*, in "Thoughts of an EcoTheater Performer," Haywood deftly illustrated one of Maryat's principles about reality on the stage, writing: "My feelings about the character Hal are mixed and contradictory. The part calls for much hostility, which I have somewhat suppressed since my

written here on the spot as the other EcoTheater plays were, the play was about certain men who might leave home--Kentucky or West Virginia or rural anywhere--to go to the city. Such departures were an event that many low-income families had experienced. So we announced we would do this play along with John Henry. We had a choice of three other men in the company for the male roles. One was an intern who had many years of community theater experience. Before he was hired, we had a long conference about the problems that trained theater people would have with EcoTheater. Several people warned him that he would go through an ordeal and have to give up a lot of habits and cherished notions about theater. He was eager, however, to get "cleaned out" of a lot of phoniness, and he was brimming with enthusiasm. Another Intern, John Gulley, who was to be an assistant director, was a theater major at a southern university. A third Intern, a young man from thirty miles away, was a theater buff, unusual for West Virginia.

> "His mind got drowned without him."

So we decided on Charles Haywood, who lived across the road in my hollow and who had never been exposed to the theater, to be Hal, the leading role. The actor from community theater and the theater buff took the supporting roles. Only Haywood lasted the entire season. The community-theater actor was so programmed that we could not cut away the intonations and role-playing and find a core in so short a time. He was replaced a week before opening by one of the original EcoTheater members from this hollow, Mike Buckland. Mike was young for the role, but his accent and understanding were right. The theater buff also did not last, but on his own initiative left halfway through the summer. It was not his cup of tea. However, John Gulley, the assistant director, was so open to this approach to theater, and so sensitive, that little by little I let him take over the directing.

In the play two of the characters have pulled the third one, nearly drowned, out of

---

tour in the Marine Corps. It is a little scary to bring forth these feelings because there's always that chance that some of the 'acting' will be incorporated into my real behavior...One never wants to acknowledge the baser feelings of one's nature, but when one acts it can not be denied." July 1, 1980 at 5.

the river and saved him. One morning, from my window in the house I saw the four actors down at the creek, hovering over Robert Anderson, who was in the creek, with the other two pulling him out, wiping him off, and presently heaving him up and heavily trudging back to the barn. This was the beginning of a lot of exercises that would normally be difficult for men--treating Upjohn, the mentally challenged, like a child or pet dog, touching him simply and absently. The feeling of family among them--without any inference of sexuality--has to be very strong for the play to hang together. On one occasion we blindfolded Upjohn to help him realize his dependence on the others and their instinctive protectiveness of him.

It was during a rehearsal that the new ending came to me, while John was directing. I wondered how it had taken me so long to find it. The original ending, in the 1969 Samuel French edition, has Hal shooting through the hole:

> He's dead. Hal and Upjohn put Tot's hands together and put a spread over him. Each man hums a low tone. After putting Tot together properly, they squat and look at one another. Upjohn pulls out his primer and pulls down the spread and puts it in Tot's hands, and then he quietly exits. Hal watches but does not move. The next DOOR opens and shuts. Hal nearly follows Upjohn, then goes to the calendar and removes it and puts it on the original wall and tries to look in there once more and then he looks for the pistol and goes to the hole and now slowly looks. After appraising the scene in the next room he puts the pistol to the hole and fires. At first there is no sound. But then the ROOM seems to move, tremble, the WALLS shake, DUST flies, LIGHTS flicker, with deep thunderous NOISE. MUSIC starts [Suggest second movement of Bach's Second Brandenburg Concerto.] He fires again. The MOVEMENT ceases. LIGHTS come on, but then dim. Hal goes to the bed and lies down in tremendous final exhaustion.)
>
> CURTAIN

Maryat Lee

JOHN HENRY

Introduction
Dr. William French

Laying down the track for *John Henry*. *West Virginia and Regional History Center*.

John Henry is based on folk legends about a Black steel driver alleged to have died following a contest with a steam drill. The Black man was pitted against the machine during construction of the Great Bend tunnel on the Chesapeake and Ohio Railroad mainline between 1870 and 1872. This tunnel is located in the rugged Allegheny mountains of Summers County, West Virginia, about nine miles east of Hinton and one mile west of Talcott.

Before the introduction of the railroad, this country was virtually inaccessible and

The Appalachian Plays

The backdrop for the Big Bend tunnel, site of John Henry's fatal triumph over the steam drill, was a scrim strung up on a flatbed truck so the play could presented anywhere a few people could gather. *West Virginia and Regional History Center.*

only sparsely settled. Charles Nordhoff, commissioned by the railroad to report to New York City newspapers on construction progress, called the region a "howling wilderness"

(*New York Weekly Tribune*, Nov. 1, 1871), probably an accurate phrase.

About half a mile west of Talcott, the Greenbrier River, which the rail tracks follow through the mountains, bends sharply south into a great ten-mile curve and returns to a point little more than a mile from its original turn at Talcott. "Big Bend," as it is locally known, therefore both describes the river's course as well as names the mountain that diverts this course. The tunnel through Big Bend Mountain spares over ten miles of railroad track.

Construction of the tunnel was extremely hazardous work, and to this day no one knows how many men died underground of suffocation, lung disease, roof falls, explosions, and other accidents. This high incidence of mortality is apparent in a popular work chant about the building of Big Bend Tunnel (found in Louis Chappell's book on John Henry at 34):

Killa mule, buy another;

Kill a nig---, hire another.

Construction workers lived at Talcott, a crowded camp near the tunnel where frontier conditions prevailed. The 1,000 or so laborers were predominantly black, most not more than five years out of slavery. Drunkenness, murder, brawling characterized this rugged life. The camp attracted all manner of itinerant people: prostitutes, gamblers, peddlers, fortune-tellers, musicians, and "at least one pagan beauty" (Chappell, p. 8)--Lee works them all into *John Henry*. Understandably, tension existed between tunnel people and the few farmers scattered thereabouts who saw themselves as the original settlers and rightful inheritors and saw the tunnel people as gypsies.

Most tunnel labor was manual. Steel drivers like John Henry used a nine- or ten-pound hammer on a leather handle to strike steel bits (called "steel") held by "turners" or "shakers" between their knees. The shaker would turn and angle the bit between strikes to make the cutting edge effective. The "steel" was hammered into shale rock, making a deep hole for an explosive charge. Once exposed to air, the hard, red shale was prone to crumbling, and roof falls often occurred.

Inside the tunnel shaft heat was intense, smoke thick and poisonous, and light from lamps burning tallow or blackstrap very dim. The men worked almost naked. Pete Sanders, whose uncle worked there, said that the "Big Bend Tunnel was a terrible-like place, and many men got killed there. Mules, too.

The "Great Bend" tunnel, twin to the Big Bend, under construction. Both were well over a mile long and the brittle shale in the mountain made for frequent rock falls. "Hard as iron. 'Course when it hits the air, it gets soft, crumbly-like, and she'll drop on ya." *Library of Congress*.

And they throwed the dead men and mules and all together there in the fill between the mountains." (Chappell, p. 33).

This dangerous work was accompanied by work songs or chants the men used to establish a rhythm for hammering. Black people's labor in this period--cotton picking, steel driving, rail laying, digging--almost always was accompanied by work songs. The rhythmic fluidity and adaptability of the tempos of the songs eased the tiresome labor. Singing made driving steel safer; men were encouraged to sing as they worked so that the steel driver's blows would be rhythmical and regular. A strike even slightly.1ut of time obviously was shattering--if not fatal--to the shaker. It is said that the accompaniment of the "weird and monotonous chant (sometimes pitched in a minor key) to the sound of clinking steel made an unforgettable impression." (Chappell, p. 80).

Steam drills--later supplanted by pneumatic machines--were just coming into widespread use during the 1870s, being more efficient under certain circumstances than hand labor. Conditions for a challenge of man vs. machine were set.

Whether the contest celebrated in song and legend and dramatized by Maryat Lee actually took place, we may never know. Such literal truth matters little. John Henry's story carries its own "truth" that transcend facts and is more important than facts. The "truth" of fiction, poetry, and drama conveys and reveals the human spirit acting in a particular time and place. In this play Maryat Lee has attempted to recreate the sights and sounds--the "feel"--of a hard, physical way of life that, except in rare instances, has passed forever from the earth, but that endures whenever we work together to achieve some special goal against heavy odds.

It is no wonder that the name of John Henry is to this day honored by working people everywhere--not only among Blacks--as a model of strength and courage and endurance. He performs a heroic feat; he triumphs over technology. Yet as a "natural man" he does so without presumption; he "ain't nothin' but a man," and his modesty is perhaps his most endearing quality.[41]

---

[41] Readers interested in pursuing the subject should consult the following: Edward Cabbell, *Like a Weaving: References and Resources on Black Appalachians*, (Boone, North Carolina Appalachian Consortium, 1983); Louis Chappell, *John Henry: A Folklore Study* (Jena, Germany: Fromannsche Verlag, 1933); Guy B. Johnson, *John Henry: Tracking Down a Negro Legend* (Chapel Hill: University of North Carolina Press, 1929); Ezra

One of the fight scenes in *John Henry*, rendered in slow motion. *Courtesy West Virginia and Regional History Center.*

Keats, *John Henry: An American Legend*. New Yok: Pantheon, 1965; and John R. Kellens, *A Man Ain't Nothin' But a Man*. Boston: (Little Brown, 1965).

JOHN HENRY

Scenes

> Prologue - Impressionistic far off future time.
> Scene 1 - 1920's - near Big Bend Tunnel, Talcott, W.Va., laying the tracks for the second tunnel.
> Scene 2 - 1871. On the way to the tunnel
> Scenes 3 - 13 - 1871-72. The Big Bend Tunnel
> Epilogue - Same as prologue

MUSIC

The first scene can be very simple percussive sounds, using bottles, bells, sticks, any objects that have primeval sound. Classical music may be used subtly as indicated, but is not necessary.

The John Henry song has any number of variations, most of them equally valid. The version used here does not have to be any one version. Depending on the words, it can be varied. The tune is found in most folk song books. This play starts with the birth of that folk song--tentative phrases sung and experimented with by different characters as they pass time. They are creating it together. It gains confidence, flair and gradually power.

The hymns, "Some Glad Morning" ("I'll Fly Away") and "Glory, Glory Hallelujah" are in most old-fashioned gospel hymn books. *The Last Ride of Billy Richardson* was written locally and the music is unavailable at this time.

PROLOGUE

> The far-distant future is painted on canvas flats or projected impressionistically on a scrim. The sounds of seemingly random percussion are heard: woodblocks, assorted bells, triangles, plucked. strings, etc., punctuate time and speech as if a breeze causes objects to softly touch, tinkle, or knock. These sounds are coordinated with speech appropriately. These sounds are indicated at the beginning of this scene and continue to about mid-scene. Thereafter only key places are noted for sound.

(Random percussion sounds start before entrance of Mountain)
Mountain appears, slides on feet flat on the floor toward a box or promontory, - upon which it slowly takes its place. As Mountain surveys the distant ridges, Tree enters, branches waving, circling the Mountain. Then Tree discovers the audience with surprise, curiosity, and apprehension.

TREE

(Examining audience)

What is this?

(Bell)

I've seen ants before, but they don't look like ants. I've seen squirrels, foxes, rabbits,

but they don't look like them, either. Mountain?
    (Block)
    (Waits for Mountain's recognition, and then waits further until they establish a greeting of real eye contact. Peaceful sounds persist.)
Mountain, do you see this?

(Mountain resumes peaceful contemplation of the distance.)

TREE
Well?
    (Small bell)
    (Tree moves closer to audience, examines front row)
What kind of thing is that?
    (Returns, nudges Mountain's side gently)
Mountain? Mountain!
    (Block)

MOUNTAIN
    (Not wanting to see audience)
For many years now, I've been at rest. (Block) Soothed by the air (Bell), fed by the sun (Triangle), and bathed in clean rainfall. (Bell. Block)

TREE
Well, I've been through many a season, myself. But I never saw anything like that. In my life.
    (Small woodblock)

MOUNTAIN
    (Smiles)
Tree, when were you born?

TREE
Sixty years ago.
    (To audience)
I bet she was born at least 2,000 years ago.
    (Goat bell)

MOUNTAIN
200 million years, Tree. (Large Block) And, I wasn't born--in the way you think. (Chime)

(The following is punctuated by the Block) The earth was hot, seething, day and night, steaming and cracking, sending out eruptions.
    (Block. Bell)
And then the heat passed away. (Metronome beat at 60; continues to cue) It began to cool, got cooler, Then the ice came.

TREE

My.

MOUNTAIN

And (Block) the earth wrinkled (Tick) shrank (Tick), folded up into valleys and mountains (Block).
    (Several ticks)
    (Very slow)
I was one of those mountains.
    (Pause--several ticks)
Those years were but a day. (Block)
    (Metronome out)

TREE

My goodness.
(Small bell) Can you remember much over all that time? 200 million. years? (Pause) I started from a little--this big!
    (Approaches audience, shakes her branches suddenly as to chickens) Whooosh. Git.

MOUNTAIN

They won't hurt you now, Tree.
(Block)
What does a mountain remember?
    (Cowbell. Block)
I remember groaning, as we shifted and pushed and settled into place. I remember the sea washing my feet, and knees. I remember the day of the giants, gigantic lizards, monstrous birds.

TREE

Oh, my.

MOUNTAIN

I remember the day of--of the –
    (Plucked string, banjo or guitar)
    (Mountain indicates audience)
I remember their day--the little ones. They lived a short while. They were lords over the earth, (A reed sound as though stirred by air) while they were here..

TREE

What does that mean?

MOUNTAIN

They ruled everyone else.

TREE

Ruled?

MOUNTAIN

    (Ruminates)
They had special powers, Tree. They not only could see me as a mountain, but they saw the

meaning of a mountain. They not only looked up to us, climbed us, mined us, but they saw us-- as –

(Music starts; section from Bach double violin concerto)

Close to the eternal.

TREE

(Whispers)

Eternal?

MOUNTAIN

They were the only ones who ever had any inkling of it. (Pause) It can't be explained, Tree.

TREE

What were they like?

MOUNTAIN

I saw them first rise out of the dust. (Triangle) Saw them take their first steps on two feet. (Block) Make things with their two hands. I saw them scribbling and drawing on stone walls, tablets, and then paper. I saw them tame all the living things, saw them cover the earth, except the mountain tops, frozen wastes, and seas. They were very beautiful (Deep bell). They were (Block) haunted. (Three different bells)

TREE

What were they called?

MOUNTAIN

(Nodding at audience)

Sometimes their ghosts come back.

TREE

That? That's what they are? Ghosts. Hello?

(To audience)

Hello.

(If anyone answers)

They can talk!

(If no one answers)

They can't talk!

(To Mountain)

What's the matter?

MOUNTAIN

Oh, they had a language all right. Nonsense, poetry, stories--truths, lies, side by side all mixed together! Excuse me, I get all filled up. (Pause) They used to climb all over me with their axes and hoes and scratch around, planting all kinds. of little things. Built little dwellings in the crook of my arms. The fog came up in the early morning, and threads of smoke used to come out of their houses like lace mixing with fog. They'd sing sometimes and nestle me at night looking and whispering at the moon. (Triangle) Then they'd go back into their houses for the night.

TREE

(Not fully understanding)
That sounds real nice.

MOUNTAIN

Oh, it was nice.
(Bell)

TREE

What are houses?
(Block)

MOUNTAIN

Well, they'd cut down--trees.
(Block)

TREE

(Taken a back)
Oh?

MOUNTAIN

They'd saw them up, nail them together and live inside them.
(Block)

TREE

Saw? Nail? They lived inside--trees?
(Look at audience)
Did they live inside mountains, too?

MOUNTAIN

(Percussion continues as appropriate)
They lived on us, usually. The only time they went inside us, they took out something that gave them heat and light. They were very fragile. Sometimes we were so emptied, we collapsed on them, buried them.
(Flute begins)
Most of the time they'd get on top of the taller mountains to look out and see where they came from and where they were going next. Some spent their whole lives to climb us and with agonizing effort reach the summit of the tallest mountains where they felt like gods. They didn't do this to me. I'm not tall. I'm a midget, and stooped. But I certainly had my share of their attention. They made a long tunnel through me--for a railroad. I remember that most of all. It was the longest anywhere, it was longer than I'm tall.

TREE

A tunnel? What's)

MOUNTAIN

A tunnel is a long empty space inside for going somewhere directly without having to go out of the way.

TREE

Maryat Lee

What?

MOUNTAIN

A tunnel goes from one side straight to the other. Hollow, dark and dank. A lot of them died inside me. They really wanted to move me –
>(Sound of steel)

Always trying to move everything. Never content. It's all gone now, the people, the houses, the tracks, everything except the tunnel.

TREE

The tunnel? Where is it? Down in that overgrown pit. What's a railroad?
>(Hears the music)

MOUNTAIN

It's a road made of two rails.
>(Tree does not comprehend)

A way of getting from one place to another.

TREE

You hear that?

MOUNTAIN

Yes--yes, I hear it. That's how they were. Pushing, driving, restless--full of themselves. Oh, their music could light up the night and make the day dance.
>(Ballad fades into section of Holst's "The Planets" where human voices and orchestra suggest space and timelessness)

MOUNTAIN

There's no question that they knew the long term plan, Tree. Those sounds are still in the air on a quiet day. They had to know.
>("The Planets" fades into a section from Casal's unaccompanied Bach sonatas for cello, or a Bach flute sonata)

The sounds they could make made mountains want to touch their foreheads to the ground.
TREE But what happened to them?

MOUNTAIN

Tree--they could overcome matter, space, time, other systems in the universe. They could overcome everything but--greed, and death.
>(Triangle, Block. Triangle. From the distance one can hear "Some glad mornin'... I'll fly away")

TREE

What's that?

MOUNTAIN

Sssh.
>(They listen)

Nothing before or since ever made sounds like they could. The variety staggers mountain's imagination.

TREE
It makes me feel strange. Gives me the shivers.
MOUNTAIN
Tree, there was a time when they brought life to every thing around them. Even when they were rough and had nothing to work with, they spun things out of nothing but thin air. Pushing, driving to the utmost limits. There was a time that fifty-five huge trains a day roared through me--through my tunnel--operated by these small creatures. Tree, even their ghosts are strong and linger.
TREE
Can--can they--show me--how it was?
MOUNTAIN
Yes, ghosts are always trying to relive the past, if you just give them the slightest encouragement.
>(Ponderous exit)
>
>(Scenery is silently removed for next scene as Tree finishes. This may be done by railroad crew)

TREE
>(To audience)

You could really live inside me?
>(Scampers off alarmed by all the people moving in around her)

SCENE ONE
TIME: The 1920's
SCENE: The C & 0 line near Talcott, West Virginia. The Great Bend Tunnel, known locally as the Big Bend Tunnel, is seen at a distance of one-half mile, with tracks and ties leading into it. A new tunnel is close to it, with freshly-laid track. The crew is laying this second track to allow two way traffic.
MUSIC: Banjo or guitar music: "Billy Richardson's Last Ride"
ACTION: Slick the foreman and the rail-laying crew of five to eight pairs of men enter, laughing and talking as they begin to line up, facing front, on either side of a long piece of rail. The crew is matched as partners, tall ones in rear. One section of rail is seventeen feet long and very heavy; several lie alongside the ties. The crew must move them several feet to their exact place on the ties and butt them up against the preceding rail, where later the "gandy-dancers"; another crew, followed the steel laying crew and pinned rails down in place. To move the rails requires at least two concerted moves by the whole crew, though often more moves were needed to accomplish the job. This exacting work was con ducted by the foreman, often a Black man, who sang the laying of the rails (chanted orders). The tone and timing kept the crew in unison, with crew members grunting or singing answers as they

worked. The last in line was able to see if that end of the rail made a neat joint with the last one. There is no single way to sing the chant, because each foreman sang his own orders to his own rhythm, words, and sense of the action. This set of calls is based on Mr. Jesse Green's call (a Foreman in the 1920's) and was recorded in 1978 during an interview with Jim Costa of Hinton. Mr. Green lived in Talcott. The action, which can be mimed, is as follows. The Foreman is Stage Right. Pairs of men line up Stage Center, facing front, an imagined rail between them about one or two feet from their own feet. Each holds one leg, whose jaws clamp around the rail. The men lean over. The jaw of the dog is open to fit over the top of the rail. Their knees • are bent in anticipation of the lifting. As the men pull up together, the jaws close around the iron, and the men feel the dead weight as knees straighten and arms are pulled straight from the shoulder. The rail is now about a half foot above the ground. On the word "bed" they take a big step left and set it on the ties at the word "boys." They lift again as above and now try to get it in the exact spot. "U--p" is sung as an extended sound, to cover the actual time it takes to lift. "Be--d" is an extended sound to cover the step to the side. "Boys" is sung to cover the setting-down time. The men walk in place to the next rail and await the next orders, alternating to left and then to right for each rail. Essentially the movement is a highly controlled heaving of heavy material. Any deviation or carelessness could--and did--result in broken bones or mashed feet. The men's answers to the Foreman are also sung out in the Foreman's rhythm.

SLICK

(Chant)
Put your dogs on a ir--on.
(Crew bends, hook dogs over rails)

CREWMAN REAR

We got seven do--wn.

SLICK

Raise up--
(They pick up the rail in unison)
And sit him on a head, boyyyah.
(Crew lift n unison and step sideways about three or four feet, lay it down)
Raise up –
(They lift again)

CREWMAN

Don't be late, boys.

SLICK

And get it in the bed--boayah.

CREWMAN #1

Got a good joint made?

CREWMAN #2

Got a good joint made.

CREWMAN #3

Move on down the line, boys.

(Crew stands up straight and, continuing to carry the dogs, they walk in place, to the next rail and wait for Slick to sing the next call. They stoop in unison and strain as they lift and jump it onto the ties and bed. It must be exactly rehearsed: all do the movements at the same instant. This action is repeated over and over in the background through Scene 2. Ad-libbed remarks and calls can be added within the overall rhythmic cycle. Also the pattern can be varied occasionally if Slick spots some- one not prepared to move in unison)

SLICK

Whoa, boayah, won't ya set down, suh!

(They lay the rail down)

CREW

Done got down.

SLICK

(Giving Crew time to settle down)

Line up, boys, line up right. You gotta go to friends tonight.
Line up boys. Put ya dogs on a ir--on..--etc.

(The rail goes too far, as it sometimes does)

CREWMAN #1

I gotta bad joint made. Jump it back to me.

SLICK

Whoa, boayyah.

(They get set to lift again)

Won't ya swing and change here, boyyyah.
Swing it and change, don't get lost.
We don't need no second boss. Swing!

(They lift with same movement as before but with no side step)

And change.

(They put the rail down one inch to the rear)

CREWMAN #2

Gotta good joint made.

CREWMAN #4

There ya go!

Maryat Lee

CREWMAN #3

Move on down the line, boyyys.
> (The cycle is repeated until cue for Exit near end of Scene 2, but quietly so that the dialogue can be heard)

SCENE TWO

(Scene continues. Rail-laying continues. A Black female reporter appears after third or fourth rail is laid. She watches the rail-laying action intently from side, busily taking notes. She is dressed in 1920s city clothes, purse, and hat, and is not used to the outdoors. The chant and rail-laying quietly continue through the scene)

SALLY.

> (Waving)

Hello. Hello there. Mister! Hello!
> (Tries to get Slick's attention from a distance)

Hello. Hellooo. Could....Excuse me--
> (Shouting)

Could I ask you a question?

SLICK

Urn? What's that? Oh, yes, ma'am.
> (He is uncertain about leaving. Picks one of the men to call the chant. Chant continues)

SALLY

> (Crossing closer to him with difficulty)

This ground is rough! I'm Sally Duchee. I hope you don't have snakes! I'm Sally Duchee--from the Pittsburgh Courier. (Slaps at gnats) Uh, how d' you do. Uh--I came all the way from Pittsburgh--to (looks at notes) Talcott? (pronounces it *TALcut*)--on an assignment.

SLICK

> (No response)

SALLY

I need to find what--I could about John Henry? Something new about him. His--uh family? Friends? Women?
> (No response. Slick sneaks a look at her notepad)

Have you ever heard of John Henry? (Pause) You were born here?

SLICK

> (Nods)

Well, I don't know, ma'am.
> (Sneaks look at the men)

But a round here, we call it "Tawkut."

SALLY

Oh, yes. Tawkut. Thank you. What was Tawkut like back then? When John Henry lived? Fifty years ago?

(She thinks Slick might be mentally slow)
(As if to a child)
What--what was it like when your father was young?

SLICK

Well, I don't know much about them days.
(She writes down something. He is fascinated with note pad)

But it wasn't Talcott in them days. It was Rollinsberg--yon side of the river.
(Looks at men who, in between actions,-.are watching him with amusement)
But I'll tell you one thing. In my daddy's day people knew what work was.
(Deadpan, but makes sure the Crew overhear)
Not like the young fellers anymore.

SALLY

But those young men are working very hard.

SLICK

Ssss. That gang?

SALLY

(As if stung by a bee)
Gang?
(Puts Slick between herself and the Crew)
Chain gang? (To herself) Um! They use prisoners down here.

SLICK

Just a bunch of loafers. Why, these boys is so slow, you 'most have to set stakes to see if they're movin' at all. (Pause) Excuse me, but did you say chain gang?

SALLY

Uh--

SLICK

You say you be a reporter?

SALLY

Yes, I'm from the Pittsburgh Courier.

SLICK

(Laughs)
Wait till I tell 'em they gonna be writ up as a chain gang.

SALLY

(Embarrassed)
You were saying something about your daddy's days?

SLICK

(Politely)
Was I? Uhh...

SALLY

Maryat Lee

About working hard. Was it quiet in those days, as it is now?

              SLICK

Not to hear tell of it. They was buildin' the tunnel, and it was pretty wild, they say. They had a big camp of shanties--right here. All kind of things goin' on.

              SALLY
> (Scribbling)

Yes?

              SLICK

Things got right quiet once the tunnel got built, and all them furriners and folks left--over a thousand of 'em! Working for $1.25 a day. Yessir, the knives and fists flashed. Lots of drinkin', singin', swearin', gamblin', they tell of.

              SALLY

Did your dad work in the tunnel?

              SLICK

My dad helped with the survey for the short cut.

              SALLY
> (Writing)

Short cut?

              SLICK

Through Big Bend.
> (Watching her write it down)

Chain gang! You got it down that I work with a chain gang? (Laughs)

              SALLY

Where is Big Bend?

              SLICK

You're lookin at 'er. That little mountain yonder. That's her name 'cause the river, see, goes almost teetotally 'round her in a loop ten miles, and comes back to little over a mile away. They called it Big Bend, and the mountain, too. Some of the big railroad brass came along, thought they'd fancy up the name. Over the portal it reads "Great Bend." Sounds sorta grand, don't it?

              SALLY
> (Writing)

Good. What was the survey for?

              SLICK

For the tunnel.

              SALLY

I mean, it was for a railroad?

              SLICK
> (As if she were a little slow)

Well, the railroad follows the river up to here. So C & O decided to put in a tunnel 'stead of goin' ten miles around? That was eighteen and sixty-nine they started it and, buddy, it wasn't only the longest tunnel of those times--a mile and a quarter--it was the baddest. Nobody ever knew how many peoples died in there--hundreds C&O kept it quiet.

SALLY

You think John Henry died in there?

SLICK

That ole mountain--she's funny. Some died 'cause they was careless 'bout blasting powder. Some got in the way of the hammers. But most peoples was killed because of the roof.

SALLY

(Writing)

Roof.

SLICK

It's red shale. (Pronounced "shell")

SALLY

Red shell?

SLICK

Hard as iron. 'Course when it hits the air, it gets soft, crumbly-like, and she'll drop on ya.

SALLY

(Baffled, changes subject)

Did they run into any coal?

SLICK

Sssst. Coal in shale rock! Chain gang! Now coal in shale rock.
(Glances to see if Crewmen heard)

SALLY

(Embarrassed again)

Didn't your dad ever mention John Henry?

SLICK

No, ma'am. Not much.

SALLY

Not much?

SLICK

(Looks at the Crew)

People say there wasn't no John Henry.

SALLY

No John Henry?

SLICK

(For Crew)

There wasn't no John Henry. (To her) Well, my dad once said he had two nine-pound hammers with nineteen-inch handles and a leather strop. Some say he had just one striking hammer.

Maryat Lee

SALLY

He knew him? He knew John Henry?

SLICK

(Uneasily)

Well, I wouldn't say that

SALLY

He saw him hammering?

SLICK

Drivin', you mean? I reckon he did. He was a driver and a shaker, too.

SALLY

A shaker? That's interesting. He was a Shaker! There were Shakers here! (Writing) Shaker influence at Big Bend Mountain! There was a group of Shakers?

SLICK

Well, yes, ma'am, quite a lot. They was pretty busy 'round here.

SALLY

And I thought you people were Baptists.

SLICK

(Stops dead)

Baptists?

SALLY

Were there as many Shakers as Baptist, would you say?

SLICK

(Looks around, picks up stick politely)

A shaker don't necessarily believe nothin'--except stayin' clear of the hammer. See, a shaker is a turner. A shaker holds the steel--that's the drill bit--for the driver, like this, all different lengths.

(Hunkers down and puts stick between legs as if it were a bit)

SLICK

Wham!

(Turns it one quarter)

Wham! He turns it so it won't get hung in the rock. Drivers like John Henry gotta drive steel twelve, maybe fourteen feet, into shale rock so powderman can stuff blasting powder in. Sometimes fifty holes for one blast. It would take a whole day or more.

(Exit Crew, end of day's work. Slick takes note of their departure)

Shaker shakes the steel, see, turns it again and again between the blows. Steel gets dull Shaker gives it to the tool boy, boy hands him a longer bit, takes the old steel to the smith. Shaker puts new bit in the hole, huh, holds it between his legs, huh, keeps his eyes on the steel, huh, turn and shake. Barn. Turn and shake. Reach it to the walker, walk it to the smith, huh. Barn! Rings the steel, till it goes in deep. More' n twice a man's height. Then starts a new hole; then another. Then they stuff the powder in all the holes and blow her up.

> (During this speech, faint sounds may be heard in in the distance; emerging from the tunnel, at first very indistinct. Gradually, steel-driving chants from the 1870s may be heard, with sound of random hammers clinking on steel along with the chants. By the end of the speech, the hammer chants are the dominant sound, coming up in volume. One chant may be accompanied at lower volume contrapuntally by as many as three or four chants sung randomly at the same time. Several crews are at work. These rhythms are also punctuated by other sounds: a strain of a spiritual sung perhaps slightly out of key. Rhythmic slaps of leather on wood; low, indistinct rustlings and moans, a muffled explosion, perhaps a fragment of banjo or guitar music. The single hammer chant dominates).

And so like that. They all sang, same as me, laying the rails. John Henry, they say, was the singin'-est man in these parts. That's why he was the best steel driver around, if you ask me.

> (The hammer flashes down and the sound of steel is heard at the end of "Huh." The other words accompany the wind-up for striking)

> (Slick sings the first two lines of the chant, after which the voices of the drivers take over the chant at a distance. He continues to talk to her over the following)

DRIVER #1

(Huh and clink are simultaneous)

Ain't no hammer, huh (Clink)
In these mountains, huh
Ain' t no hammer, huh
In these mountains, huh
Ain't no hammer, huh
In these mountains, huh
Rings like mine, huh
Rings like mine, huh

SINGER

THIS IS THE- HAMMER
THAT KILL OLE JOHN HENRY
BUT IT WON'T KILL ME
NO, IT WON'T KILL ME
OH, IT WON'T KILL ME..

DRIVER #2

I tole Hattie, huh (Clink)
To whippa that chile, huh

Maryat Lee

I tole Hattie, huh
To whup that chile, huh
I tole Hattie, huh
To whup that chile, huh
Make 'em mind, huh
Make 'em mind, huh

DRIVER #3

Take this hammer, huh
Give it to the walker, huh
take this hammer, huh
Give it to the walker, huh
Take this hammer, huh
Give it to the walker, huh
For I'm goin' home, huh
I'm goin' home, huh
> (Repeat under rest of scene)

SALLY

Why, Mister, uh, uh, I believe your men are gone.

SLICK

> (Looks at watch. They start slow exit)

That's a fact. Oh, they was a lot goin' on here in them days. A lot of different peoples, outside peoples come here to work on that tunnel--comin' here on a job--like you. All kinds. Loggers, preachers, peddlers, gypsy-like people of all ways of life. Along with the drivers, shakers, powdermen, an' all.
> (Tunnel speech, Three people begin entering during this altering the playing area for Scene Dialogue and scraps of music and. other sounds may be heard under the scene, sotto voce)

SALLY

Tell me, did John Henry have the contest with the machine?

SLICK

Well, if it was you puttin' in a tunnel through this mountain, and you knew they was a machine drillin' through other tunnels and doin' it three times faster 'n hand labor, what would you do?

SALLY

I'd bring the machine drill here and test it. To see if it would be faster.

SLICK

Uhhum. And suppose they made that first test when they first begun the tunnel, and suppose it broke down or got hung up in the rock?

SALLY

Why, I'd go ahead with hand labor. But--I'd be waiting to see if they made some improvements on the machine. And maybe later. But the question is, did John Henry have a contest with the first drill, or later?

SLICK

Lady, what would you think?

SALLY

Let's say he won the first contest, and he kept on working. He didn't die. But then, one day they brought in a new, improved drill, and he--Oh, this is very exciting. (She is madly writing) That could make sense of all the stories. Oh, yes, before I forget. What did the country folk think of all these strange people coming in here to work on the tunnel? Were there any country people who already lived here--like farmers?

SLICK

Oh, my, yes! (Continuing slow exit) There's a story about my mother. She was just a young girl, and she told me a story about the tunnel--

(Exit)

SCENE THREE

SCENE: The mouth of Big Bend Tunnel, 1870- 72, with scaffolding and timber at the portal, upstage center, constructed to allow entrances and exits. The tunnel personnel (or the rail-laying crew, who may double) sets stage for 1870 and bring in props. When Slick mentions his mother, a crew brings on a sign that reads "ON THE WAY TO THE TUNNEL" and places it in the tunnel opening.

MAUD

(Pulling Lucy onto stage from stage right)

I want to meet 'em. I want to meet this man that's gonna take care of you. I want to meet the man that's gonna take your wash off the line. I want to meet the man that's gonna eat on your dirty dishes. I want to meet the man, honey!

(To audience)

I want to shake his hand. Where is he?

LUCY

(Pointing offstage left)

That's where he is, Mama.

MOTHER

(Appalled)

At the tunnel?

LUCY

Yes'm.

MOTHER

You didn't mention the tunnel When did you get to the tunnel? One of those people? How did you ever get to the tunnel, girl?

Maryat Lee

LUCY
Well...
>(Mother yanks her)

Owww. Mama when you give me permission, you know...

MOTHER
I never give no permission to go to no tunnel. I'll swan, anymore y' never know what the young's goin to do.
>(Asks audience)

Ain't that so?
(Points Stage Left)

MOTHER
Look at that. All that lost, godless, tattered, raggedy-tag ends of human souls, forgotten but not even gone yet. This tunnel's brought the bottom of the barrel of the whole world right in on us. How come, Lucy Anne?

LUCY
I told ya', Ma. They ain't that bad. They ain't bad people. They're real nice And they been everywhere. They been to Alabam' and Virginnie, and they seen oceans and big cities.

MOTHER
They may be from somewhere, and they may be goin' somewhere, but they got no shingles for a shelter, no porch to patch, not to mention (whispers) no pot to piss in. Now, how come?

LUCY
I told ya', Mom. I was avisitin'. You give me permission to spend the day with Emily, and--

MOTHER
Emily don't live at no tunnel. Emily lives with her family up in Clayton where she belongs.

LUCY
You axem, Mama. Mr. Axel Gill was atakin' me to Emily. And he was belt up here half a day talkin' to a stranger. I was just settin' in the wagon, steamin' in the sun, and some real nice folks tell me to come and set in the shade. Couldn't hardly turn it down, Mom, it was so hot the steam was pouring up o:ut the river, like it was boilin' on the rocks. And you told me not ever to be stuck up.

MOTHER
Axel Gill! I might've known. Lettin' you out of his sight. I told him about that. C'mon, let's find this man
>(To audience)

And then I'll find Mr. Gill.

LUCY
>(Looking Left)

He ain't there just now.

MOTHER

Lucy Anne, I taught you to say "He isn't."

LUCY

That don't make no difference. He isn't there, Mama. Don't it sound funny? Me sayin it? Isn't it? Sounds uppity.

MOTHER

I don't care how it sounds I want to see this man. Let's find where he is! I want to see this man you agoin' to marry--my least baby. I want to see him right now. And I'm just agoin' to tell 'im you can't marry--at thirteen.

LUCY

Why not?
    (To audience)
I don't see why I can't live my life the way anybody else does.

MOTHER

    (Shocked at impertinence)
Lucy Anne! I'm a 'tellin' you why.
    (Changes strategy. Lucy gathers wildflowers)
You marry now, you won't never see none of the world you been talkin' about. You end up here, puttin' diapers on the line till you're tired and so old you can't even take a walk up in the woods anymore to see the May flowers, much less dance out in the moonlight 'tween the two oak trees like I seen you do last week when you didn't think no one was spyin'. You're my only one that--
    (Pulls Lucy to face her)
You're my only 'un that got some dreams, that can read books. You ain't growed up yet. You just wait till you got some adult in you.

LUCY

Why, Mamma, you told me I just come an adult this spring! You told me, when I first got my--

MOTHER

Lucy Anne!
    (Yanks her hard. Looks around to make certain no one overheard)
I told you 'bout that bein' secret.

LUCY

    (Pulling back)
Ma, there ain't nobody listening! What about the kids, Ma?

MOTHER

Your dad can watch the place.

LUCY

What about the eatin'?

MOTHER

They'll make out. C'mon. You worried about them now?

Maryat Lee

LUCY

Well, Mama, it's like this.

(Gets some distance. Winces at expectation of wrath)

I'm expectin'.

(Silence)

MOTHER

Oh, Lordy Oh, my saints. Oh, no. Oh, Lord, please keep me near the cross. Please don't let it--Please! Oh! Wait

(Controls herself)

Now just wait a minute! Wait a minute. Let me think a minute now. Oh, Lardy, my little girl, only twelve.

LUCY

Thirteen.

MOTHER

Ain't she got a chance to spread her wings a little bit? Is she gonna just spread her belly?

LUCY

Ever'body else, Mama, ever'body else.

MOTHER

Fool You're not ever'body else. You got people that care. You got people that want you to do somethin' besides set around and have babies with some old fly-by-nights, and be stuck up in an ol' shanty. We want to see you do somethin' more with your life than hoe potatoes on land that you could fall off of.

LUCY

Ever'body. They all in church, they all gettin' married. I'm already thirteen. I want to get married.

MOTHER

Lucy Anne, listen, honey, it ain't wrong to be different. Bad as the world is, it's right to be different. Can't listen to ever'body--Are you sure you're expectin'?

LUCY

Yes'm.

MOTHER

How you know?

LUCY

I just know.

MOTHER

(Carefully)

Lucy Anne, certain things have to happen, honey. (Pause) What makes you think you're gonna have a baby? I mean, maybe, honey, maybe you heard if you kissed a boy you'll get pregnant. Did you kiss a boy?

LUCY

Yes'm.

MOTHER

And then--'?

LUCY

Yes'm.

MOTHER

Yes what?

LUCY

(Hesitant and nervous)
Mama, he kissed me.

MOTHER

You didn't do no more'n that?

LUCY

Huh?

MOTHER

(Pause)
Oh, my soul. Thank you, Jesus I surely thank you, Lord. Honey, you ain't 'spectin'.
  (Hugs her)
You ain't gonna have a baby--not just yet.

LUCY

I can go 'round kissin' and--

MOTHER

Now, I didn't say that! You can get pregnant easy enough once you start kissin'.
  (Lucy is puzzled)
Now, you didn't really want to get married yet, did you?

LUCY

Yes'm.

MOTHER

(Starts walking)
Then let me go and meet this man. C'mon.

LUCY

Ssssh. There he is, Ma.,
  (Points about 100 yards away--Stage Left)

MOTHER

Which one? That big ole brute?

LUCY

Oh, no, Ma. He's the little one. C'mon!

MOTHER

That--that little switch?
  (Hides her relief)

Honey, what would you like to do with your life? Oh, I know. You said you want to get married. Let's forget about that part right now. What is it you're awantin', when I see you dancin' out in the moonlight? Oh, I know you're dreamin' about a boy comin' down the path on fleet feet. But--there's always somethin' behind that--somethin' else--for a girl--that she'd like to be adoin'.

LUCY

(Stops)

Mom--you mean that? You really want to know? I want to get married 'cause you wouldn't let me do what I want. Sounds crazy, but I just love to dance! They's a dancin' lady at the tunnel--

MOTHER

Dance? Honey, dance? What would the preacher say?

LUCY

Mama, you said, don't pay no 'tension to what people say.

MOTHER

Oh.

(Stopped. Looks at her)

So I did. Dance? Dance. Um.

(Shakes head. o audience)

What do I do now?

(Gunther Mann, a peddler, enters with suitcase)

LUCY

Let's just set awhile, Mama. C'mon.

(Lucy leads Maud off left and around in front of stage to a point of observation Stage Right)

SCENE FOUR
SCENE: Crew removes "ON THE WAY TO THE TUNNEL" sign, and the stage is now set with all the various paraphernalia to be found in that period where there was digging, blasting, boring holes, eating, drinking, waiting, smithing. A portable anvil, down Left, with a small tripod down Right that can hold kettle to cook or heat food, etc.

(Gunther pauses with suitcase as Lucy and Maud cross Left)
(To Mother)

'Scuse me, Ma'am. You know a place where I can stay overnight in Talcott?

(Mother loftily shakes her head, snubbing him, as she and Lucy pass him. Gunther follows at a distance. As Mother and Lucy Exit, a midwife, Rosa Mae Adkins and Dreama, a landlady, enter, talking. They bring stools and their sewing and sit together upstage Right)

ROSA MAE
She told me herself they was goin' to let me deliver. So, when I heard she started labor, I just quit shellin' the peas, cannin' the corn, told the children I'd be gone and set 'em to pickin' and shellin' and took my basket and went over to set with her, and, Law, there was Dr. Bray in his vest, watch chain, sleeves all rolled up, lookin' hot and bothered. I didn't know if he was all blisted up at me or at the mother or what.

DREAMA
My goodness. Anymore he really don't like our old ways of doctorin, I can tell you that since that boy...

ROSA MAE
Johnson?

DREAMA
No, he was a Smith. Lost his leg and the old Doc, without cleaning it, slapped vinegar, mostly, and a bunch of herbs--pepper and spit. Dr. Bray was fit to be tied.

ROSA MAE
But he's right about bein' real careful, cleaning with boilin' water and all.

DREAMA
But you haven't lost one baby or mother since you been here.

ROSA MAE
If it was me, I wouldn't use them tongs if I could help it. Why, they can mar a baby's head that quick. Well, I got to get back to the children.

DREAMA
But what happened when you showed up at the bornin' this mornin'?

ROSA MAE
You know me, I just said, "Mornin', Doc Bray. Don't reckon you need any help today." And he said, "Mrs. Adkins, come in here a minute." He was out on the porch like he was t:rying to cool off. I said, "I didn't know you was deliverin' this baby." He said, "Oh, yes, delivered her about an hour ago." Then he looked sideways. "Come on in. Maybe you can give her a hand. Mother won't stop hemorrhaging," says he. So I march in. And, Lord, that woman was just about dead. So I roll up my sleeves, washed up and--well, she's up and walking.

DREAMA
Well, my. Did he--?

ROSA MAE
Not a word. Not a cent.

DREAMA
(Sees Lucy and Maud sitting on Stage Right)
Say, that looks like that country girl that was here last fall awhile. Let's see, they was from up at Clayton. That's her Mother. Let me see, I used to know her from church years ago, before the tunnel came. Don't they change?
(Gunther re-enters, followed by Tina, a young girl. Tina watches everything

Gunther does)

GUNTHER

(To women)

'Scuse me, ma'am, I'm new here and wonder if there's a rooming house or overnight somewhere close by.

DREAMA

You probably know I run a boarding house.
(Looks him over)
But I'm full up right now. What are you sellin'?

ROSA MAE

Dreama, I'll be goin' on back to the poorhouse.
(Starts Exit)
Come with me, Dreama.
(As a parting goodbye)

GUNTHER

I've got knives, spices, 'n brushes, patent medicines. I've got one or two pots left, and sieves, and, let's see, soap powder and cheese cloth, and some muslin, and a bonnet for a little girl.
(Rose Mae stops to look)
(Tina sees bonnet and loves it)

ROSA MAE

Why, have a nice place for you to stay. I keep some of the men. It's not right here where it's noisy. But it's close.

GUNTHER

Oh, thank you.
(Tina asks Gunther in mime if she can touch bonnet. Touches it reverently. Lifts it up.)

DREAMA

What's your name?

GUNTHER

Gunther Mann.

DREAMA

Oh, we've got a lot of Manns here. You're not from here?

GUNTHER

No, ma'am, I'm from White Sulphur.

Dreama

Umhum. Well, I just remember I have one of the men leavin' this morning, if you'd like to stay here.

ROSA MAE

Dreama, I'd like to invite the young man to stay as a, guest. I think I need quite a few things he's got.

DREAMA

Well, Rosa Mae, I do have a room right here, which is where he's doin' his business. You'd like to be right in town, wouldn't you?

GUNTHER

Why, I thank you both. Uhh, why don't I stay the first night here, and then stay the second night with you. Then early next morning I could go on back home.

(Tina folds bonnet carefully and gives it back to Gunther)

ROSA MAE

I could use some of your merchandise. You wouldn't have to pay for lodging. What kind of knives?

GUNTHER

Paring knives, butcher knives, pen knives, pocket knives, scalpels.

(Tina picks up bonnet again)

DREAMA

But here he could make more money, Rosa Mae. Gunther Mann, you just pack that up, and I'll show you a nice room, with a window facin' the tracks. You can see just when the men come out of the shifts. They get their pay today.

(Tina puts bonnet back)

GUNTHER

Ladies, now, please, don't get upset. Maybe I can stay there, with her, and then come here.

(Rosa Mae and Dreama now start pulling at him)
(Rosa Mae notices lump on Gunther's neck)

What's this?
What's what?

ROSA MAE

A swelling here.

(To Dreama)

Look at that! Listen--don't move.

DREAMA

Maybe he ought to see the doctor.

GUNTHER

Doctor!

DREAMA

We've got a English surgeon lives four houses down.

ROSA MAE

Doctor? Why, I can fix that up. Here let me see those knives, it's nothing, hold still.

(Tina looks for knife. Brings out bonnet again)

GUNTHER

Oh, I've had that lump--it's been with me since birth.

ROSA MAE

Hold still It really doesn't look good. Tina, just bring one of those knives. Quick girl. Fetch it.

GUNTHER

Oh, I don't want to lose it. I've always had it.

ROSA MAE

Any knife, Tina! Now, just wait--just be still. It'll only take a minute.

GUNTHER

I'm attached to it. Wait!

ROSA MAE

I'm not going to hurt you. Where's that knife?

GUNTHER

(Squirming, trying to talk to Dreama)

Ms--uh, you do run a boarding house?

DREAMA

I do, I'm one of the two boarding houses here for years.

(Tina hands Rosa Mae a knife as Witchy Waters enters)

ROSA MAE

(Holding Gunther down)

Just one minute. Don't jump like that.

(She grapples Gunther slowly to the ground)

GUNTHER

Help! Don't! That's my knife. Put it down. Help!

ROSA MAE

Help me, Dreama!

WITCHY

What's goin' on?

DREAMA

(Holding him down)

Rosa Mae, that boy wants up.

(Gunther's legs are flailing. Tina finally helps hold Gunther's feet to the ground. Then Witchy helps)

ROSA MAE

Dreama, I don't like the looks of that lump. He needs to get rid of it.

DREAMA

He just wants a room, he says.

ROSA MAE

Hold him, Dreama, he could die.

(At this, Gunther flings them off, gets up in disarray, collects his clothes, baggage, etc., and snatches back his knife)

DREAMA

Rosa Mae, I've got it.
    (Catches Rosa Mae before she renews her efforts)
He don't want no doctorin'. But...
    (Whispers)

TINA

Here, Mister, here's your bonnet.
    (Puts bonnet in his bag)

GUNTHER

    (To Witchy, hastily)
Excuse me, I'm new here, and I need a place to lodge overnight.

TINA

Can I help you carry your things?

WITCHY

There's an ole flea bag over there in Rollinsberg, 'cross the river.

GUNTHER

    (To Tina)
Why, yes, thanks.
    (To Witchy)
That sounds fine.
    (Tina picks up part of bundle, with bonnet on top)

WITCHY

But you have to take the ferry.
    (Points)
There's a flop house on this side.
    (Nods at Dreama)

GUNTHER

Oh, I'd rather go to the flea bag. Goodbye, ladies. Where's the ferry?

TINA

I'll show you.
    (Tina and Gunther hastily Exit)

DREAMA

Oh, Mr. Mann Shoot! Wouldn't you know he didn't have any manners.

ROSA MAE

Well, then, I've got to go on home. See you tomorrow, Dreama.
    (Rosa Mae Exits right, Dreama left)
        SCENE FIVE
        SCENE CONTINUES
(Ansel Bragg, a romantic youth, 15 or 16, enters carrying daisies. Sits and begins picking the petals),

Maryat Lee

LUCY

There he is, Ma.
> (Maud holds her back)

BRAGG

She loves me,
She loves me not,
etc.

LUCY

See Ma, he's talkin' about me!
> (Maud holds her back)
> (Witchy Waters enters, watches Bragg)

BRAGG

> (Continuing to pluck daisies)

She loves me,
She loves me not,
etc.

LUCY

Ain't he beautiful

WITCHY

> (She has been watching Bragg. She now approaches)

What are you doin', Ansel Bragg?

BRAGG

> (Continues plucking daisy petals)

She loves me,
She loves me not,
etc.

WITCHY

Who's "she"?

BRAGG

A girl.

WITCHY

A girl? You don't mean it.
> (Bragg gives her some daisies. She plucks petals too)

This year, next year,
Sometime, never, etc.
> (They pluck and recite the rubrics alternately)
> (Enter Tina, skipping, with bonnet on. She stops, listens to Bragg and Witchy. She can't decide whether to interrupt. Finally she gets Witchy's attention)

TINA

Witchy, you know numbers. Teach me, please?

(Witchy hands her a daisy and counts as she plucks petals, demonstrating for Tina)

WITCHY

One, two, three, four, one, two, three, four, (etc.)

TINA

(Slowly)

One, two, three, four, (etc.)

(Continuing in same rhythm and plucks petals for each number)

WITCHY

(Resumes her rubric as she plucks petals)

This year, next year,
Sometime, never,

(Continuing)

BRAGG

She loves me, she loves me not.

(They are all counting and reciting and plucking quietly in counterpoint)

TINA

(Tiring)

Witchy? I wanna learn letters.

(Witchy hands her a daisy and calls out a letter for each petal and Tina repeats the letter)

WITCHY

A, B, C, D, etc.

TINA

A, B, C, D, etc.

(They all resume)

BRAGG

(Finally exasperated)

Well, I'll be--She doesn't love me. Every time.

WITCHY

I can fix that.

BRAGG

How?

WITCHY

Do it with your buttons. You know how to do it with your buttons?

BRAGG

(She starts him counting the buttons of his jacket or shirt, top to bottom)

She loves me, she loves me not etc.

(Repeats until it ends with "She loves me not". Bragg is disgusted)

WITCHY

Maryat Lee

I can cut it off.

BRAGG
What?

WITCHY
(Points)
The bottom button.

BRAGG
(At first misunderstands, horrified. Then sees)
Oh, that's right.
(Enter Brenda and Vicki. Brenda carries basket)
(Bragg jumps up)
There she is.

LUCY
(Jumps up. Maud holds her back)
Why that ornery thing.
(Witchy drops the daisies, takes Tina upstage, sits and gives her a counting lesson on the fingers--sotto voce, sing-song and rhythmically while scene continues)

BRAGG
You need some help?
(Reaches for her basket)

BRENDA
Hello there. No, no. It ain't that heavy.

VICKI
Who's that?

BRENDA
You know Ansel Bragg.

VICKI
He sure has growed up since my last visit. But he's sorta puny, ain't he?

BRAGG
(To Brenda)
Is this your sister?

VICKI
Boy you sure like the girls, don't ya.

BRAGG
Oh, ever'body knows I'm the best man that ever walked on two feet on Greenbrier Bottom.
(Enter, Toby)

VICKI
He might be the best man; but the way he's agoin', he'll never be a groom.

WITCHY
(Who has become more interested in the exchange than in teaching Tina counting)

One of them braggedy Bragg boys.

TOBY
(Approaching)
Say, buddy, will you say that again? What you said?

BRAGG
Uh, which?

TOBY
I heard ya. Say it again.

BRAGG
Oh, I just said I'm the best man that ever walked on two feet on Greenbrier Bottom. An you be surprised what kinda strength I got!
(Tries to leave)

TOBY
Now, you know you're talkin' sorta biggety, ain't you? Now, where's this little lady
(Indicating Brenda)
come from? Ma'am, I ain't much for handsome, but I'm sure the he--heck for strong.
(Catches Bragg as he escapes)
And this young feller knows I'm the best man that ever walked "on two feet on Greenbrier Bottom." And if he don't, we can prove it right here and right now.

WITCHY
Oh, goody, let's have a fight.

LUCY
(Breaks away from Mother and runs to Witchy)
Me too! Let's have a fight. What's your name?

WITCHY
Hi. I'm Witchy Waters. And what's yours?

BRAGG
(Recklessly now)
All right. I'll take him on. I'll take on anybody. I stand good on what I say. Ever'body knows that.
(Stalls)
How much do you weigh?

TOBY
I weigh in about 170.

LUCY
(Looking around)
Listen, where's the dancin' lady?

WITCHY
Oh, she's still here, poor thing.

BRAGG

You think so? Where'd you weigh in at? You look a lot fatter'n that.

TOBY

Tobacci scales.

BRAGG

Why, ever'body knows they ain't true.

TOBY

How long you know me? I run that shed. Them's my scales, and I'll put your mouth in the back of your head so you can tattle on your own whereabouts. Son of a gun!

> (Toby winds up and spits in Braggs face. Bragg deflects it with a whip of his head and it hits Brenda, who deflects it to Vicki who deflects it and it hits Lucy square in the face. They all scream and Lucy shrieks and attacks Bragg)

BRAGG

Ow, ow. That's not my spit. Help. It's his dirty ole tobacci spit.

LUCY

You flang it at me.

BRAGG

> (Finally recognizes her)

Oh--it's you. Lula May!

LUCY

LUCY! Lucy Anne. I'll Lula May you!

BRAGG

> (Holds her swinging hands)

Right. Just what I was sayin', Lucy. Oh, honey, where've you been? I just almost died broken-hearted. Honest. I did everything to get you out of my mind. Tied rocks to my feet, jumped in the river.

LUCY

Yeah? Really?

WITCHY

> (Nudging Lucy)

Where it was about waist-high, and his feet got stuck in the rocks and he just stood up an' hollered.

BRAGG

It wasn't my spit.

LUCY

But you flang it, you dumb jack-cracker.

WITCHY

Ansel Bragg is a dumb jack-cracker.

> SCENE SIX
> SCENE CONTINUES
> (Phil, the shaker, enter. Little Ben enters from tunnel with empty water pail)

PHIL

Hey, what's goin' on?
> (Gets between them)

BRAGG

Yeah, he's tryin' to show off by pickin on me. He's 170, and I'm only 130.

TOBY

That little rascal says he's the best man on Greenbrier Bottom.
> (Little Ben mimics the men behind their backs, making caricatures of their belligerence)

PHIL

And I say.!'...ill the best man on Greenbrier and the New Bottom.
> (Phil and Toby circle around each other. Group gathers egging them on. Bragg, suddenly off the hook, gratefully backs out of this fracas and joins the women. Lucy attacks him again)

BRAGG

> (While Lucy is shaking him, he remembers)

Oh, Oh! When I saw you that day, it tuck the breath clean outa me.
> (Little Ben mimics lovesick Bragg)

BRENDA

He ain't got much breath to begin with.

VICKI

He's sure got a thimble of hot air somewhere.

LUCY

An' you told me all those beautiful things, and you
> (Whispers)

kissed me! And you can't even remember my name!

BRAGG

> (To Lucy)

Don't you understand? I had to make myself forget you. See? Please don't be mad. I'll kill myself.
> (To Little Ben)

Get outa here. Oh Lucy Anne!

LUCY

Don't Lucy me!

TOBY

> (To Phil)

You workin' up a row?

WITCHY

There. There they go.

BRAGG

(Fickle, now he turns to Vicki)

What did you say your name was? Vicki? That's the name of the queen Victoria!

    (During this dialogue the preparation to fight between Toby and Phil has been developing. Now everybody watches the fight, egging them on. Little Ben shadow boxing in the background)

PHIL

Try me.

WITCHY

Hey, Shake, there's a snake behind you.

    (In slow motion, when Phil looks around, Toby knocks him down with a sucker punch and pins him. Cheers and comments)

PHIL

(Normal time)

Hey. That's dirty fightin'.

WITCHY

It's true. I just said somebody's behind you.

    (In slow motion, Toby lets him up. Toby prances, shows off. Phil takes off vest, glares at Witchy. He exchanges blows with Toby. Phil knocks Toby down and pins him)

TOBY

Enough I--

    (Normal time motion. They get up. Phil struts.. The fight seems over)

LUCY

(Catching Bragg flirting with Vicki) Let me tell you one thing. You ain't any better than a rabbit.

BRAGG

    (Alternately addressing Lucy and Vicki)

Oh, you're the prettiest--you're the sweetest thing. I feel like I'll just about kill myself, or run away, leave this hole--there's no life here--but you. You keep me going. Keep my nose above the water.

    (Little Ben teases Bragg)

Little Ben. I'm gonna tell your dad! Yow!

    (Toby aims blow at Phil, who ducks, and the blow lands flat in Bragg's face. He falls straight back. The women catch him and lower him to the ground. He clutches his jaw and yelps. Little Ben imitates getting socked and falling. They all laugh)

LUCY

See? That'll teach you a lesson.

BRAGG

Ow, ow, my tooth!

WITCHY

Oh, Ansel Bragg got tagged on the tooth. Oh, oh, here's the ol' Doc. He'll help you good. Little Ben they'll be hollerin' for water.

    (Little Ben takes his bucket and exits to get water)

SCENE SEVEN
SCENE CONTINUES

    (Ole Doctor rushes in)

DOCTOR

Now, now, what is it?

WITCHY

I'll tell you! Ansel Bragg opened his mouth on both sides the head at the same time.

DOCTOR

Now, son, be calm. What is it?

BRAGG

Ow, ow, it hurts.

    (Ida Red enters.. She crosses and takes her seat on dynamite box, Stage Right. Box big enough to allow two or three to sit)

DOCTOR

Where?

    (Bragg points to jaw)

IDA

Oh, oh, somebody got punched. Ansel Bragg, I bet.

DOCTOR

    (Poking)

Here?

BRAGG

YOW!

    (Little Ben enters with water bucket - exits tunnel)
    (Fortune teller enters. Gets out crystal ball. Sets up a sign, "Palms read.")

DOCTOR

I have it. I have a remedy.

    (Low voice)

Do you have some money?

BRAGG

A little. Yow.

IDA

You won't have it long, honey.

DOCTOR

Listen carefully. Take a little pepper.

FORTUNE TELLER

I see--I see the rear end of four horses. One's black. One's--

Maryat Lee

                              DOCTOR

Hot pepper and mix it with

                         FORTUNE TELLER

White.

                              DOCTOR

Mustard.

                         FORTUNE TELLER

One's--

                              DOCTOR

Then rub it--

                         FORTUNE TELLER

Red.

                              BRAGG

The money?

                              DOCTOR

The pepper and vinegar!

                         FORTUNE TELLER

I see things howling!

                              BRAGG

Rub it on the tooth?

                         FORTUNE TELLER

Outcries The end of the world!

                              DOCTOR

Pah on the tooth. Rub it into your bum.

                       FORTUNE TELLER

Doom!
    (She throws crystal ball away)

                              BRAGG

Gum?

                              DOCTOR

No. (Points) Rub it into the bum and the pain in your tooth will go away in no time.
    (Bragg exits in a hurry)

                              WITCHY

Wait! Better than that, take an apple. Cut it into five pieces. Put it into your mouth and hold your head in an oven till the apple bakes. You positively won't have a toothache after that.

                              LUCY
    (Shyly)
Are you a real doctor?

                              DOCTOR

Yes, yes, little lady. I practice medicine--for the love of it, you might say. I operate, snip,

dissect, sew, slash, split, smash, break, extract, tear, trim, slice, locate, dislocate, and. also I deliver babies--like someone else here tries to do.
    (Glares over his shoulder)

LUCY

Oh, I'll have to tell my mommy. She--

DOCTOR

Yes, tell her. I chase away. chills and fevers. I remove gravel, stones, treat measles, plague, ringworm, catarrh, colic, bad wind.

LUCY

I could go get her.

DOCTOR

Unlike the quack who just arrived, tell her I treat all forms of disease. And tell her this! When I find an incurable disorder, I go so far as to exterminate the whole patient to get rid of it! I'm known here--for my success in relieving many people of all discomfort, past and future.

IDA

Oh.
    (Mourning Glory enters. She sees Doctor Bray and stares after him angrily)

DOCTOR

Ah, I forgot my patient on Pea Ridge. Excuse me, please.
    (Doctor exits)
    (Witchy holds Lucy, who has started toward Mourning Glory)

WITCHY

Sshh. Don't. That's poor Mourning Glory.

LUCY

That's the dancin' lady. What's wrong? Why's she crying?

WITCHY

She lost her son in there.
    (Indicates tunnel)

LUCY

Oh. Poor thing.

FORTUNE TELLER

    (Passes from one to another, offering to read palms)
Fortune? Tell your fortune? See your future. Call up your past. Ah, fortune? Pretty thing. Tell your future? I can conjure. Make potions. Love potions? Future? Fortune. Flotsam. Pretty baby. Pretty love, some one is behind your back, sticking pins in your behind.
    (Approaches Toby and Phil and teases them. They insult her)

PHIL

Get outa here, you two-bit, flat-footed floozie.

FORTUNE TELLER

>   (Backs off, hurls a curse. Little Ben continues imitating her)

Dominus regitarita. Pig pox on your head, and let your hair fall out before Harvest Moon. Flesh flap all over your feet. Fah. Faaah.
>   (She approaches Mourning Glory, who is patiently waiting with her hand out)

FORTUNE TELLER

Ah, Glo--always this sad hand.
>   (Looks again)

Glo! Wait--something new--I see a child--no, a young woman looking to you, reaching out her hand. Follow--yes, follow her to a new life.
>   (Enter, Little Ben from tunnel)

BRAGG

What about me?
>   (Approaches Fortune Teller, extending his hand)

What about me? Tell me what's my future. Is she thin or fat or just right?
>   (Exit Brenda, Vicki Toby, Tina and Phil)
>   (Fortune Teller waves him away. Bragg goes to one of the men to borrow a coin)
>   (Little Ben extends his hand insistently. Finally she looks, casually, then closely at his hand)

FORTUNE TELLER

Little Benjamin. Something's about to happen. It'll change your life honey. It seems to be happening soon. And you better go back to work or the boss'll holler,
>   (Little Ben exits)

BRAGG

>   (Handing her a coin)

Now--tell me. Which one? I'm about to go crazy. Which--

   SCENE EIGHT
   SCENE CONTINUES

TIMEKEEPER

>   (Enters, running, from tunnel)

Fire in the hole!
>   (Explosions are heard from inside tunnel. Sal and Mary Magdalene enter. Mourning Glory starts to weep, wail, and gnash teeth. Little Ben exits tunnel at a run)

MARY MAG

Come here, honey. It's all right.
>   (Mary Magdalene comforts her. Mourning Glory passes from one to another for comfort)

IDA RED

How long you gonna carry on like that, honey? She thinks she's the only on. I just wish they' d fix that tunnel roof. Scares me half to death, every time they set the charges.

SAL

They got it shored up as good as they can.

IDA RED

Shoot fire they do. You never know when somebody disappears in there. They never tell you. Now, I don't mean to bad mouth the carpenters, y'all, but it just seems like the more they dig, the more it falls where they already dug. That ole shale.
    (Patting Mourning Glory)
Scaffolding don't help at all.

SAL

Ida, you all the time complainin'. What else can they do?

IDA RED

Now, Glory, come on, stop that.

SAL

Listen, if I was bossin' the job, I'd put brick in it--as they go along.

SAL

'Cause her daddy's a mason, that's why.

WITCHY

If it was me, I'd put somethin' else in it, and have done with it once and for all.
    (Tina enters, wearing new bonnet and carrying lunch bucket)
Come here, Tina. You brung me some dinner!
    (Takes bucket, looks in it, looks at Tina as she turns the bucket upside down. It's
      empty.)
Well?

TINA

I got hungry.
    (Witchy slaps her bottom. Tina runs and hides where she can watch Lucy and
      Mother)

IDA RED

I'd just make a long, brick sleeve like, all the way long, and shoot fire! I'd just throw out ever' last one of them stinkin' timbers.

MARY MAG

Stinkin', smelly timbers is right.

IDA RED

Holdin' up nothin' put empty hope. Why, half the time, it's the timbers fallin' on the men as much as the roof.

TINA

Men? Well, my sister's in there, too.
    (Makes faces at Lucy and Mother)

SAL

Yeah, always talkin' about the men. Like no woman was bustin' her behind, too.

IDA RED

Maryat Lee

I don't want to think about that. Tina, what are you doin'?

         WITCHY

Tina!

         TINA
  (Points at Lucy and Maud)
What's that?

         WITCHY

Stop that, Tina!
  (Slaps Tina's hand down)
Mustn't point.

         IDA RED

It's just country folk. From up in the hills. Can't hurt you. And it ain't polite to point. Now, Glory, listen here. Tears ain't gonna get a woman nowhere. Best way for you to get over it

         WITCHY
  (Scolding Tina)
They'll think you're putting a ha'nt on them.

         TINA
  (A running Exit)
I am! I witched 'em!
  (She and Little Ben go to the side and quietly plot)

         MARY MAG

Yeah. Glo, listen to Ida.

         IDA RED

And that's to get back to dancing again. It's time you took off the crepe.
  (Victor enters, carrying guitar. All greet him cheerily, ad lib, glad to see him, eager
  for him to play guitar)

         WITCHY

We been missin' music. Used to put some cheer at this ole hole.

         IDA RED

Come on, Glo. Shake a foot or two. Show us!

         SAL

Seein' you do some of them furrin dances, we used to die 1aughin' at you. But I got. so I miss it an awful lot. You know somethin', I feel bad about makin' fun of you, the way we did, but you never seemed to mind. Y'all re-member them Spanisher dancins'?

         ALL

Yes. Yes. Hooray! The Spanisher dancins'? Come on, Glory!

         SAL

An' that Frenchy dancins'? Whooee! An that--what kinda dancin' was it?
  (Sal dances around Mourning Glory to get her going. She puts Mourning Glory's
  arm overhead, but it drops. She tries again, failing again. Finally, on the third try,

Mourning Glory's arm remains aloft, and she suddenly begins to dance a Flamenco (or other dance of choice). Victor plays guitar, accompanying the dance. Gradually several becomes involved in a spontaneous dance, the tunnel people shuffling in time. The dance is ended with fervent applause, laughter, movement)

IDA RED

Right! Listen, y'all, what we ought to do is get everybody out of that hole for a few days. Stop workin' and live a little bit.

MARY MAG

Quit workin', and maybe they'd do something 'bout it in there.

IDA RED

The men won't quit.

SAL

And women.

MARY MAG

Not 'less we do somethin' else.
    (Someone snickers)

IDA RED

    (Noticing Lucy and Mother)
Y'all waitin' on somebody?
    (Lucy and Mother are too embarrassed to answer)
Honey, it's just like te rest of us. All of us is just awaitin' An' fussin'. An' cookin'. An' washin'. An'... Um, hum. Y'all come from up in the hills?
    (Lucy and Mother nod)
Well, I don't. I couldn't live in a wild place like this. How do y'all manage? Snakes 'n wolves 'n catamounts 'n.....? Why, I heard these corn patches is so steep you 'most have to put seed in a shotgun to get it planted. Just let me go home to the flatland soon. I'm just awaitin' 'til them tracks is put in, and I'll be ridin' out of here in style. But now I'm happy here in a funny kind of way. Got to know some folks, all kind of different folks, and we all hang together, work, play. Like her--just look at that.
    (Indicates Mourning Glory)
Never would have seen nothin' like that at home. Not in five lifetimes.
    (Lucy has been watching Mourning Glory, who tries to get various ones to dance with her. Lucy' begins to move her move one arm rhythmically to Victor's music, which is starting again quietly. Then Lucy begins moving her head, a foot, then both feet. Mourning Glory, noticing Lucy, gently draws her into a dance, observes her, and then fits her own dance in with their two styles together by showing her a movement, or by extending one of Lucy's movements further. They dance while everyone watches and encourages. Maud is in a spell to the conclusion of the dance)

IDA RED

    (To Mother)

Maryat Lee

Why, that's the best thing that's happened 'round here in a long time. Mourning Glory lost her son and ain't been herself since. There's nothin' to keep her here now. but she hangs 'round the tunnel anyways. Every day. Say, didn't I see your girl here last spring?
    (Mother glares at Lucy)
Wasn't she that nice country girl a settin' up in a wagon waitin' half the day in the hot. sun.
    (Maud glares at Lucy, comes back to life and goes after her)

MOTHER
Lucy Anne.

IDA RED
Uh oh.
    (Mother starts to fetch Lucy. Ida Red intercepts her)
I was just sayin' what a nice country girl she was, settin' out in that wagon in the sun.
    (Mother pushes past Ida)

IDA
Uh oh. I done it this time.
    (Mother grabs one wrist of Lucy and pulls her. Mourning Glory pulls her other arm. They play tug-of-war in slow motion. Mother finally yanks her loose. Mourning Glory collapses in slow motion)

MOTHER
    (Returning to normal pace)
Now you come home.

LUCY
But, Ma, you axed me what I wanted to do. Yoww. You axed me. Ma.
    (Mother pulls Lucy offstage. Mourning Glory weeps as she watches Lucy go)

WITCHY
    (Suddenly grabbing Mourning Glory)
Glo. Say! 'Member what she said, Fortune Teller, about a young girl? 'Member?

MOURNING GLORY
Oh--
    (Sudden ecstasy)
Oh, that's right. That's her. A new child. Follow her. That's what she said. Oh, yes!
    (Calls to Maud and Lucy)
Wait. Oh, wait for me! May I come? Don't leave me.

MOTHER
    (Offstage)
No, Ma'am! You wouldn't' like it up there. You're not like us. It's wild--

LUCY
Oh, Mom, Mom, Mom. Please. Please let her.

MOTHER
Ssshh. She wouldn't like it, Lucy. No!

LUCY
Yes she would!

MOURNING GLORY
Oh, yes. Yes, I would

MOTHER
There's nothing but chores, hoeing, washing, building fires, and...

MOURNING GLORY
I'll help you. I will.

MOTHER
Humpf.

MOURNING GLORY
Yes I'll do some chores. But she'll have to practice dancing.

LUCY
Oh, Mom. I'll run away if you don't let her.

MOTHER
Hush. Just stop that.
    (To Mourning Glory)
Miss? You think you could teach the other young'ns too?

MOURNING GLORY
    (Ecstatic and nodding, she turns to say goodbye)
Bye. Oh, bye bye. Thank you, thank you. I'll come see you!
    (Mother, Lucy, and Mourning Glory Exit hand in hand, Mourning Glory dancing.
    Little Ben and Tina follow them part of the way out through audience)

WITCHY
    (Waving)
Bye bye, Mourning Glory. I sure am gonna miss her, but maybe now she'll have a real family, more than with us, with a house and a well and things like that. She's been to so many places, strange lands, across the sea, she might not like stayin' here in the hills. Now take me, I like here. 'Course I ain't never been out of the mountains, don't know what flat country be like, or the sea.
    (To audience)
I'm an orphan. Tunnel people just 'dopted me. I stay with this'n and that'n, it's just like havin' a big family. John Henry told me once that this was the hardest country he'd ever seen. Said you had to spend two, three years just to go one mile. What I want to know is, what for is the tunnel. It ain't gonna do me no good. I ain't never goin' anywhere. Just knocks a hole in the mountain. And mountain'll get you back, you'll see, if you live long enough.
    (Witchy Exits)
    (Little Ben and Tina return)

SCENE NINE

Maryat Lee

SCEE CONTINUES

IDA RED

Witchy, now come on. Let's just hope she finds a new home and that old woman won't kick her out or make her feel like trash.

MARY MAGDALENE

Yeah, now. How'd that song go we started the other night?

IDA RED

'Bout John Henry?

SAL

Yeah. How'd that go? I was thinkin' up a verse last Polly made one, too. She got a good verse.

(Group starts warming up, hesitantly trying out keys and tunes, getting key that all can sing. For the first verse, Sal begins, and a different person thinks up each line)

SAL

(Pause)

WHEN JOHN HENRY WAS A LITTLE BABY

ALL

(That's right. That's good, etc.)

SECOND VOICE

SETTIN' ON HIS DADDY'S KNEE

THIRD VOICE

(Pause)

HE TUCK A HAMMER AND A LITTLE PIECE OF STEEL

FOURTH VOICE

STEEL GONNA BE THE DEATH OF ME, LAWD, LAWD

(Sal stirs pot. Tunnel workers, Gilpin, and Captain enter from tunnel. Contractor, Gill, a Salesman, and PollyAnn enter from Left. Tunnel workers talk with Captain and Time Keeper, reporting time.

IDA RED

There's Polly. Say Polly. Pol.

POLLY

Just a minute.

(Stage movement, ad libbing, everyone doing his business)

IDA RED

Say, what're those men up to now?

MARY MAGDALENE

(Crossing to eavesdrop near Captain)

I'll find out.

CONTRACTOR

(To Gill)

Hey, Gill, what about goin' over the shed.

GILL

Which shed, Captain?

(Captain points)

CONTRACTOR

Can the boys carry it?

SALESMAN

It's on wheels. It's easy--portable. Once you see how easy it is, you'll wonder how you ever done without it.

CONTRACTOR

(To workers)

The big shed. There's a crate at the door. Fetch it over, and mind you don't drop it.

GILL

Yes sir.

(Gill passes Gilpin. Hands him a steel bit)

Hey, take this back, will you? I got an errand.

GILPIN

Who's it go to?

GILL

Old Turkey Shooter. They're 'bout to put in powder. This'll be the last one.

GILPIN

Just wait a minute 'till I get back.

LITTLE BEN

I'll take it! I'll take it in!

(They give him a long steel bit 8-10" long. They Exit Left. Ben Exits at tunnel)

GILL

Well, come on then and give me a hand. They got a real machine over here.

(As Gill and Gilpin exit, they nearly bump into Victor, who enters carrying an instrument)

MARY MAGDALENE

(Crossing to Ida)

Say, you know what? That one skinny-legged man with a cigar, he says it goes three times faster than hand labor. Three times cheaper. Then Boss says he's not sure machine can bore through shale rock. Then they say, let's try her out. Then the one with the paunch says, let's try today. I gotta get back home tomorrow.

(Meanwhile Victor is asking Contractor questions. He has a new guitar, wrapped carefully. He points to it proudly, as if selling something. The men point to the women across the stage. He moves.)

VICTOR

Ladies, excuse me. I'm on my way west. And I just won this new instrument over in

Maryat Lee

Lewisburg. I wasn't gonna show anybody
> (Gesture indicating someone might steal it)

but I'm sorta proud of it and I just can't hold back any longer. And I know you don' t get a chance to see new music instruments much. Would you like to see it?
> (They all gather around, curious, as Victor opens the case, takes out new guitar. Sighs and compliments as they marvel at it)

IDA RED
Look at that! Now listen. Who can play such a thing! That don't look much like a banjo.

VICTOR
It's not a banjo! It's a guitar! Look--I can pick it a little. I'll show you.
> (Victor tunes up. Strums a little Ad libs as they see he can play it)

MARY MAGDALENE
He could play the song maybe?

IDA RED
Yeah! See if you can make up somethin' for this:
THEY TOOK JOHN HENRY TO THE MOUNTAIN
> (Victor tries several chords until he finds the right key. He begins to pick out the tune)

IDA RED
THAT MOUNTAIN WAS SO HIGH
MOUNTAIN SO TALL
AND JOHN HENRY SO SMALL
HE LAID DOWN HIS HAMMER
AND HE CRIED LAWD LAWD

POLLY
> (Who has sung the last lines)

I like that. I like that.

THREE VOICES IN TURN
JOHN HENRY HAD A LITTLE WOMAN HER NAME WAS POLLY ANN
WHEN JOHN HENRY LAY DOWN SICK ON HIS BED
SAY, I DRIVE STEEL LIKE A MAN, LAWD, LAWD

POLLY
I gotta get home, wash up, do some laundry and get some cookin' done, girl.

MARY MAGDALENE
You done enough today.

SAL
Turnin' nice, now the gnats is gone.

MARY MAGDALENE
Ain't you gonna wait for John Henry?

POLLY

Not with ever'body else waitin' for him, too. Y'all been settin' out here in the cool all day.

ALL

Cool?

POLLY

It's so hot in there and all that smoke, a person can't hardly breathe.

IDA

Cool? It was so hot out here, one of Miz Hedrick's chickens laid a hard-boiled egg.
>(More workers emerge from Tunnel, smudgey and blinded by the light. They gather upstage left. talk softly. Music comes up. The women's voices take turns at the stanzas)

WELL IT'S HONEY AND IT'S DARLIN' WHEN I'M HERE
AND IT'S A BIG NASTY MAN WHEN I'M GONE
AND WHEN YOU SEE ME COMIN' WITH A TWENTY DOLLAR BILL
IT'S BABY WHERE YOU BEEN SO LONG, LONG, LONG?

IT'S WHERE DID YOU GET YO SLIPPERS FROM
AND THE DRESS YOU ARE WEARIN' SO FINE?
I GOT MY SLIPPERS FROM. A RILROAD MAN
AND MY DRESS FROM A DRIVER IN THE MINE
MY MAMA GONNA SHOE MY PRETTY LITTLE FEET
MY PAPA GONNA GLOVE MY HANDS
MY SISTER GONNA KISS MY RED, RUBY LIPS
AND JOHN HENRY GONNA BE MY MAN

MIZ HEDRICK

>(Has entered during song)

Now what is this! You girls oughta be singing hymns, 'stead of shoein' pretty little feet and kissin' ruby lips. That's just what's wrong today. Now, take a good song, beautiful song, like--"Rock of Ages." Now that's a song for this camp.
>(They all politely agree. Miz Hedrick starts to sing it)

ROCK OF AGES, CLEFT FOR ME
LET ME HIDE MY SOUL IN THEE.

OTHERS

Umhum, that's true. Oh, we know all bout that.
WHILE I RISE TO WORLDS UNKNOWN
AND BEHOLD THEE ON THY THRONE
>(Some join in)

ROCK OF AGES CLEFT FOR ME,
LET ME HIDE MYSELF IN THEE
>(At the last note, the John Henry music starts up again, as she starts the second

Maryat Lee

verse, the two melodies are in counterpoint, but not with antagonism. Her duty done, Miz Hedrick joins the John Henry song with spirit, and she sings stanza three, below, as if making it up on the spot)

SINGERS

(Different women sing)
JOHN HENRY HAD A PRETTY LITTLE WOMAN
HER NAME WAS JULIE.ANNE
SHE WALKED THROUGH THE LAND WITH A HAMMER IN HER HAND
SAYIN', "I DRIVE STEEL LIKE A MAN, LAWD, LAWD"
  (Men join in)
OH WHEN I WANT GOOD WHISKEY
WHEN I WANT GOOD CORN
BABY WHEN I SING THAT LONESOME SONG
HEY, DOWN THE ROAD I'M GONE, LAWD, LAWD

JOHN HENRY HAD A LITTLE WOMAN
HER NAME WAS.MARY MAGDALENE
EVERYDAY SHE WOULD SING FOR JOHN HENRY
JUST TO HEAR HIS HAMMER.WHEN IT RANG, LAWD, LAWD

JOHN HENRY HAD A LITTLE WOMAN
JUST AS PRETTY AS SHE COULD BE
THE ONLY OBJECTION I'VE GOT TO HER, LAWD,
SHE WANTS EVERY MAN SHE SEE

JOHN HENRY HAD A PRETTY LITTLE WOMAN
THE DRESS SHE WORE WAS BLUE
SHE WENT DOWN THE TRACK AND.SHE NEVER LOOKED BACK
SAYIN', I DON'T WANT NO MAN, LAWD, LAWD,
NOT AFTER MY STEEL DRIVIN' MAN
  (Miz Hedrick exits)

SCENE TEN

SCENE CONTINUES

CAPTAIN
There he is: Hey Hey, John Henry!
  (On cue everyone is in slow motion)
  (John Henry and Phil, the Shaker, and Little Ben enter)

IDA RED
  (Sings slowly. Entire cast in slow motion)
CAPTAIN TOLD JOHN HENRY

GONNA BRING MY STEAM DRILL 'ROUND
GONNA TAKE MY STEAM DRILL OUT ON THE JOB
GONNA BEAT JOHN HENRY DOWN

IDA RED

CAPTAIN TOLD JOHN HENRY
I BELIEVE THIS MOUNTAIN'S CAVIN' IN
WELL JOHN HENRY JUST LAUGHED AND HE SAID TO HIS CAPTAIN

JOHN HENRY

IT'S JUST MY HAMMER SUCKIN' WIND, LAWD, LAWD
IT'S JUST MY HAMMER SUCKIN' WIND, LAWD, LAWD

    (Return to normal movement. Ad libbing, stage movement all around him. He is central to them)

MESSENGER

    (Offstage)

Hey!

    (Everyone freezes. Messenger enters running)

Hey! Man's trapped.

    (Murmur, movement. Captain and Contractor try to silence him)

CONTRACTOR

Who is it?

MESSENGER

Man's trapped. Up in shaft one.

    (Messenger stops as he sees Little Ben)

Where's John Henry?

    (John Henry steps up to him)

Take his boy--it was Powderman. Take him for a walk.

    (John Henry steps to Ben, whispers to him, puts arm around shoulder, they move to stage rear and then to down stage left. Everyone picks at Messenger to get the details)

MESSENGER

    (Speaks so that Boy doesn't hear)

It was Powderman.

    (Crowd responds)

And his wife had their baby just last night--two weeks early.

    (Crowd responds)

Couldn't get the midwife in time, so he done it himself. He told me how he shouted when he first saw the crown of the head coming through the arch as he brought his own into the black mornin' of this world.

CROWD

And killed the same day!

Maryat Lee

Oh, what is she going to do?
God help them.
What can we do?
Is her mother there helpin'? etc., etc.
    (Continue ad lib, under)

LITTLE BEN

    (To John Henry)
Is somethin' wrong?

JOHN HENRY

    (Facing him)
How old are you, boy?

LITTLE BEN

Fourteen.

JOHN HENRY

How many brothers and sisters?

LITTLE BEN

Just got a new sister last night. We was up all night. My daddy delivered her. He yelled when she came out right. He kept whirlin' me around. She's alright. Ain't she a beauty. She looked like a ole wrinkled somethin' to me. And all the dogs startin' howlin'. Midwife said he done real good. As good as herself. She don't have a name yet. My daddy wants to name her. He said he'd come home with a name tonight. I'd call her Hortense.

MESSENGER

So he went out to work without sleep. Boss wanted that air hole blown open. Drivers were suffocating down in the tunnel. So he put Amos on it and he went down the hole, said, "We'll knock her open today, boys. I was a midwife last night, brought my own baby into the world, and today I'm goin' in and blow this hole to kingdom come."

JOHN HENRY

How many brothers and sisters that make?

LITTLE BEN

She makes six. Besides me.

MESSENGER

So he was down in there, got the charge ready, lit the fuse, and started right back up. The rope got taut. A ways up we seen a frayed place in the rope begin to turn, 'bout halfway between him and us. "Take your weight off," we yelled. He looked up and saw where it frazzled. His face was an awful sight, his eyes reachin' out like hooks to us.

JOHN HENRY

Boy, you be the oldest? You're the first one.
    (Ben nods)

MESSENGER

Then he shouted, "Hey, tell my wife"--it was his last words and he knew it--"call her,

Felicity." Then he made a grab up to a rock, missed, and fallin' back on the rope, it broke. He cussed as he scraped on down to the bottom again. We couldn't see a thing. We heard him wrastlin' around with the fuse, tryin' to put it out with his bare hands, like it was a great snake about to strike. Then it struck The biggest charge he ever set. It went through all right, him with it. Stale air from the tunnel and smoke poured up like smoke out of Hell.
    (Starts Exit)
Won't do no good to hunt for him now. Man's trapped.
    (Exit Messenger)

JOHN HENRY

    (Gently)
Son, your daddy--
    (Ben draws back confused hearing Messenger's last words)

BEN

My daddy?--Where?
    (Ben tries to run away. John Henry holds his arm)
Nigger, leave go!
    (John Henry holds him tighter as Ben struggles to run. Then Ben's head tilts backward, and with a howl he throws himself on John Henry, who holds him gently)

IDA RED

    (To the Captain and Contractor and other men in a group)
You gonna tell us "No Casualties" like you done last week when Hamlet Jones got trapped? Y'all seen him this week?

MARY MAGDALENE

No casualties. The man's all right under the mud and stone, right, Ida?
    (Crowd murmurs and gestures in disgust)

LITTLE BEN

I gotta go to my mom.

JOHN HENRY

    (Holds him)
Not yet.

LITTLE BEN

    (Looks at John Henry)
How we gonna live?

JOHN HENRY

You're a man now.
    (Ben shakes head, tries to leave)
Boy, you can't go to your mammy. Can't hang on her no more. She got six hangin'. Can't be Mommy's boy. Can't be water boy. Can't be tool boy no more. Understand what I say?
    (Pause)

Maryat Lee

Now, don't move.
> (John Henry turns his back as if leaving, and then suddenly throws two or three lightning punches that barely miss the boy. Ben doesn't flinch)

Good. You do all right. Be a good shaker.

LITTLE BEN
> (Startled)

Shaker?

JOHN HENRY
> (Severely)

Now, if you ever flinch, you finished. Your head, or hand or knee be pounded into sausage.

LITTLE BEN
> (Long look)

Can I be your Shaker?

JOHN HENRY
> (Quietly)

You be where Foreman puts you.

LITTLE BEN
> (In shock)

Whew.

JOHN HENRY

Now, before you go home, you want to find out ever' thing for your ma.

LITTLE BEN
> (Nods)

I think I'm ready now.
> (They look long at each other. John Henry nods. With one last gesture of childhood, Ben hugs John Henry, then backs off)

LITTLE BEN

Thanks.
> (They grasp hands, like men. Crowd is silent as Ben and John Henry cross to Ida Red. She and Ben have an intense, silent dialogue)

LITTLE BEN

I gotta go tell my mom.

IDA RED
> (Long look at him)

Ben?
> (She holds out her arm. Ben wants to cry, but holds her hands a minute)

LITTLE BEN

Tell me--I didn't hear all of it.
> (They talk)

SCENE ELEVEN

SCENE CONTINUES
(Boss enters, confers with Captain)

CAPTAIN

Hear this We've got an announcement.
(Crowd quiets in anticipation)
Y'all heard about that drillin' machine they got over at Lewis Tunnel?
(Crowd stirs, murmurs)

MIZ HEDRICK

(Entering with first aid basket)
Mercy. Who got hurt? Where is he?

BOSS

Nobody's reported hurt, Miz Hedrick.
(Ben exits, waving. The women and John Henry wave, but the men do not see this departure)

MIZ HEDRICK

Nobody to me. He may be nobody to you, but he's somebody. Where is he?

CAPTAIN

(Conferring with Boss)
Miz Hedrick, it was a little accident up in shaft one.
(The crowd repeats "little accident," bandying it about)

MIZ HEDRICK

Oh, no, not up that high. What happened?

CAPTAIN

They say a man trapped in the shaft. We haven't verified it yet.

MIZ HEDRICK

Did they get him out yet?

CAPTAIN

We're workin' on it. We haven't found him yet.
(The men try to keep her from talking to the women)

MIZ HEDRICK

You're workin' on it, hungh.
(To audience)
The only thing I see they're workin' on is snuff, 'baccer, and cigars. The only thing workin' is their mouths, ain't that so?

BOSS

(To Miz Hedrick and the women)
The crew is up there workin' on it. It may not be as bad as--

MIZ HEDRICK

They better be, and you better be workin' on it so's it stops happening up there and in there. All o' y'all. And I mean it!

Maryat Lee

IDA RED
Miz' Hedrick, he's worse'n hurt.
MIZ HEDRICK
(Pause)
I guess I'll just have to go up there and see for myself.
(Calls off)
Son, saddle up the mule.
IDA RED
Miz Hedrick, it was Brown, the Powderman. He's gone.
MIZ HEDRICK
Brown? With a baby on the way? Dead?
(Shakes her head. Calls off)
Son--don't saddle nothin'.
IDA RED
(The women gather around her and complain, ad libbing)
Baby come last night

SCENE TWELVE
SCENE CONTINUES
(Enter Gill and Gilpin, pushing a large wooden crate on a wheelbarrow or suitable wheeled means of conveyance. The steam drill is inside. They push it to center stage, where it becomes the center of attention. Crowd responds with "oohh" and "ahhh," murmurs of admiration. Someone flies off to get a crowbar. The crate is dismantled to reveal the steam drill, a big, unwieldy engine with many pipes and valves. The drill itself is attached to the engine by a thick line. It is heavy and awkward, but the whole is very impressive and commands attention. Everything else is momentarily forgotten as everyone looks at it, touches it, admires it, etc., with mixed pride and apprehension. Gill, Boss, Contractor are beaming. Captain is not so sure)
(Enter Bookie)
(John Henry, who has been holding back, talking with Shaker, has watched from a distance, now in curiosity comes forward to look at the machine. He and Shaker assess it as a tool. John Henry touches it, tries to lift it slightly. As everyone studies it, the people on all sides cannot help but speculate. The machine grows in their minds as a competitor to John Henry even before the Captain speaks)
CAPTAIN
There she is! We got the steam drill like they used at Lewis Tunnel Right here at Big Bend. Now, what do ya say?
PHIL
Won't do no good in shale rock, Cap'n.
GILL
That machine there? Why, it'll beat the best man you got, three times over!

BOOKIE
You say, three times faster'n drillin' by hand?
CAPTAIN
That's what they say.
SALESMAN
That's right. You can put your money on it.
PHIL
Depends on who's drivin' steel, don't it, Cap'n?
CAPTAIN
They say, it'll beat our best man three times over.
PHIL
I say, it won't beat our best man, three times over.
 (Crowd murmurs im agreement)
IDA RED
I say, it won't beat John Henry one time over.
 (Crowd cheers, ad libs: That's right. You said it, etc.)
What about it, John Henry?
JOHN HENRY
 (Laughs)
Look at that thing!... Now I'll tell ya...I ain't made of steel. I'm just flesh and bone. Ummm.
IDA RED
Flesh and bone is right! John Henry, let me tell you something. If it works like they say, that means a lot of men be out of jobs.
JOHN HENRY
What I'm thinkin', too.
IDA RED
Right, Captain?
CAPTAIN
 (Exchanges looks with Boss and Contractor)
Well--that's right, Ida.
 (Silence)
You got to understand, the company has to--uh--
SAL
 (Prattling)
Get the work done cheap as they can, right, Cap'n?
MARY MAGDALENE
 (Going to machine)
Um hum, no matter what it costs.
 (Everyone laughs)
POLLY ANN

Maryat Lee

Soon's they can get all jobs ever' where done with stuff like this, we won't need to work at all. We can go on back to Easy Street.

IDA RED

Uh huh.

MARY MAGDALENE

At least there won't be as many men hurt and killed.
    (Laughter)

IDA RED

They'll just die of hunger.

TIMEKEEPER

Let's stop talkin' and do somethin'. Let's have a contest.

PHIL

Easy for you to talk. You wouldn't lose no job least not now. Not from somethin' like that. But they'll make a machine for you, too, Mister, some say. Wait and see. A time-keepin' machine. We just stick in a piece of paper and it'll snap out the exact minute you come and go, and it'll keep its' mouth shut, too.

GILPIN

Aw come on, let's see how that thing works.

GILL

Let's have a contest, Cap'n.
    (Crowd cheers in agreement, ad libs encouragement, though a few express worry)

CAPTAIN

What do you say, John Henry? If you beat that steam drill, I'll lay $20 in your hand.
    (Cheers, mixed with a few expressions of doubt and anxiety, as crowd becomes
    more and more excited to see what the machine can do. They encourage John Henry
    to take the challenge. He hesitates)

JOHN HENRY

I ain't sure, Cap'n.

MARY MAGDALENE

Come on, John Henry. You can't lose.
    (They urge him)

JOHN HENRY

Listen--a man ain't 'nothin' but a man. A machine could beat a man. Easy. Sure it could.
    (Walks from one worker to another, looking at each)
And, if it beats one man, it'll beat all of us. You know what I'm sayin'? I heard this here machine could do the work of fifteen men. Fourteen out of fifteen of us men have to ride out of here. If the machine wins.

MARY MAGDALENE

Do it, John Henry. You can't lose.

JOHN HENRY

You mean, I better not lose?
>(Looks at machine)

We got a year more on the job here. More'n a year. We like a family. The onliest I got. Now, what we gonna do? Where we goin' if a machine wins?
>(Crowd murmurs agreement)

We gonna lie down and pray?
>(Crowd: No, that's right, etc.)

IDA RED

We gotta stand up and pray.
>(Crowd cheers)

JOHN HENRY

>(LAUGHS)

Well, they always did say, hammer'll be the death of me.
>(Cheers)

But let me say this. How long we live don't matter. We can die any time, any year, any minute the Lawd wants, right? Whenever I go in there
>(Indicates tunnel)

I might die, Cap'n. Whenever I drive the steel, my Shaker might die. Whenever I come out to the sweet light of day to my friends, I just might die that night.
>(Someone wails)

So I says to myself: We live while we live, as lovin' as we can. We play while we play, as playful as we can.

SAL

Don't do it, John Henry.

JOHN HENRY

And most--mostest of all--
(Building to a crescendo)
--we work while we work as good, hard, as proud as we can.
>(Cheers)
>(To Captain)

So! 'Fore I let that steam drill beat us down, I'll die with my hammer in my hand, Brothers and Sisters, Amen
>(Crowd joyous, cheers. John Henry laughs, signals for attention. Crowd quiets)

Hey. Hey, come on, y'all. Don't ever'body look like I done got beat already. This here gonna be a big day, maybe proudest day in this man's life.

CAPTAIN

John Henry, you beat that steam drill, I'll lay it in your hand.
>(Whistles, calls, cheers, preparation for a contest begins.)

IDA

>(Sings)

Maryat Lee

JOHN HENRY TOLD HIS CAPTAIN
SAYS, A MAN AIN'T NOTHIN' BUT A MAN
AND BEFORE I'D LET YOUR STEAM DRILL BEAT ME DOWN
I'D DIE WITH THIS HAMMER IN MY HAND, LAWD, LAWD

>(Gill and others prepare the steam drill. They roll it close to one side of the Tunnel facing a rock wall and hover around it. They start it up a couple of times. It sounds like a miniature locomotive. Gill takes off coat, tinkers furiously to get the machine going. Timekeeper and Bookie start taking bets. They stand on boxes. The bets are recorded while crowd buzzes around, ad libbing and miming betting. John Henry and Phil station themselves on opposite side of Tunnel. They choose the right place to drill, as Gill and others choose a spot for the machine. When the betting is finished, the crowd gathers around the adversaries, concealing the drill and John Henry and Shaker. Ida remains downstage on box)

>   TIMEKEEPER

On your mark!
>(Crowd quiets)

Get set!
>(Steam machine picks up momentum)
>(Pistol shot)
>(John Henry's hammer head can be seen flashing above the heads of the crowd and the sound of steel can be heard as he strikes. Simultaneously, the steam drill bites the rock, with a loud jackhammer sound. The rhythm and noise of the two form a beat that the crowd falls into)

>   JOHN HENRY
>(Starts singing in time with his driving)

This ole hammer, huh   (Clink)
Gonna beat dat drill, huh
This ole hammer, huh
Gonna beat dat drill, huh
This ole hammer, huh
Or I'm all done, huh
Or I'm all done, huh
This ole hammer, huh
Gonna beat machine, huh

>(Repeats with variation)
>(Crowd joins in on the "huh" with him. Suddenly the steam drill falters. Gets hung up in the rock, spits and coughs and goes dead. Crowd laughs, cheers, boos, breaks up, collects bets. Steam drill is loaded onto wagon and pushed offstage to general merriment and derision as Ida sings)

IDA RED
JOHN HENRY LAUGHED WITH HIS CAPTAIN
FOR HE WON FOR ALL TO SEE
YOUR DRILL DONE BROKE, YOUR HOLE DONE CHOKE
YOUR STEAM DRILL COULDN'T BEAT HER MAN, LAWD, LAWD.

CAPTAIN
Won easy that time.
    (Everyone freeze)
        SCENE THIRTEEN
        SCENE CONTINUES
    (Everyone remains frozen as a sign is carried across the stage reading "SIX MONTHS LATER")

IDA RED
The man that invented that ol' steam drill
Found it couldn't beat their man
So he put it on the rack and then he brought it back
Sure it's faster'n any man's hand, Lawd, Lawd.
    (Normal stage action resumes, crowd murmuring, talking, ad libbing various actions)

CAPTAIN
Hey, ever'body. Remember that steam machine? The day John Henry beat it down? Well, what do you know. Steam drill is back.
    (crowd boos and laughs)
Now, I'll tell you one thing. John Henry makes people think there's a storm when he throws the hammers, that the mountain is catchin' on fire. But listen. Steam drill has done gone to school. Steam drill was just a baby last time. Steam drill is growed up. What do you say now, John Henry?
    (Crowd breaks into several groups, miming different actions simultaneously. The actions are separate but orchestrated. Crowd flows together again when the Bookie starts the betting)

(Mourning Glory, Lucy, and Maud enter, returning for a visit. They are warmly greeted. Enter from other side Witchy and Phil and join crowd. Mourning Glory confers with Victor about music. A dance breaks out. Mourning Glory is anxious to show off her pupil of six months. Mourning Glory looks more like a country person now, but tell-tale remnants of her gypsy life of the past remain. Lucy dances with her, at first reticent, then enthusiastic. Mother watches half-proud and half-embarrassed)

(Ida Red, Victor, others sing and try new versions of their song)

Maryat Lee

JOHN HENRY TOLD HIS CAPTAIN
DO ME JUST ONE THING
BRING ME ROUND A TWELVE-POUND HAMMER
SO I CAN HEAR IT WHEN IT RINGS, LAWD

JOHN HENRY'S CAPTAIN TOLD HIM
I JUST WENT TO TOWN
I BRUNG YOU BACK A TWELVE-POUND HAMMER
SO YOU CAN DRIVE THIS STEEL ON DOWN, LAWD

THE MAN THAT INVENTED THAT OLE STEAM DRILL
FOUND IT COULDN'T BEAT THEIR MAN
SO HE PUT IT ON THE RACK AND THEN HE BROUGHT IT BACK
SURE IT'S FASTER'N ANY MAN'S HAND, LAWD
  (They argue about verse)
           MARY MAGDALENE
Ida, that don't sound right. Try this.
"Said it's faster 'n John Henry's hand, Lawd."
It lays better.
             IDA
  (Sings)
Said "it's faster 'n John Henry's hand, Lawd."
You are right, Maggie, it sure enough lays better.
  (Enter Little Ben, The Boy, now very adult. He approaches the steam machine, stares
  at it soberly)
  (John Henry, Captain, contractor, Gill, Gilpin, Boss, others set up machine for the
  contest, in the same place as first contest. They ad lib and mime, arguing about
  placement of machine, length of bits, etc. John Henry examines machine again)
            CONTRACTOR
Who's gonna be your shaker?
            CAPTAIN
Who you want for shaker, John Henry? Choice is up to you.
            PHIL
I'll do it.
            JOHN HENRY
Phil, thanks, but I want to give a young feller a chance. Hey, Little Ben
  (Little Ben, The Boy, looks up)
            JOHN HENRY
Come over here, man.

(Ben goes to John Henry. They mime John Henry's invitation to be shaker. Ben is about to burst with happiness. John Henry and Little Ben confer quietly, while the other men laugh and welcome him into their midst)

(Gill and Gilpin enter, rolling in the refurbished steam machine)

TUNNEL WORKER ONE

Hey, there it is. There's Gilpin, with his big baby.

WITCHY

Baby that makes so much noise.

TUNNEL WORKER TWO

Hey, Gilpin, you got your big, bawlin' baby out for a ride in its carriage?

(Crowd laughs and hoots. Someone approaches the machine, strokes it and talks to it like a baby. General derision)

GILPIN

Cut it out. I'm just doin' my job.

(Crowd picks it up: I'm just doin' my job--he's just doin' his job, etc.)

TUNNEL WORKER THREE

(Shoving Gilpin from behind)

Let's see if your fists can do the job.

(Gilpin shoves back. They start a slow-motion fight, a natural preliminary to the contest. Everyone watches, cheering and rooting and laughing. The fight goes on uninterrupted until it becomes so vicious that the Boss jumps in between them. This signals the end of the slow motion, and the Boss nearly gets torn to pieces as the crowd moves in to end the scrap)

TIMEKEEPER

(Up on box)

All right, folks. Let's have your bets. Five more minutes to lay your bets. I said, we got five more minutes. You hear me? Is the steam drill ready? Well, get her ready. Place your bets. I got the book. Set it down. Won't get cheated. Don't count 'less it's down in the book. Come on, put your money down now. After that rock fall last week, may be your last payday. Put your money down.

(During this spiel, crowd comes up to Bookie or Timekeeper and places bet in cash box, gives name, etc. Witchy may act as assistant helping organize, etc. Timekeeper pauses during spiel to write down names and amounts. Captain makes a $100 bet. OOOHHHS and AAAHHHS all around. Betting becomes very serious).

TIMEKEEPER

Put your money down. Put it where your mouth is. Steam drill or John Henry. Come on, don't be bashful. Only got one more minute, folks. Come on, tell your children you was 'round to watch. it. One minute to go, folks.

(Ad lib)

(Steam drill, starts up)

One more minute, folks. Can you hear me over that racket? Hey, Cap'n, I can't hear my bets. We can't hear nothin' with that contraption. Gill got the steam drill goin'. John Henry-- got his hammer ready. Half-minute, folks.

IDA AND VICTOR

JOHN HENRY SPOKE TO HIS SHAKER
SAYS SHAKER YOU BETTER PRAY
CAUSE IF I MISS WITH MY TWELVE-POUND MAUL, LAWD,
TOMORROW'LL BE YOUR BURYIN' DAY, LAWD, LAWD

(John Henry and Little Ben are ready, steel between Ben's legs, people gather around as before, talking, cheering him on)

TIMEKEEPER

John Henry got his feet set. Little Ben, you ready for the ride?

(A woman wails)

Steam drill ready? Gill ready. Got your steam ready?

WITCHY

You got your. hot air more'n ready!

(Crowd laughs)

MARY MAGDALENE

What we laughin' about?

SAL

I just know he's gonna kill hisself.

TUNNEL WORKER ONE

Let's go!

(Pause. Crowd tenses)

TIMEKEEPER

Ready. Cap'n? Ok. Ready. Set.

(Fires pistol)

(Steam drill that was idling now starts up with a burst of sound and jack-hammering. This sound comes in counterpoint to John Henry's steady chant and the ring of the steel as his hammer flashes down)

JOHN HENRY

(Chanting)

This old hammer, huh   (Clink)
Rings like silver, huh
This old hammer, huh
Rings like silver, huh
This old hammer huh
Rings like silver, huh
Shines like gold, huh

Shines like gold, huh
Ain't no hammer, huh
In these mountains, huh
    (Repeat)
Rings like mine, huh
Rings like mine, huh
    (During the contest, Ida Red wanders downstage. Her singing comes up in volume as the hammer chant and racket of the steam drill decrease, though they can still be heard as counterpoint to her singing)

                        IDA RED

JOHN HENRY'S SHOULDERS IS A SHAKIN'
LAWD, A SHAKIN' I SAY
PULL MY HAMMER FROM MY SHOULDER
BOUND TO HIT HER WHEN SHE RINGS
    (Others join the singing)
JOHN HENRY HAMMERED IN THE MOUNTAIN
'TIL HIS HAMMER CAUGHT ON FIRE
VERY LAST WORD I HEARD HIM SAY
COOL DRINK OF WATER BEFORE I DIE.

                        JOHN HENRY
    (Chanting)
Ain't no drill,. huh   (Clink)
Gonna beat John Henry, huh   "
    (Repeats)   "
While I live, huh   "
While I live, huh   "
Take me home, huh
Let me sleep, huh
    (Repeats)
Let me sleep, huh
On Jesus' sweet chest, huh

                      IDA RED AND OTHERS
JOHN HENRY HAMMERIN' ON THE RIGHT-HAND SIDE
STEAM DRILL DRIVIN' ON THE LEFT
JOHN HENRY BEAT THAT STEAM DRILL DOWN, LAWD, LAWD
BUT HE HAMMERED HIS FOOL SELF TO DEATH

THE MEN THAT MADE THE STEAM DRILL
THOUGHT IT WAS MIGHTY FINE
JOHN HENRY SUNK A FOURTEEN FOOT HOLE

Maryat Lee

AND THE STEAM DRILL ONLY MADE NINE

SOME SAY GIVE JOHN HENRY SILVER
SOME SAY GIVE HIM GOLD
BUT HIS MAMA SAID GIVE HIM JESUS
FOR HE'S PRECIOUS TO EVERY MAN'S SOUL
>   (All turn to watch the final stages of the contest)
>   CAPTAIN

Time!
>   (Crowd cheers wildly, congratulating each other, etc. They lift John Henry on their shoulders and march around celebrating. John Henry enjoys the ride, then gets a pain in his head and falls back. They continue for a moment to celebrate. Someone in rear shouts. Cue for slow motion, change to silence, fear, and reverie. They try to set John Henry on his feet, but he slumps onto his knees. They lay him down tenderly, one arm falling lifeless. They kneel, Ben holds his head next to John Henry's head, consoling one another. They lift him up again, on their shoulders, place hammer on his chest, carry him off in slow motion and silence. All exit except Ida Red)
>   IDA RED
>   (Sings unaccompanied. First verse is sung sadly, slowly)

GLORY, GLORY, HALLELUJAH
SINCE I LAY MY BURDENS DOWN
GLORY, GLORY, HALLELUJAH
SINCE I LAID MY BURDENS DOWN
HEARD THE VOICE OF JESUS CALLING
THIS IS WHAT HE SAID TO ME
I WILL TAKE AWAY YOUR TROUBLES
AND I'LL LET YOUR SOUL GO FREE
>   (Crowd re-enters in normal motion. Two or three carry shovels. Pace of song picks up, is syncopated, finally crowd is keeping time, clapping, singing)

I'M GOING HOME TO LVE WITH JESUS
SINCE I LAID MY BURDENS DOWN
I'M GOING TO LIVE WITH JESUS
SINCE I LAID MY BURDENS DOWN

I'M ON MY WAY TO GLORY
GIVE ME STRENGTH TO MAKE MY ROUND
I'LL SING PRAISES E'ER AND EVER
>   (Slows) SINCE I LAID MY BURDENS DOWN.
>   (Pause)
>   CONTRACTOR

It's over, folks.
> (No one moves)

BOSS
Let's go home, y'all. It's another day tomorrow.
> (No one moves)

CAPTAIN
What ya waitin' for? Go on home.

IDA RED
Say it, Cap'n.

PHIL
Say somethin Cap'n.

CAPTAIN
Yeah, I guess somebody ought to say it.
> (Looks for someone else)

We got a preacher?

IDA RED
Say it. You can tell it, Cap'n.

CAPTAIN
Brothers and sisters, it's rough and it's wild in this wilderness.

VOICE
That's right!

VOICE
Tell it, Cap'n.

CAPTAIN
And all we got for a roof is the sky.

IDA RED
Or a roof that falls in on us all the time.

VOICE
And all the family we got is this here little camp.

VOICE
On a river.

VOICE
That's right!

CAPTAIN
Rough.

VOICE
Awful rough, etc.
> (Other voices ad lib similar words and phrases)

CAPTAIN
Hard.

Maryat Lee

VOICE
Lordy!

CAPTAIN
Wild.

VOICE
Way too wild.

VOICE
It's home.

VOICE
It's all we got.

VOICE
Tell it.

CAPTAIN
Our family is cut down today.

VOICE
That's right.

CAPTAIN
Struck down.
    (Tell it, ad lib)

CAPTAIN
You might say.

POLLY
The heart is stopped.

VOICE
Stopped!

CAPTAIN
The heart drove and pushed (That's right!) til it 'sploded like a great charge of dynamite.

VOICES
Yes, Lord. Tell it. Say it, etc.

CAPTAIN
He don't need me to say rest, rest, ole man. We never knew a man like you.

VOICES
And never know another.
Rest, rest. Rest in peace, John Henry
He don't need any words from any of us.
He don't need me to explain.
He don't need no words to pretty up his life for judgment.

CAPTAIN
But I'll tell you one thing. John Henry said he wasn't nothin' but a man.

VOICES

That's right.
A man.

IDA RED

But, John Henry, if you wasn't nothin' but a man, how come we see you aridin' up across the river now on wings!

VOICES

How come we see you ridin' up on the clouds (How come?) How come ridin' up to where the gates'll be open wide? (Yes, Lord) How come we see wings shinin' in the glorious rays of evenin' sky?
How come, how come?

BEN

John Henry, if you was--nothin' but a man, I just wish and pray

OTHERS

I hope and pray, too.

BEN

Someday, I can be a man

VOICES

Praise God. That's the truth. Tell it.

BEN

Someday, I can be a man, too. And, when the day comes mount up with wings' as eagles.

VOICES

That's right!
That's just right.
Amen.
Amen.

CAPTAIN

Let's go home.

IDA RED

(Starts singing slowly, unaccompanied. As others join, the tempo picks up)
SOME GLAD MORNIN' WHEN THIS LIFE IS O'ER, I'LL FLY AWAY TO A HOME ON GOD'S CELESTIAL SHORE, I'LL FLY AWAY I'LL FLY AWAY, OH GLORY, I'LL FLY AWAY WHEN I DIE, HALLELUJAH BYE AND BYE I'LL FLY AWAY.

(Cast spreads into audience, singing, greeting members. During this the stage is cleared and the stage is set as for the Prologue. At the end of the hymn the cast reassembles at or below the stage. They face the stage)

WHEN THE SHADOWS OF THIS LIFE HAVE GROWN, I'LL FLY AWAY
LIKE A BIRD FROM PRISON BARS HAS FLOWN, I'LL FLY AWAY
    (etc.)
JUST A FEW MORE WEARY DAYS AND THEN, I'LL FLY AWAY

Maryat Lee

TO A LAND WHERE JOYS SHALL NEVER END, I'LL FLY AWAY
    (etc.)

EPILOGUE
    (Mountain and Tree enter with quiet percussion noises. They wait till cast is collected at their feet)

MOUNTAIN

Tree? Are you still there?

TREE

Oh yes. I listened to every word, but where are they? What happened after? Did the machine finally win? Where's Little Ben now? Did he become a man?

MOUNTAIN

Yes, Tree.

TREE

Where is he, Mountain. I'd like to talk to him, or see him, or watch him. Or just shelter him.

MOUNTAIN

Tree, they are dead.

TREE

How! How could. they die! Mountain, where's the boy--the man? Mountain, I have a longing I never had before.

MOUNTAIN

Tree, they are dead.

TREE

But not the boy!

MOUNTAIN

The boy died.

TREE

The boy died.
    (Pause)
Mountain, was he like John Henry?

MOUNTAIN

A little.

TREE

Did he die like that?

MOUNTAIN

Something like that.

TREE

How long ago did he die, how long ago did John Henry die, when did all this happen?

MOUNTAIN

I was trying to figure it out, Tree. It must have been
    (Percussive sounds)

Yes, about 50,000 years ago.

    (Mountain descends from box. Slowly moves off stage)

    (Tree tries to understand. Mouths the last words of Mountain silently. Notices a bird or butterfly that lighted on her arm. Waves arm slowly, watches the bird fly off over a mountain. Long hold)

    (Tree skips off stage)

END

Maryat Lee

Approximation of rail calls. JOHN HENRY, scene 1.
M. Lee

Foreman: Put your dogs on a iron —
Crew: we got seven down.

Foreman: Raise up an set 'im in a bed boy —

Foreman: Raise up an set 'im in a bed boy
Crew (front person): Why dontya make a joint on me —.

Crew at rear: got a good joint made —.
Another crew: got a good joint made —.

Crew: Move it on down the line boy.

NOTE: The pitches are all relative.
Each "crew" is a single voice.

Author's Note on *John Henry*
Maryat Lee

A celebrated historical personage is always hard to deal with in a play without falling into romanticizing (or sentimentalizing). This lesson was brought home to me in writing *John Henry*. My farm includes one shoulder of the Big Bend Mountain through which the great C&O railroad tunnel is bored. This tunnel was the longest in the world when the thousand or so whites and recently-freed slaves dug their way through the red shale with steel-driving and powder-blasting in 1870-72. John Henry, one of the liberated slaves, met his fate at this tunnel in 1872, and became one of the major folk heroes, not only in this county but over the world. Obviously the hero of this county should be the subject of our first play. That his feat in life was due to his muscles made it difficult for me, a woman, to deal with. Yet for a single man, and a Black, to have stood out and be remembered in legend and song when hundreds of men were killed in building that tunnel says something of the kind of man he must have been that goes further than brute strength. But I fought the idea of a play about him.

Fran Belin, who was co-producing with me that first year, suggested that we center the play in Talcott, the little town five miles from my farm that straddles the tracks at the east end of Big Bend tunnel. She insisted that we should celebrate John Henry and get fresh material from old people who still might have interesting bits of passed-on information about him. That's how we started.

In our first summer of producing *John Henry* we had fifteen youths from a federal employment project called in West Virginia the Governor's Summer Youth Program. When the kids showed up, we asked them to go back home that night, especially those who lived in Talcott, where the workers' camps and shanties had been located during the tunnel-building, and ask their grandparents and descendants of the tunnel-workers who had settled there, about John Henry.

The "Great Bend" tunnel, twin to the Big Bend, under construction. Both were well over a mile long and the brittle shale in the mountain made for frequent rock falls. *Library of Congress.*

Jimmy Costa, a local historian, also did some interviewing, and while looking for nineteenth-century material, turned up quite by accident an account by a local man named Jesse Green of how the laying of the steel tracks was sung when he was Foreman during the 1920s. This particular tape was very exciting. It revealed how the foreman "bossed" the crew of eight pairs of men to pick up rails and set them on the ties, with all the directions "sung" or chanted, and the men singing back answers. I had to find a way to incorporate this material into the play. This became scene one, and a transition back to 1870 was easily managed. A young reporter arrives at the tracks to interview the foreman and get a story on John Henry. She comes across a gang laying the second set of track at the new tunnel only a hundred yards to the left of the old tunnel, thus allowing simultaneous two-way railroad traffic through the mountains.

The roles of the Foreman and the Reporter have been interchangeably white and Black, but in general throughout the play, the actual color of the characters is of little importance, except for John Henry himself. In fact, in the first summer, when we had no Black male, the company and I agreed that it would be better for a Black female, rather than a white male, to play the part. This set a precedent for considering gender for roles less important than other qualities. That same Summer, Jimmy Costa played the part of Miz Dacey, an old mountain woman. Over the years, the female John Henrys were not in the

John Henry triumphs, briefly, over the steam drill. *West Virginia and Regional History Center.*

least distracting. Ossie Davis, who came one year as an observer, found himself curiously not aware of the gender at all. Billie Jean Young, a Black poet from Mississippi, amplified this: while ordinarily very conscious of who is Black in a play, she found, halfway through, that she wasn't even aware of what color the actors were. The company in the first year was, incidentally, almost equally mixed, with a few more girls than boys.

We did not have an actor of either gender with the size and stature that a hero like John Henry should have. We adapted to this by intensively developing the life around the tunnel within a few feet of the portal. This primitive environment in which John Henry lived allowed unlimited scope for the people who lived there: a country doctor, peddler, landlady of a boarding house, captain, contractor, salesman, water boys, blacksmiths, women who gather during the day to gossip and sing and make up a song and comment while they wait for the shifts to change.

The first year the EcoTheater company was also very primitive. But it was not "amateur" in the corrupted sense in which the word is often applied to theater today-- "amateur theater" equals awkward, poor acting and an embarrassing performance. But something appears "amateur"--in this negative sense--only when one is attempting to copy something that is professional. If people present something that reflects the integrity of their own persons and place--no matter if things be spelled or pronounced "wrong"--as long as it can be heard, it has its own strength, its own integrity and style. One need think only of primitive sculpture or painting to understand that they have qualities that can be judged only on their own standards, not on ours. This concept in theater has not yet been accepted. But since primitive dance and primitive music as well as primitive art long since have been accepted in their own right, we may hope that it is only a matter of time until the concept is accepted and practiced in theater.

> With improvisations about things that had just happened to them, perhaps on the way to work or school, they began to see how exciting their friends were when momentarily they lost their shyness.

The most important feature of rehearsals was to build the confidence of the actors. Not all of the kids wanted to act in the first place. This was for me an asset. It meant I was spared the embarrassment of star-struck people who wanted nothing better than to pretend for awhile to be someone else. But it took time for them to understand that I did not want them to pretend to be anyone else than who they were. They could simply be themselves, but not the roles that they, too, play in everyday life. This is more complicated, of course, than the telling of it here. I spoke to them about how we all play roles and that the stage is a safe place to take off the roles and be some aspect of what one really is. With improvisations about things that had just happened to them, perhaps on the way to work or school, they began to see how exciting their friends were when momentarily they lost their shyness.

While they were getting this introduction to theater for an hour or two in the morning, they did various jobs--stretching canvas, painting, helping in the office, clearing a field to make rehearsal space. Meanwhile, I was writing the *John Henry* script, knowing now who we had to work with and tailoring the script to them and what I perceived was within their reach. As a scene was finished, we started casting and rehearsing, with Fran Belin directing. I might say that we were the only two who had any concept of what we wanted. The rest of the staff were quite able but as much in dark as the kids were. We spent at least one hour each day singing and playing music with them, teaching them "old timey" songs. Soon we were to have *John Henry* rehearsals in the mornings, and *Ole Miz Dacey* in the afternoons. Many of the kids were in both plays. That summer both plays were quite short and on a double bill. We opened August 2, 1975, with *John Henry*, and a week later added the other play. Starting from zero, we had whipped up the company in three weeks to do this back-breaking, nerve-snapping thing. We had no stage, just the grass with painted flats braced from behind. Any other spare time we spent making patchwork banners to decorate the space we performed in--at the courthouse lawn, or the Pence Springs flea market, or Alderson Prison, or back in some hollow.

After that summer I folded up all the plans and had no intention of trying it again. I had proved that the idea worked. But it was a nightmare in the short, six-week period we had with the company. However, over the next year a local woman came and gave an impassioned plea for me to continue and said she would help. That encouragement was all I needed. We produced *John Henry* again in 1978 and each summer thereafter until 1981.

Maryat Lee

With each season, the play became longer, more complex, and more interesting. The Mountain-Tree scenes were added the second year. The Mother-Daughter scene was added the next year. The scenes also became more challenging and difficult as the troupe each year became more expert and confident. Each year, I also revised it as I myself grew in my confidence of them. We never had the same company as the year before; but usually about seven returned from the year before, and they made the work much easier for the other twelve or fifteen. The new kids seeing the other kids already swimming were much quicker to jump in the water and take risks. This play has been revised yet once more for this published version. It may be too demanding for a group starting from scratch. But it can be cut down--just as it was built up--leaving some of the scenes out, and simplifying others. John Henry himself does not appear until the latter half of the play, and yet in this version it is clearer why the people at the tunnel really love him--not just because he was a muscle man--but because he is big in compassion and absent of the usual ego of the strong man. He is not a superman, as he says when faced with the competition. "A man ain't nothin' but a man." And, of course, when a man is just himself--what a man he is!

> "Maryat was inspired by her location, by Summers County itself: the swift, white rivers running through gorges over rock shelves; the water racing between looming, mysterious mountains; the morning mists that cling to the mountains: these things filled her with awe. The wild beauty of the place infused her with the need to write about it...John Henry is not her real subject. Her real subject is the spirit of the people who came to live in this wild, forbidding, beautiful place. These people had to adapt to the mountains that crushed and killed many of them. To give the descendants of these tough, hard-living pioneers--farmers, tunnel people, laborers, blacks and whites, male and female--a sense of their ancestors was her real purpose. She wanted to render the struggle for survival in this tough and beautiful place that becomes part of the very spirit of the survivors and their descendants."
>
> -Bill French, writing in "Drama for Appalachians," *Appalachian Journal* (Summer 1984)

A formidable statue of John Henry now stands just outside the Big Bend Tunnel near Hinton. *Courtesy Michael W. Harding.*

Maryat Lee

OLE MIZ DACEY

A Comedy in One Act

> AT RISE: Unnatural bird sounds may be heard. Stage is empty. Presently Miz Dacey opens door, steps out of her porch. She appears troubled. Bird sound s are heard only when she is inside house. She sweeps and mumbles to herself. She peeks through screen door, looks around corner at something in living room. She continues to mumble and pick at her plants. Finally she opens the screen door and hesitantly steps inside, and the bird sounds are heard again. She steps back on the porch; the sounds stop; she puts a foot on the threshold and they start again. After several such experiments, she comes downstage and stares at audience, perplexed.

Dacey

Now, just what do you suppose? I just don't know what to do. If I could just talk to somebody about it.

(Sweeping.)

Here I am. Lived here for many a year, through all kind of things since my old man died, and then this year I finally decided to sell out and move to a little place in town. Felt the old place was gettin' too much for me. My granddaughter tells me to sell it and move in with her in Cincinnati. My son says not to sell it, he'll do the work. But he lives in Charleston. Anyway, since I began thinking about sellin' the place, things--queer things--all kind of things I never saw or heard of--begun to happen.

Well, first it was the television set. 'Sploded that night when I was in the kitchen cookin' up some apples. Just went in there to see if they was stickin', and I heard this big noise and come runnin' to see what in the world it was. And there they was--beginning to kind of drip out of the back of the set--little green things. And, Lord, when they hit the floor, they began to crawl around, then got up on their feet. Yessir, they was standin' up, millin' around, turnin' cartwheels and all. I went to the kitchen and got my broom--this here broom--and went after 'em like they was a bunch of bats a' flyin'. I turned the broom around and hit 'em with the handle, but them little buggers just danced out of reach.

"What are you doin' in my television set?" I says. "Now, you all go on back to wherever it is you come from. Shoo," I says. "Go on, Shoo." But it wasn't 'til I turned off the set, they climbed back up the legs and into it again. Next day I didn't turn on the set for an awful long time. Then, in the evening, kind of accidental, I turned it on and, Lord, it jumped up and down, you know, and then out they come again. "Well," I says, "I'm going to sick the 'sterminator on you. I can't keep my set off all the time."

(Swats at a fly.)

Well, I get on the phone. "Mr. Yancey," I says, "I got some terrible trouble up here today. Little men, little things, are a comin' out of my set." And 'fore I could finish tellin' it, he's already here with his old blue and green truck. Well, he looked all around and couldn't find nothin'. So, I asked him to squirt some of his bug stuff 'round the legs, which he did, and he said they wouldn't bother me no more. But that night, I set down, turned it on, and down the legs they come again and start wandering all over like they owned the house.

Well, I says, I'm goin' to call the television people and put them on it. So I called and told that lady there about these little things, I don't know what to call 'em. And she asks me, "Are they bugs?" And I said, "Well, no, they're men, little men, and they're kind of greenish-like. " "My gracious, Miz Dacey," she said. I says "Why, one of them taken to climbin' up my rocking chair last night to pull at my apron." She says, "Does it act like it wants to do something to you?" I says, "Lordy, honey, no--if you mean was they tryin' to get under my skirts." Then she left the phone--you know, covered it up a minute--and then she comes back and says, "Are you up there all by yourself?" I told her I was, and then she says I ought to see the doctor. I said, " don't want no doctorin'. It's that TV that's broke that I bought at your store--let's see--last August 28th it was." I told her I adjust the what-you-call-them-ears, turkey ears, that you pull out and around. But all she could say was call a doctor, call a doctor.

(Picking dead leaves off the potted plant.)
Well, the long and short of it was, she finally sent out a young man from the store to look at it.

(Sits down and swings or rocks vigorously and fans herself.)
And that was just the first thing--the beginning of a streak of good luck or bad--can't say yet.

First it was the television set. Then it was the television man, Orfin Furlow, one of them Furlows over there on Pea Ridge. His mother was a Bragg, his father a railroad man that took off the Cleveland, and that's where Orfin was born. Now he likes it back here in the hills. Just a boy. Well, Orfin couldn't see 'em--the green men. He said they was in my head, you know.

But then--
(Pause)
He started comin' back. Sort of a lonesomey boy--younger than my youngest boy. Come out of a Saturday, doin' some of the chores, fixed up the fence. Took a notion to take out the straggly old posts and put in new locust posts, by jackies. Knows how to lay a tree down, and how to lift a hammer. There just ain't nothin' dooless about him. Lately in the evenin' after work he come ridin' out just to visit. I had some old railroad soup or something, and he sit down and said it was the best food he's had for the longest time. Yep, he comes out again a day or so later. And that's the way I got to fixin' real meals again.

(Peering some distance away, behind audience.)
Lands, here comes somebody now.

Maryat Lee

   (Looks hard,)
But it ain't Orfin. Now, who is that? Some town lady, looks like. Steppin' this way and that, not wantin' to get her feet dirtied up. Ooops - she nearly fell on that old rock. With them fancy heels she'll have a time on this old porch.
   (Watching her advance.)
Evenin'.

         Goodbody

   (From path.)
Good afternoon, Miz Dacey.
   (Pause.)
   I believe you are Miz Dacey?

         Dacey

Ever since I got married, that's what they call me. Come on in.

         Goodbody

   (Opens imaginary gate. Slight worry about dog. Professional smiles. From bottom of steps.)
Well, I'm Letrosha Goodbody, from the Outreach Office? And I just thought I'd come by to see how you're doing. your dog?

         Dacey

He can't even hurt a flea. Well, come on up, if you don't mind gettin' stuck up between the porch boards,

         Goodbody

   (Teetering up steps to porch she walks with extra care to chair.)
I shouldn't wear these old heels when I--one shouldn't ever wear open toes in the country, should one?
   (She takes off one shoe and shakes out a pebble.)

         Dacey

   (Studies the shoe.)
Beats me why a person would wear 'em anywhere. I had a pair once. My old man brought 'em home and I put 'em on one time. He brung me a corset with pink flowers on it, and fine stockings, too, I tried on the whole outfit but never even bothered to put a dress over it. I felt like sausages: one bit sausage and two little ones in high heels tied to the end of it. I took the whole thing off and wrapped up the shoes in the corset and give it back to him. He dropped it behind the door and later when I went to town, I put it in a poke and left it in a shoppin' cart at the old A & P. Never knew what happened to 'em.

         Goodbody

   (Laughs.)
Well Miz Dacey you tell a good story.
   (Stifles belch.)
And you've got such a nice view. Are you feeling well these days?

(Digs in her purse)

Dacey

I'm gettin' along tolerable well. Now I don't mean to butt in, but are you feelin' all right?

Goodbody

(Twisting and turning bottle.)

I just can't get this cap off my pills. It's so aggravatin'.

Dacey

Oh, I know 'bout them caps! Why, it 'most takes a blacksmith and a little boy to open up them ornery things. But I'm on to 'em now. I found a sure-fire way of doin' it.

(She puts bottle on floor and stamps on it. They pick up pills. Ad lib.)

Now, I don't know when it was I took my last pill, anymore, but it was in one of them new bottles. The ones old folks can't get into. So I threw 'em in the burn pail, and they really lit up the sky that night with fire-works when I burned my trash.

Goodbody

It's nice to meet somebody who's in perfect health and doesn't need any pills.

Dacey

Nobody's in perfect health, I don't reckon. You say you're from the Outreach Office?

Goodbody

Yes, I'm an aide to the Director of the Community Nutrition and Health Bureau, Mr. Abscess?

Dacey

No. I don't believe I know who that is. But wasn't it them that told us, long time ago, to buy those little rose bushes for fences a rabbit couldn't pass?

Goodbody

That's not my department. I'm in Nutrition and Health.

(Looks around for water, then decides to swallow pill dry.)

Dacey

What exactly would that be for?

Goodbody

I've got this condition.

Dacey

I mean your nutriation work.

Goodbody

Oh. Would you be interested in our recommended diet with high protein and low cost. The menus are all made out, depending on the number of people in your family--even for one per son. And one need s a diet that has variety and lots of vegetables and fruits and, of course, your protein. We encourage folks in better diets, better food s, so they'll be healthy and live to a good age.

Dacey

Seventy-seven seems like a good age to me. Wouldn't want to stick around here long. And,

Maryat Lee

oh, I've got plenty to eat.

Goodbody

That's wonderful. Now, for instance, what did you eat yesterday?

Dacey

Law, I can't remember. Cornbread, soup beans, I expect. And I cut up some of these old yellow onions. Didn't have no green ones.

Goodbody

Now corn and beans together are very good. Together they make up a protein. But it would be good if you had a little meat, too.

Dacey

A little bacon is all.

Goodbody

Umhum, good. Now, do you can, Miz Tracey?

Dacey

Dacey

Goodbody

(Giggling)
Oh, excuse me, Miz Dacey. I don't know what's botherin' me. I just couldn't get to sleep last night with a headache? So I'm doing silly things today.

Dacey

(Gently teasing.)

Couldn't have been somethin' you et?

Goodbody

No. I went to the doctor this morning, and he gave me a prescription for tranquillizers. My headache is a little better, but I do have a little heart burn.
(Teasing now sinks in. Pause.)
But to get back to you, Miz uhh –
(Nervous laugh.)
Do you have any trouble preparing meals for one person--you are alone, are you now?

Dacey

Well--you might say so. No, can't say I have any troubles at all, no sirree.

Goodbody

(Makes checks on list.)
Good. Good.
(Rocks. Pause.)

Dacey

No, don't have no trouble.

Goodbody

That's nice.

Dacey

No troubles. Least, not way.

Goodbody

(Looks closely at Dacey.)

Dacey

(Pause.)

Well, come to think of it, maybe you could help me.

(Pause.)

I have some little green men that's been botherin' me an awful lot.

Goodbody

Some little green--?

Dacey

They started first in the television set, you see, and they seemed to live in it at first and come out only when it was turned on. Now they begin to come whether it's on or not.

Goodbody

Oh, they do?

Dacey

Why, yeah, they taken to pulling at my quilt last night, 'way after I turned off the set.

Goodbody

(Trained smile.)

Really? My sakes, Miz Macey, you do have a lot in your life, Well, I think I'd better go on down the road. But you might be interested in reading--you do read?--this here literature, I mean, this literature, here. I'll just leave it with you. See, it has the menus and diets for the old people, so we can keep them, not only around for a good, long time, but in good mental health, too!

Dacey

Say, you wouldn't want to see 'em before you leave?

Goodbody

The green--uh--

Dacey

Yep, I'd like to see if somebody besides me can see 'em. Orfin can't see' em. The 'sterminator couldn't. Maybe another woman could, you know.

Goodbody

Orfin, did you say? Orfin Furlow, that boy that works at the TV store?

Dacey

Yes, that's him. You know him? By crackies, I'm glad to hear that. Some- times I just wonder if I was makin' hit up. Yeah, he come out to fix my set. An awful good -turned young feller, ain't he? Even if I'm old, I can see that much. I mean he's got an awful good character about him, kindly serious. A little bit of every kind of nature to me that's good. Why, he took me out in his car, the prettiest car. Just rides like a bunch of feathers. We went to the preachin' last Sunday and, boy, I set up so high in that car and seen these other old women out there lookin'. After it, we was sittin' right here on the porch, and--oh, well –

(Thinks better.)

Anyway, how long you know Orfin?

Goodbody

I don't mean to butt in, Miz Dacey, but you got to watch these young fellows nowadays.

Dacey

Oh, I watch him all right, and he always looks so good and always clean, too. Why, last Sunday he dressed up in a new shirt--one of them they use to write messages across--and shiny pants, all slicked up, like a bunch of spring flowers.

Goodbody

(Nervous.)

Miz Dacey, have you every thought of seein' a doctor?

Dacey

Doctor? Don't you know about them doctors, honey? I don't mean to be down on 'em, but if there's one thing most doctors want to cut out and sew up anymore, it's your money--yours or the government's and I'll tell you somethin'. You watch. People are gonna go back to the country medicine--like golden seal and comfrey and sassafras root. And to tell you the truth they'd be better off. Why, anymore, the doctors dose you up with pills so good you don't know what hit you. Try and talk to 'em sometime.

Goodbody

Miz Dacey, I'll just leave these little booklets.
And here's a number if you need help. Now, you take care of yourself.

(Tottering on high heels, EXITS in a hurry.)

Dacey

(Peering in distance.)

Don't hurry off! Here comes somebody. Who is that--Orfin? No, some man. What's he looking at, like I'm some old target at a turkey shoot. Now he's looking at my mountain' above the house like there's timber in it. Ain't nothin' much but buckeye and brush--and them federal roses that took over. He can have them, Buddy. Always thought a feller'd do good to start a mail order business on them daggone roses. All them rose bushes the state wanted us to plant years ago, and me and the old man put 'em in, and now you can't hardly find a place big enough for a cow to drop a pie on, with all them rose bushes trying to take over your garden, pasture, house and home. Now they want you to buy stuff to get rid of what they had you put there in the first place. Now he's lookin' at the old barn. He's gonna try to beat me out of something, oh, I can tell.

(Dacey goes to her door, opens it, pulls out a hand gun,)

Can't know 'bout folks these days, what they'll try with a widow woman. Now everybody knows I can shoot the head off a copperhead, crow, or squirrel from this porch all the way to the barn.

(Albee Hood enters down path.)
Howdy, Mister.

Albee

Howdy, Miz Dacey.

Dacey

Afore you come through the gate

Albee

Miz Dacey, you remember me? Albee Hood. A. A. Hood.

Dacey

From where? You one of them Hoods up at Split Rock?

Albee

You remember, I met you and your husband some time back at a ramps supper in True when he used to fiddle.

Dacey

I can't seem to remember that far back.

Albee

Me and him used to do some loggin' in the old days. And squirrel huntin'. He was a fine feller. But most of all, ain't nobody 'round could ever play a tune like he did.

Dacey

Come on in the yard. What you standin' around out there for?

Albee

(Opening gate.)
I see you got a.38 in your lap. Feared it just might go off accidental.

Dacey

It ain't a.38. It's a.32. And it don't ever go off accidental.

Albee

It ain't loaded?

Dacey

It's loaded, Like I don't want to hurt nobody, but if anybody knocks on my door and they don't answer me, I shoot right through the door. If anybody steps in, he won't step out,

Albee

You can reload it real quick?

Dacey

It shoots five times. But I don't ever shoot more'n once. My old man give it to me before he died and told me to keep it right with me.

Albee

It's better than a new one, I reckon,

Dacey

(Handing over gun.)
Here.

Maryat Lee

Albee

That's an old Owl Head, yep,

Dacey

Yeah, I had that gun for years. I was just sewing my other dress because it split where I carry it.

Albee

Yeah, that's a good little gun.
    (He's slow in handing it back.)
How's your water, Miz Dacey?

Dacey

Want some? I got good water.
    (Dacey goes in house. Bird sounds are heard. Albee takes out notebook, makes notes, puts book away. Within, Dacey mutters and scolds: Scat, go away, etc. Dacey enters with pitcher and glass, looks at Albee to see if he hears what happens in house. Then shuts door.)
Thanks, Miz Dacey.
    (He tastes water carefully.)
You got a well, Miz Dacey?

Dacey

Yessir, it's ninety-five feet deep under a rock shelf. Eleven foot down through solid rock. And the water ain't druggy or nothin'.

Albee

Uhhum, it's nice.

Dacey

It's soft all right, no minerals mixed in it.

Albee

I see you got some nice chickens. Rhode Island Reds.

Dacey

No, they're Red Jersey or something.

Albee

Red Hampshire?

Dacey

One of them things. But they won't hardly set. Now, if you want a chicken to set good, you just get you an old mixed-up hen. They'll set real good. You throw one off the nest and they'll crawl back on it. Something's d one killed one of my hens. They go down there of a day, and the foxes is gettin'' em.

Albee

You better go down there and set your gun on 'em.

Dacey

I'll get 'em one of these days. What's the matter?

Albee

(Dodging her gestures with the gun.)

Like the little boy says, a feller can get a little nervous with a lady with a gun.

Dacey

A lady? Like that old woman[42] used to say, Mr. Hood, the Lord made woman, and the city bunch of thieves and braggarts made the ladies.

(Puts gun away.)

Albee

I know what you mean, Miz Dacey. It's all a feller can do to figure a living with all them people tryin' to skin you out of somethin'.

(Sits down.)

Dacey

(Pause.)

So what's your business, Mr. Hood? It be real estate business, I believe.

Albee

I sometimes fool around with it. Boys, it sure is pretty out here. You got such a nice view with them mountains across here. It's so peaceful. Must get kindly lonesome?

Dacey

Not hardly. I got my chickens and pig and garden and dogs and,

(Looks toward house but thinks better of mentioning the green things.)

well, I ain't never lonesome.

Albee

Didn't you all have three children?

Dacey

We had four, two boys and a girl.

(Pause as he ponders.)

And they're all livin'?

Dacey

Yeah, and all gone.

Albee

Guess sometimes it's hard to keep up with a farm, with only one person.

Dacey

Well, I was giving a little thought to sellin'. I guess word was goin' around?

Albee

I guess everybody talks about people in a sellin' mood. But I don't never bother 'til they come to me. It's no use 'til they're ready. You know, it's a shame about that music. None of your sons ever took it up, did they?

Dacey

No sir, none of 'em had the hankerin' after it.

---

[42] Mary Jones (popularly known as Mother Jones), 1830 - 1930, labor agitator in southern coal fields.

Maryat Lee

Albee
I suppose you don't still have his fiddle? (Or guitar.)

Dacey
It's hanging on the wall.

Albee
Ain't that a shame, after bein' played so much? Just to hang on the wall? I knew somebody who'd love to buy it. Feller in town. Fixes up old instruments. Plays on 'em too.

Dacey
That Costa boy?

Albee
That's the one. You know him?

Dacey
He comes around. Sort of talky, ain't he? But he sure likes the old ways. Likes this old farm. Thought I'd see if he wanted to buy it sometime.

Albee
(Eagerly.)
I'll tell you something, Miz Dacey, you want to be sure to get a good price. Land ain't cheap anymore. You could get a fine price for this land.

Dacey
What do you call a good price, Mr. Hood?

Albee
Just call me Albee, Miz Dacey. Nobody calls me Mr. Hood.

Dacey
Well, the question is still there, however I call you.

Albee
I'll have to think about it. Let me see. My goodness, Miz Dacey, you got a nice little bottom Even if it's wore out. A feller could lime and fertilize it. And the barn needs a new ridge pole, and the house a new roof. New fencing, I would guess.

Dacey
You don't make it sound like it's worth pickin' up in the road.

Albee
Oh, it is. It's a good little farm. I bet you a feller could get
(Pause.)
say, uhh, near $10,000 for this pretty farm.

Dacey
Mr. Hood, you're a little behind times, ain't you? That was a good price ten years ago.

Albee
(Laughs.)
Miz Dacey, if you could get more, with all the work needed on it--the road, everything, plumbing, and all--more power to you. What's wrong, Miz Dacey? You look all rosy like.

Dacey

I just seen a car drivin' up.

Albee

Is my car in the way?

Dacey

No--yes, it could be in the way.

Albee

I'll be goin' along anyway.

Orfin

(From back of audience)
Anybody home?

Dacey

Orfin: Come on up, Orfin. Well, I declare.
    (Orfin comes to gate, opens, and enters. For version two, he carries guitar in case.)

Here's Orfin. Uh, I guess you don't know each other.

Orfin

Orfin Furlow.

Albee

Albee Hood.
    (They shake hands.)

Orfin

Albee Hood. Ain't you the real estate man?

Albee

Some people call me that.
    (Orfin looks at Dacey.)

Dacey

He dropped by. He give me an offer on the farm.

Orfin

He did?

Albee

We was just talking about it. I come by for old times' sake. We known each other from way back, haven't we?

Dacey

Mr. Hood, I'm sorry, but I've got to get some supper on for this young man.

Albee

Don't you worry. I gotta be getting on home. It's real nice to get over here and talk with' you. And I'll be back this way soon,
    (Goes down steps.)

Dacey

Maryat Lee

Yessir, you come back.
    (Aside.)
When you can't stay so long.

Albee

    (Off.)
Come with me.
    (Further off.)
Say, Miz Dacey, maybe you ought to try to play that old guitar (or fiddle). Shame for it to just collect dust.

Dacey

    (When Albee is out of earshot.)
Afore I'd ever sell the farm to you, I'll see it a stripped, naked, rock bare, in the other place.

Orfin

I'm glad to hear that.

Dacey

    (Still fuming.)
How's that? You awantin' the farm at a cheap price, too? Get out of my way.

Version 1 - for a fiddle-playing Miz Dacey	*Version 2 - for a non-playing Miz Dacey*
(She rushes in the house, comes out with fiddle, waves bow at Albee.)	(She rushes in the house.)
Listen to this you old cross-eyed mangy hound dog. I could set my old man back on his heels any day.	(Orfin, undecided as to whether to go after her, takes guitar out of case and plays a few bars of country song.)
(Plays expertly.)	(Dacey comes out with apples and bowl and knives and listens with shining eyes. Orfin pauses, looks at her.)
A shame for it to collect dust. That's the one truth in all your dadburned lies.	

(Dacey returns fiddle inside. Comes out very quiet.)

Orfin:

I didn't know! You can really play that thing.

Dacey:

Anymore I hardly ever do.

Orfin

Could you teach me?

Dacey:

Aw, Orfie, you don't have the time.

Orfin:
Sure I do.
(Dacey studies him, then goes inside, returns with pan of apples and knives.).
Hey, I thought you're gonna learn me to play.

(They start peeling.)

Maybe I could learn. I liked to sing.

Dacey:

(Starts peeling.)

I'm sorry, Orfin. I didn't mean to get my blood up like that, Why I haven't done that in years. He really pushed a button. I once upon time played myself, before I knew Jake.

Why I wanted to say to that gypper, Listen, you old cross-eyed mangy hound dog, I could set my old man back on his heels any day. A shame for it to collect dust.' That's the one truth in all his dadburned lies. The truth is--I can't play anymore. Or I woulda showed him.

Orfin:

You played music: Maybe you'll take it up again. You could learn me some new things.

Maryat Lee

Dacey:

Bless your heart. That's an awful nice thing to say.

(He plays.)

Dacey

Singin' is a good thing. What do you sing, Orfie? Do you know –
(Sings verse, quavering falsetto.)
She goes in house again, and this time brings out an old banjo, and they sing, gaining more confidence.)

Orfin

Oh boy, Let's do some more.

Dacey

Just a minute. Got to catch my breath.

Dacey

Orfie, that's the one thing I never forgive my husband for. He could fiddle good, and he knew a good fiddle when he heard it. People always brought out their instruments when he come around. We got married 'cause of it. And then, anybody ask us to fiddle, he always done it, and then after that no one ever remember I ever played. He was a good man. Never drank. Worked hard. But I never could forgive that. Now, isn't that terrible to hold a grudge that long? I never told anyone 'til right now. I felt so mean when he sold my fiddle for that cow, that I traded a quilt for a banjo. I never told him and kept it hid and figured how to play it myself and was agoin' to play with him fiddlin'. And then he died, and never knew I had it. We never did play together.

Orfin

(Pause.)
Murble, have you had any more thoughts about us--about what I said?

Dacey

'Bout gettin' married?
(Pats him.)
Orfie, now ain't it a little funny? Don't look thataway. I don't mean no hurt. But why would a pretty young feller marry an old woman like me? Lis- ten, you know I'm aseein'

things nobody else can see. And now I'm hearin' things, too! Today they begun to whistle. Law. I forgot all about tellin' you. Yessir. They're chirpin' like birds. Ever' time I go in there, whistlin', singin'. Yessiree, I must be headed out for the wide open spaces.

              Orfin

Like I told you, maybe it comes from bein' alone too long. You want some company, and that's why they're there!

              Dacey

I want five-inch green men for company?

              Orfin

I want to marry you, Murble:
  (Takes her hand.)
  (Telephone man enters from side of house, off porch at back.)

              Telephone Man

Uh, 'scuse me.

              Orfin

  (Jumps.)
Hey!

              Dacey

Oh!
  (Grabs her heart.)
My goodness! What are you doin' here? Mercy

              Orfin

What you think you're doin'?

              Telephone Man

I'm sorry. I was just tryin' to find some trouble in this party line. Have you had any trouble makin' calls?

              Dacey

  (Fanning.)
I just been too busy today to notice.

              Telephone Man

Ok. I'll just keep testing 'til I find it.
  (Exit to side)

              Dacey

Mercy me.

              Orfin

Scared me, too.

              Dacey

Like a snake adroppin' out of the rafter on you.

              Orfin

Yeh. Listen, I want to marry you, Murble. I like how I feel. I like makin' music. I like to pick berries with you. I'd like to come home here every night. I'd like to fish in the pond with you, set down to your table, listen while you fiddle, and learn to play with you. I want to fix this farm, put in a ridge pole, fix all the fences, put some lime on the meadow, cut down the brush. It's like I'm free here. Like I can spread my wings, like I do what I like to do, and I want to take care of you.

Telephone Man

    (Enters from side.)
'Scuse me. Do you mind if I try to ring your number? Just don't pay any mind.
    (Exits.)

Dacey

Mercy! Well, Orfie. What about the little men?

Orfin

That's what I mean. That's what I like. No girl I ever knew had little men with whistles and chirps. I like it.

Dacey

What in the world makes you like this?

Orfin

I don't know. I'm--Murble, I'm--

Dacey

Queer!

Orfin

Uh, no--not exactly.
    (Laughs.)
Well, the way you mean it,
Yes, I am.
    (Dacey reaches out her hand tenderly, smiles.)
    (Orfin takes her hand.)
Murble, you're old. I'm young. And I feel comfort when I'm with you. And wise. And I feel I can give you something. I can't even talk like this to anybody I ever knew. Maybe you won't live five years--or even one. Maybe I won't, either.

Dacey

    (Pause, Shyly.)
Why don't you just live here? Why get married?
    (Studies him.)

Orfin

    (Pause.)
Someday I'd like to have your farm.

Dacey

    (Shocked.)
Oh!

(Walks to other side. Turns to put him in his place, then reconsiders.)
I--I like that. That's just exactly what I'd say. And that's just what my children'll say--you marryin' me to get the farm.

Orfin
What do you think? Do you think that?

Dacey
Yessir. I think you are awantin' this farm. Well, why not? I had my use out of it. I believe you already care for it like you loved it, every stick, stone, every tree and bush, every bench and swag of it. But it's more than that. Things is never so simple, Orfin. You make me remember how I used to love it, care for every creepin' vine, thorn bush, every old mushroom and odd thing that growed. How I used to wander off into the mountain, never a worry about snakes nor nothin'. And nary one ever bit me. But living with Jake, anymore it got so I never walked out alone, nor hunted, nor fished, and without ever knowin' it, well, I just forgot, just lost the feelin'. Then, I started to think about sellin' the farm. To any old body that come up to the door with a check. And none of the children, none has that love for it anymore. Maybe their children. Maybe they'll see it like you do. So--

Orfin
You'll marry me? Listen, you can leave the farm to your grandchildren--if I can have it as long as I live.

Dacey
Now, Orfie, you might marry some young woman and have your own children someday. Don't be foolish. Yet--I'm a'feared once we marry it'd be like it was with Jake--never askin' me to fiddle again and then sellin' my fiddle 'cause it ain't used. Yessir, by jackie, he traded my fiddle for a five-titted old cow! 'Cause I shoulda' kept on playin'! But, I never thought of it then.

Orfin
I'd wrung his neck. That's what I would have done.

Dacey
But I'll tell you one thing. The other Sunday when you took my hand out here, I felt the shivers. Yes, I did. Didn't know I had that kind of spark left. And--that's another thing. I ain't mindin' the idea of having you live here, sharing the chores, the roof, the food, and all. But I don't know about the other thing.

Orfin
What's that?

Dacey
Orfin, I don't know about sharin' my bed. I'm used to having my own bed for years now, and I don't know--

Orfin
The only thing I'm nervous about is people laughing at us.

Dacey

Maryat Lee

That's something, too.

                         Orfin

Gimme another handful of apples.

                         Dacey

Orfin, we done finished 'em!
    (They could have more music or simply smile. Then he gently reaches for her hand. They are shocked by the next interruption.)

                         Telephone Man
    (Pops around corner of house.)
Excuse me. I found the trouble, Miz Dacey. But, uh,
    (Scratches his head.)
there's some funny whistlin' and chirpin' goin' on inside, and I don't know if it has to do with the phone or not.
    (Exits.)

                         Dacey
    (She vigorously fans.)
I'm glad you got it fixed. Oh, he's gone already. He sure does act like a jack-in-the-box. Whistlin'! He heard it? Orfin! He heard chirps and whistles. But if there's anything I hate it's to be jumped out at!

                         Orfin
    (Looks at her, goes to door to listen, notices visitor.)
Who Is that?

                         Dacey
    (Squinting.)
Who?

                         Orfin

A girl.

                         Dacey

Yep, it is.

                         Orfin

Never saw her.

                         Dacey

She looks--

                         Orfin

Colored.

                         Dacey

Orfin!

                         Orfin

I mean Black,

                         Louise

(Offstage. Back of audience.)
Hello!

Orfin

(At edge of porch.)
Are you lost?

Louise

(Calls.)
I got a flat tire down the road and was tryin' to find a phone. Could you ask your granny can I use hers?

Orfin

(Mortified.)
This' ain't my granny.

Dacey

Tell her to come on in and use the phone.

Orfin

Come on in.

Louise

(Pauses, opens gate and enters.)
I sure do thank you. I just need to call my dad.
(Uneasy pause. They all look at each other awkwardly, then suddenly smile.)

Dacey

You need somebody to change your tire?

Louise

No, ma'am. My sister and I can change it, But my mom and dad'll be worried. I thought I'd just phone and say what held us up.

Dacey

You can change a tire? Do you have a spare?

Louise

Oh, yes, Ma'am. I checked it.

Dacey

Why you could probably fix a fan belt.

Louise

Yes, Ma'am. My mom taught us both how.

Orfin

What about the points?

Louise

I'm sorry to be botherin' you, but would you mind if I make the call? I want to get back to my sister.

Dacey

Why, sure, come on in, child. We just got the phone fixed, I think. I'll show you where it is.

Maryat Lee

(Dacey exits with Louise.)

(Orfin sees approach of Tatter Lee.)

Tatter Lee
(From path.)
Howdy.

(Orfin puts instrument aside.)

Tatter Lee
(Closer.)
Is Miz Dacey home?

(She opens gate, comes up on porch and peeks through door.)
Murble!

Dacey
(Within.)
I'll be right out.

Tatter
Howdy, young feller. I thought I'd drop over--just to see if she's all right.

Orfin
What's the trouble?

Tatter
You be her grandson?

Orfin
No, I ain't her grandson! Nor her son, either.

Tatter
Umhumm. I seen you here a lot, drivin' by in your car a lot lately.
(Pause.)
I just ran past a car broke down and saw "somebody" come in here and thought I'd better check up on it.

Orfin
She's a friend of ours.

Tatter
(Giggles.)
"Ours"? Miz Dacey's friend?

Orfin
What are you wanting?

Tatter
Wanting? Well, I been Miz Dacey's friend since way back. I live on the next farm, and we kind of look after each other.

Orfin
Funny, I never heard about you.

The Appalachian Plays

Tatter
I guess you don't know Miz Dacey very well.

Orfin
You know what I think?

Tatter
What?

Orfin
I think you come over here to check up on me. You live in that yellow house with the window shade that's always winkin' up and down, don't you?

Tatter
Where in the world could you ever get that idea? If there's anything I hate, it's a nosey busybody. Why, if anybody was nosey about me, you know what I'd do to him?

Orfin
Yeh. You'd drag him into some bushes.

Tatter
(Shrieks.)
Oh! You're one of those dirty-mouthed town trash, and Murble Dacey better watch out who she's seen with. And especially lettin' them come in her house. Why, she'll be' robbed-- you just wait

Orfin
(Gets up in a rage.)
Get off of this porch

Tatter
This isn't your porch, young man.

Orfin
It will be soon enough

Tatter
(Shrieks.)
I knew it! You're gonna take over her farm!

Tammy
(From path.)
Hello!

Orfin
Who's that?

Tammy
Excuse me, is my sister in there?

Orfin
Yes. She's right here. Come on up. How you doin'?

Tatter

Maryat Lee

Um-hum
> (Aside.)

Here they come!

Tammy
> (At stairs.)

Thank goodness. I was gettin' worried where she went to.

Orfin

Come on up. She's inside making a phone call. Just make yourself at home.
> (Tatter mumbles.)

Tammy
> (Enters.)

Sorry to bother you, but you never know what some people do when you're away from home.

Orfin

You had trouble with the tire?

Tammy

Oh, no. The car's down there, ready to go. Just behind the tree.

Tatter

You changed a tire?

Tammy
> (Sweetly.)

Well, what would you do to it?
> (Dacey and Louise enter, Dacey with pitcher and glasses.)

Dacey

We'll just wait a little bit. The phone man is nearly done fixin' it. You must be her sister.

Tammy

Yes, Ma'am.

Dacey

Set down, honey. I need to get some more chairs out here. I never had no Black folks visit me. Are you thirsty? (Pours water.)
And, Tatter Lee, you thirsty? And what was it you was wantin' today?

Tatter

I come to see if you was all right.

Dacey

Oh, I'm just fine. I'm havin' an awful good time. Just look what I been missin' all these years and never even knew it.

Tatter
> (Aside.)

She's--!!

Dacey

You know something? I used to think the Lord wanted us all separated and kept pure. But to tell the truth, this bunch thinkin' they can't mix or share with some other bunch--that kind of talk has just about got us a world tearin' itself to pieces. Now, look. Isn't this fine, we can set on the porch and talk and play music. All of us, young and old, and different colors. I figure it this way, now. If the Maker didn't want us to mix, he would have fixed it that way, so we couldn't mix. Like horses and cows.

Tatter

Murble Dacey.

Dacey

I tell you, Tatter Lee, the rest of my life--however long it is--I want to do some things different. First, I want my house and porch full of music. And--yes, I want you young people, you girls avisitin' me.
    (Hesitates.)
And finally I want to make another person comfortable and a little happier. Old as I am, I've got me a second turn at it, and
    (Looking at Orfin.)
I think we all need a second chance, as well as a first. And--oh, I'll fix us all a good salad in summer and soup in winter, 'til I'm ready to go on up yonder, And.
    (Tatter faints. The girls catch her.)
Mercy! My gracious sakes. Here, Orfin. She done fainted dead away. Give her some salts.

Telephone Man

    (Pops around house.)
Miz Dacey!

Dacey

Land sakes! You still here?

Telephone Man

I finished, It's workin'. (EXITS)

Dacey

Good.
    (To Louise.)
Honey, go in and make your call.
    (To Tammy.)
And, honey, you go get a cold rag out of the sink.

Telephone Man

But I never got them chirps and squeaks out.

Dacey

Umhum. Well, I know about that, it's alright. So thank you.
    (Tammy returns with rag, dabs Tatter's face. Dacey slaps Tatters hands and face.)
Serves you right, you nosy old wench.

Maryat Lee

Tatter
(Recovering.)
Oh, Oh.

Dacey
Now, wake up, Tatter Lee. I didn't even get to the real news yet. You wouldn't want to miss it.

Tatter
Oh? Oh! Oh, thank goodness, you was just kiddin' around.

Dacey
No, I wasn't foolin'. I just didn't tell the real news. Orfin--get your guitar out--we're gonna have some music. Tatter Lee, we're gettin' married.

Tatter
(Shrieks, and then faints again. The girls catch her again, give her salts, pat her face, bring her to.)

Dacey
Oh don't worry about her. Just bounce her off the porch with some good ole foot stompin' music. (Orfin starts his music, a lively square dance. Or Dacey herself gets her fiddle and starts up.) (They begin to dance around the porch. Tatter Lee wakes up and gets twirled about.)

Albee
Miz Dacey! (Hurrying down the path.) Miz Dacey, I found a buyer for your farm--the kinda price you wouldn't dream of.

Dacey
We ain't sellin'.

Tatter
Price?

Albee
Ah yes. You must be the lady in the yellow house with the window shades--

Tatter
That's my house.

Albee
Well now maybe we could sit down together and talk about it. I have some good prospects…
(They are already walking down the path, mumbling about the house. The girls decide its time to go home, and are shaking hands with Miz Dacey and Orfin.)

Dacey
Now you girls, come back. I just don't know when I had such a good time.
(The girls leave. Orfin and Dacey are left.)
Well, Orfie. What a day. It sure brings back memories. Orfie. My throat is dry as an old bean pod.

Orfin

How about some lemonade? (They look at each other, then smiling, he puts his arm around her and they go in the house.)

END

Author's Note on *Ole Miz Dacey*

Maryat Lee

As a playwright living in the Appalachian mountains, I am constantly confronted by a question that, practically speaking, overrides all others: Why don't country people want to act or go to plays? One must face the fact I that they are not only indifferent to theater but secretly repelled by it. When they are exposed to the theater, as they seldom are, they often find it pretentious or boring or artificial or contrived. Then why develop an indigenous theater in the country? There's only one answer--and it is entirely personal. Because I need it. I am drawn to the theater as a place for seeing beneath the surface, being in touch with truth and with people who have a similar vision. When I go to the theater in New York or to its imitators, I am, as a rule, alienated, insulted, left unfulfilled. In short, I feel as a country person feels toward city people because I am a country person. I need a theater that comes from a totally different place, a theater that goes back to what it was in the beginnings, something that comes not to the people but out of the people. I need to work with actors who don't aspire to act, audiences that don't attend theater as we know it.

> I need to work with actors who don't aspire to act, audiences that don't attend theater as we know it.

One day an old country woman called the local television store and complained about her set to Jimmy Costa, the high-spirited son of the proprietor. The next day, in a practical-joke frame of mind--typical of the humor of Hinton people--Jimmy walked around the corner to a phone booth and, mimicking the old woman and carrying her complaint a step further, had the store in an uproar of laughter: little green men, "she" said, were dripping out of the set and bouncing around on the floor. His prank was so successful that not even his father suspected the fraud. Carried away, Jimmy then phoned me, impersonating this old woman. I talked with "her" awhile, enjoying the conversation--until Jimmy started laughing and revealed the prank. The idea took shape right then, even before I hung up the phone, to make a play about her with Jimmy playing the part.

The phone call catalyzed an assortment of unrelated bits of things and gave a meaning and an order to hundreds of incidents in which I as a Kentuckian, in spite of my fancy education and years spent in the ultimate city (New York), never fit in to urban life and always felt conscious of my awkwardness and southern connections. I betrayed myself thousands of times as I tried to sound like and think like a Northerner. Jimmy's phone call got me started.

Jimmy, an unregenerate "country boy," has always had a deep love of and respect for the old timers, has identified so much with them that he built a log house and lives like an old timer himself in many ways. His vocation is music, and he has mastered fiddle, banjo, guitar, dulcimer, and a large repertory of the old music. It was literally an example of the actor and part made for each other--at least for the opening of the play which uses Miz Dacey talking about the little green men to get the action started.

Maryat with Myrtle Hosey, one of the models for Murble Dacey. *Photo by Fran Belin, courtesy Mary Clare Powell.*

But two other actual country women became my models, both of them neighbors on Powley's Creek, a little hollow about three miles long. One of them was seventy-nine, and her husband was in his forties, and they had been married since he was nineteen. No one else in the hollow seemed to think the union extraordinary. I gradually got to know this couple, and in a short time it did not seem unusual to me, either. This gave me the idea for the romance that develops between Miz Dacey and the television repairman, Orfin Furlow, which explores how such a thing might happen very naturally.

The third old woman had lived as a widow for a decade and was thought to be a little odd. Some of the opening dialogue of the play with the real estate salesman was inspired by my visits with the widow, and some of the other dialogue was taken from oral history gathered from my neighbor by me and others. The widow carried a little revolver, and her dress was worn where the weight of the revolver had stressed the cloth and had to be sewn up periodically. She was a good shot at snakes, and could "shoot the head off a copperhead from here to the barn." She would shoot through the door if anyone failed to knock, and said, "If someone steps in, he won't step out."

> One of them was seventy-nine, and her husband was in his forties, and they had been married since he was nineteen. No one else in the hollow seemed to think the union extraordinary.

She had trouble keeping her chickens because of the foxes. She also had a well five feet deeper than we actually used in the script. She made note of this when she came to see the play--that her well was five feet deeper. I sat behind her and heard her whisper this information loudly to her neighbor.

These were essentially the given pieces to work with, embroider, and embellish. The scene: a porch. Miz Dacey sweeps, talks to herself, trying to figure out just what's happening to herself, watching for company coming down the path. And she does have company--a nutrition aide who makes a call to help Miz Dacey eat properly. Meanwhile the aide has a bit of indigestion herself and resorts to her pills which Miz Dacey has to help her get out of her bottle. A real estate man is out looking for property to buy and sell and tries unsuccessfully to patronize her: "You're a little behind the time, ain't ya, Mr. Hood? That was a good price twenty years ago." Later her young suitor comes; a nosy neighbor takes an interest; two Black girls need to make a phone call home,

Lucinda Ayres as Ole Miz Dacey and David T. Miller as Orfin Furlow. *Collection of David T. Miller*

stranded by a flat tire.

In the original production of Miz Dacey, in a script designed for Jim Costa to play the lead role, Miz Dacey plays a fiddle. She angrily pulls if off the wall when the realtor says he feels bad that the old fiddle that Jake (Miz Dacey's late husband) used to play is now collecting dust. In a later production Lucinda Ayres played Miz Dacey. The script was modified for her, a non-musician, and instead Orfin Furlow played the guitar.

At first Miz Dacey might appear to be a cartoon. The country language leads one to expect it. But she is not simple-minded. Rather, she is simple; the only thing she wants is company. At first she creates it, live, out of her TV set, and then the "real" company comes-- most of them townspeople who, compared to her, seem unreal when they come on her turf, especially when she cuts through their routines as she tries to get to a kernel of honesty. In fact, she

> Country people as a rule do not want to act--ever. They understand what is lacking in the city folks with their airs, pretensions and roles, and they want no part of it.

began to come to life for me on paper as a person when she began to take control of her circumstances--something which cartoon people do not do. As I started putting the scenes together, the choices she made were consistently opposite to what I as writer anticipated. I realized then that she was perhaps escaping the usual fate of country people on stage. Fiction writers can handle country people with subtlety and art, especially when the writers live as Faulkner, Welty and O'Connor did--in or near the country. But fiction writers can survive in the country as playwrights cannot, because of the latter's supposed dependence on a company. Country people as a rule do not want to act. They understand what is lacking in the city folks with their airs, pretensions and roles, and they want no part of it. Certainly they do not want to act as acting is generally understood. If all this means that EcoTheater has few actors and few people attending performances for awhile, that is the price. One had to be prepared for that. It is not a commercially sound venture, nor even an accepted or perhaps culturally-sound venture. And it is not easy to develop without compromising. But when one does finally get to a place where something momentous happens and sparks begin to fly, it's worth all the long time and discouragement along the way.

A DOUBLE-THREADED LIFE (The Hinton Play)
Introduction
Dr. William French

Except for a stool at the left for the Narrator, the space is empty. The actors sit on three chairs to the left of the stage. Tonight three actors enter and sit. The number varies depending upon the actors' availability. Almost any scene in the play may be removed from a given performance, for the play has no narrative line, and its simple themes become apparent from almost *any* combination of its scenes. The complete play involves several dozen scenes, shuffled in or out of the lineup to fit the performance duration and available performers. Many scenes celebrate the old railroad days that Hinton people now romanticize. But the actors are unpaid and have other commitments--jobs, babies, house- or farm-work, family-that often prevent the performance of the complete play. The play is deliberately built of such removable "tuck scenes," as their author calls them, insurance against the uncertainties of life--sickness, a broken-down truck, a truant babysitter.

The characters in Lee's plays express the inner concerns of her performers. This makes some of them nervous. Many actors quit in self-pity. Disgust, frustration, defiance, or anger, but those who remain attest to the special meaning EcoTheater has for them. By their own testimony, the activity enhances their lives.

The Narrator rises from his or her stool, advances to center stage, and begins to speak conversationally in a soft Southern-Appalachian voice:

> *I've played my part. I've played my part-most of the lime. I've been going along quietly all these years. Unnoticed. Eating and sleeping, getting and spending. Except, once in a while, a wild little thing suddenly erupts, and disappears into the depths. Into the surface. It's all covered up again. Nobody remembers. Or at /east, they never mention it. Most people think that's the way I am. Quiet. Average. Good, fairly good looking, with a few oddities. But I did it. I've played my part. I've kept you from seeing me as I am. I've hidden. And recently-- I discovered so have you. Or most of you. That's your secret now, isn't it? To keep me from seeing you. All these years.*

Maryat Lee

The play develops episodically as a series of monologues and dialogues that characterize the people of Hinton, West Virginia, a tiny hamlet deep in the most mountainous and rural area of southern West Virginia. The scenes reveal the inner lives of these people not only because that's what the author, Maryat Lee, intended, but also because the words are--more or less--their own. They wrote them. Lee even credits them with authorship: The title page of the script reads "By Maryat Lee and the People of Hinton, West Virginia" The attribution stretches reality a bit; Lee exercises firm artistic control over the final script, infusing it with poetic touches and revising it for economy and coherence, but the script reflects her desire to create a people's theater.[43]

> "Maybe you'd be interested in this, Miz Lee. Put it in your play. I couldn't sleep the other night and just wrote down what was on my mind."

Lee creates indigenous theater for a rural, isolated people of restricted means that explores and validates their life occupations, values and speech. Virtually all the material originates in oral history: taped conversations, gossip, local newspaper items, folklore, diaries, and written reminiscences that townspeople give her.

"Maybe you'd be interested in this, Miz. Lee. Put it in your play. I couldn't sleep the other night and just wrote down what was on my mind." Retouched for economy and some diction--but little else--the monologue is by a woman whose husband has died and whose children have grown up and moved to the city. She broods about loneliness, restlessness, and her desire to establish an identity besides that of mother, wife and grandmother. She wants to give up these roles and do something to fulfill herself: make pottery, paint pictures, learn to square dance.

---

[43] O'Connor (and Lee) scholar Carole Harris has had access to some of Maryat's journals from the late 1960's and notes that "When Maryat eventually claimed sole authorship of the SALT plays, the students revolted, and Maryat prepared to step out." Harris, Review of French, "Maryat Lee's EcoTheater," in *The Flannery O'Connor Review*, vol. 18 (2020), at 171.

The Appalachian Plays

The scenes of *A Double-Threaded Life* reveal the inner lives of the people and their relation to communal life. The play clarifies the need for people to occasionally unmask themselves and each other. A woman waits for her railroad-engineer husband to come home to a cold dinner and thinks about her loneliness, his betrayal and their desolate marriage. The monologue builds to a concluding revelation:

"Honey, baby, I need you. You don't need to take care of other people's children. I'll give you some of your own. You'll be my sweetheart. Oh, honey." you said, "I can't live without you." And I was hooked--like any little old six-inch fish. Oh, you young girls, don't ever marry someone who says, "I can't live without you," because once they get you and they put you in their house and they give you the children and have you all occupied, they'll go and find someone else they can't live without. (She registers shock.) That's what he's done. He's found someone else he can't live without. You've found someone else. You say if I don't like it I can leave. You want me to leave, my house, my things. Oh, Buster, I don't have to leave. I left! (Pause.) I left? (Pause.) I left you when we were very, very young. I left. I left you the day that you put your ring on my finger and they called me Mrs. I left.

Other monologues sketch the pioneer history of the region and its geographical setting: the brooding presence of steep, forested mountains and rivers rushing through narrow gorges. (Not much over 100 years ago the *New York Times* described this region as a "howling wilderness.") Cultural mores and social attitudes are gradually revealed. An independent mountain woman will not let a contractor fix her roof until the sign of the moon is right. A Vietnam veteran broods about his war experience and reveals that his guilt issues not from the war but from a murder he committed.

A Double-Threaded Life ends with a poetic resolution of several voices weaving phrases that recall the most significant event in recent local history: the day in the 1950s when the last steam engine clanged through town. Maintenance of the steam locomotives used to haul coal trains across the steep stretches of the Allegheny mountain grade powered the local economy for over 80 years. Diesel locomotives, needing little maintenance and few workers, replaced them. The old roundhouse closed down, and the steam engine became obsolete. This technological advance destroyed the town's economy: thus, many folks have come to think of that day in the late 50's as "The Day Hinton Died." Indeed, this was Lee's first title for the play; she changed it after many people objected. While the town's population has dwindled to less than half of what it once was. those who remain refuse to accept its death. Their children aren't aware of the loss and accept their given lives. Out of the pain of adjustment came new life.

EcoTheater actors achieve an unusual intimacy with their audience. The use of local material gives them special advantages: Audiences recognize stories about local types, or figures drawn from the local past, gossip or folklore. The boundaries between character actor-audience subtly shift. Lee strives for this intimacy and arranges her theaters physically to foster it. Her audiences are often noisy, restless and inattentive. Her actors sometimes become frustrated and discouraged. But a small portion of the audience will almost always be mesmerized by an EcoTheater performance and will show their appreciation in various ways. Sometimes--especially indoors--an entire audience will be captivated. They keep coming back, apparently hungry for the material that EcoTheater has to share.

> These discussions, usually led by Lee and including her actors and guests, are astonishingly open. They become a celebration of the play and their society, and of the function of theater in society.

Most spectators stay for the discussion following the play that is an essential part of an EcoTheater performance.[44] The spectators enter the discussions eagerly. pointing out what they thought "true" or "real." or what the play meant to them. (These discussions sometimes result in an altered script the next day.) These discussions, usually led by Lee and including her actors and guests, are astonishingly open. They become a

---

[44] "[Maryat] first saw it in her street theater productions in New York City, where the people on the street watching the play 'just didn't have the audience role implanted,' and would interact with the people on stage. She found herself, instead of dealing with a few instruments up on the stage, dealing with three or four hundred instruments that were somehow in this thing together. 'In comparison,' she noted, 'an indoor audience seems to be like little papers, pretending that they're not there.'" Quoted in Powell, supra, at 123.

celebration of the play and their society, and of the function of theater in society. The discussion reveals that many in the audience are far more attentive than a casual observer might think: "Why do people in real life feel that they have to disguise themselves and wear masks?" Such a question evokes a spirited, searching discussion, as does: "What does this mean politically?" Or, "Are you aiming to 'get' someone downtown by this?" Many questions reveal an interest in the process of theater: "Where did you get the material for this?" "Could I learn to write a play like this?" "How do you rehearse?" The discussions often run longer than the plays. For a while, the alienation of the artist in our society is banished, compassion and fellowship reign, and the ritual act of theater is fulfilled.

"A door opens" is the concluding line of *A Double-Threaded Life*. It is a call to social action and to individual change. It also reminds us that decline or failure is often the prelude to a new beginning. Lee's theater helps people open doors to new lives.

Maryat Lee

Scenes from *A Double-Threaded Life*

The scenes[45] are portraits and sketches of the town and its residents, past and present, the story of the demise of the railroad as the diesel replaced the steam engine. The scenes performed depended upon what actors were available for each evening, but the most frequently performed were:

"Potsy:" Portrays the man who was responsible locally for the main line changeover from the steam engine to the diesel. He tries to save a friend from buying a new house in Hinton and encourages him to wait and see. "The (railroad yard) shops will no longer be in Hinton, they won't be anywhere, they are no longer needed."

"Young and Old Railroader": A retired railroader (Sims Wicker) recounts his forty-seven years with the railroad, his experience with steam engines, and the "romance of the railroad." Now he wonders about it: "We all told ourselves it would be better for you all. Easier work. Better pay. But sometimes a feller wonders."

Excerpt from "John Henry": John Henry says that a man has to do the best he can at whatever he does; that one must play as playfully, live as lovingly, and work as hard and as proud as he can. "You can die anytime, any day and any second the Lord wants."

"Waiting Woman: A housewife who has lived her life thinking all is well and then she finds that her husband has found someone else. She discovers that she became a "role" when the ring went on her finger and she was called "Mrs."

"The Man Who Came Home": A story of a man who left the small town of Hinton to go to the big city (Detroit) to make more money for his growing family. He was so caught up in money and buying and notes to pay off that he had to stay in the city, leaving his wife and family at home. A deadly fire takes them all and he comes back home to Hinton to work his wife's garden and give its fruits away--realizing that he traded his family for things.

"Ethel Hinton": A brief recount of Ethel Hinton's grandmother who gave the right-of-way to the C&O and who donated the 40 acres of land to be the town.

"Miz Dacey and the :Nurse": A county nurse comes to the rural are a to encourage the elderly to come into town to the clinic and have a check-up for blood and other physical ailments. Dacey explains that she takes care of herself and that she uses nature to heal all her ills, from gout with cherries to arthritis with poke weed tea.

---

[45] This snapshot of the current repertory was made in 1983 by Lee for the West Virginia Division of Humanities.

"The Businessman": A revealing scene of a businessman who thinks he has all the answers of how life should be lived. He sets himself up to preach to all his townspeople about how things should be and how they should live. He discovers--through a dream--that he has been telling others what he himself should be doing.

"Miz Dacey and the Roofer": Miz Dacey has been trying to get a roof put on her old farmhouse and, finally, the roofer shows up after a five month wait. Miz Dacey won't let him put the roof on because it is the light moon and "you can't roof in the light moon." She is able to get him off the subject of roofing and gives him some short lessons in how to plant by the signs.

"I Done Wrong": A young woman pours her heart out to strangers and is able to tell them a wrong she has done to a friend. She wants someone to listen to her as she explores how to ask, "Can you forgive me, please?"

Preamble – Narrator:

Folks, I'm not an actor, yet I act all the time. I hope tonight I can, at least for a few minutes, just be me without any roles.

(Reading:) Fifty years ago, a little railroad town down the road was a progressive place, one of the three of this state, known far and wide, a gem lying on the mountain river banks. Only fifty years before that the writer of *Mutiny on the Bounty* trudged through here and wrote back to the *Times*: "This is a howling wilderness here."

In the span of one person's life this howling wilderness became a boom town, Hinton, with three hospitals (now it has one), three opera houses (now it has none). Seven hundred men worked in the roundhouse (now scarcely a dozen). Thirty-three passenger trains a day rolled to a stop. (Now only three a week, and in the dead of night.) The streets were jammed with folks all hours of the day (now but a solitary few wander about). Hoboes came flocking to be fed in this generous river town. William Jennings Bryan delivered his silvery oratory as he ran for president and lost three times. The big road shows stopped on their way to Cincinnati, performed to packed houses at the Masonic Opera House. The elegant arches, raked stage, box seats, and the horseshoe balconies are now a shadow left on a parking lot.

> "This is a howling wilderness here."

The show people and cultured folks stayed at the Hotel McCreary, with its marble bathrooms and balconies. (Now its windows stare with the eyes of a haunted house.) Other folks went to Madam's Creek, where they could afford to dance and drink and, yes, they also gambled and-- In general shouted *hurray* for sin and the dollar. (Now Madam's Creek is a reformed, quiet, God-fearing holler.)

Yet some things don't change. The Confederate Scout--of all things--still presides

Maryat Lee

from his pedestal on Union Street. And still the floating veils of mist, the hovering mountains, like gigantic ladies peacefully reclining, dabble their fingers in fast-flowing rivers, glittering streams. They too are still there, more dignified than ever, and more mysterious. There's story--no, hundreds of stories in all this. Of which we'll tell just a few.

A ringing in my mind – Kathy Jackson

Kathy Jackson started at EcoTheater as a summer job and stayed on to become Maryat's right-hand woman and director of training. *West Virginia and Regional History Center.*

(Editor's Note: Jackson, who would eventually become EcoTheater's Director of Training, joined EcoTheater as fifteen-year-old. Her personal story is moving and improbable. A mother at thirteen, from a poor family with an alcoholic father, she also had a learning disability and hearing loss. She started taking drugs and attempted suicide. But she started working at EcoTheater with a state-funded group of teens and found her voice on Eco's stage, staying on year after year, and becoming close with Maryat. "Maryat has given me something to live for... I started caring about myself and the people around me," she says.[46] Jackson went on to share her EcoTheater experience by holding regular workshops with many other young people facing the same kind of troubles she had been through, helping them draw out their own stories. Her performance as John Henry was always moving, and the many personal scenes she created were fresh and vivid. More than any other single person, Jackson exemplifies the possibility of being on stage rather than acting a part, *as Maryat put it.)*

JACKSON: So, I've got this ringing in my mind. And we, I, go up there now--up to Powley's Creek--to rehearse, and I want to tell you I don't get a check now. I do it, well, because I love to do it. That's why. But that isn't all of it. I meet folks I'd never talk to otherwise. And I get to go places I never been. There was this woman-- she came one summer, she was what they call a Humanist. She was big, Black and from down there

---

[46] Quoted in Powell, supra, at 68.

somewhere in Mississippi or Alabam, and I reckon, she could be mean.[47] Well, that woman talk to us kids, and she open up her big mouth and out flew some poetry she wrote--and us kids with our mouths hangin' open.

Anyhow I got to go and stay, live, in this woman's house down there. I thought we had lots of Black folks in Hinton, but honey, down there, they hardly have any white folks. I coulda gone and lived with a real nice lady in Charleston. I turned it down. And kickin' myself ever since. But you see, I'm even learnin' to read. You know, you don't have any control of your life at all if you can't read. You can hardly drive anywhere outside Hinton, can't read street signs to know where you are or where you going. Ask somebody how to get somewhere, and they give you a name of a street to turn on and then where are you. But I've got a teacher, they call it a "tutor" teachin' me, just me. Over there in Lewisburg.

> I'm even learnin' to read. You know, you don't have any control of your life at all if you can't read.

And somehow or other, if I can just keep on Welfare, I think in a while I'll be making my own living. Now Welfare is fine, it's wonderful. But you know, it's well--to me, it's stupid. It's almost like they want to keep you in crutches. If you get rid of one crutch tryin to get on your feel they'll snatch that other crutch you gotta lean on till one leg gets strong, and then down you go in the dust again, and then you have to get two crutches again. And oh, does that feel bad. Lots of folks I know just decided a long time ago to forget about walking on their own.

You can see why.

The only answer I can find is--now, don't laugh--you have to find someplace that you like and work for nuthin'. You look around and find a place where you can learn something And you see if who you work for will give you enough to get back and forth. And you treat it like a job. Just as if you was gettin' paid. Don't be late. Call when you ain't--when you are not coming to work. You can always find somebody's phone if you ain't got one. And get yourself in shape. Watch how folks that you'd like to work like, eat. And they eat different. They eat foods raw, now that don't cost anything. They don't eat white bread--I read that rats die when they get fed white bread. I wouldn't touch their funny food for years. Now I gotten so I eat it I feel like a rabbit sometimes. But I got more energy these days.

If we ever gonna get outta being at the bottom, welfare ain't gonna help--'less they change it. We gotta get ourselves over that crutch business. So this is my idea.

Keep both crutches, and use 'em to hobble--not just down to the Welfare office, but to find a place you can work and learn. They got a name for it, people laughs about it. Volunteer. And don't get paid--or you lose your welfare card. Make it a two-year plan. End of two years you'll have a record of working and a reference. Then you can apply

---

[47] When Kathy was working her first summer job with EcoTheater she met MacArthur fellow and actress\poet Billie Jean Young, a Black woman, at Maryat's farm.

somewhere else if they can't put you on payroll.

And that's just what if, I was a boss, I'd wanta know: you have any job experience, and if you got some skills. Now, see, after two years you'd get a choice of jobs, cause you was an "apprentice," how do ya get the 'prentice job? You just go to the place you want a work, where you can learn something and you say, "Mr. So and So, I want to work: for you. I don't know much about your work, but I'll be glad if you'll teach me and, I'll work for you free till I learn enough to leave welfare, if you can just help me with car money." And you tell him or her, that you're serious about it and you want to make a good work record cause you need reference. And then you'll be ready to get decent wages, and you can throw away both crutches and walk on your own.

But you got to watch out. Don't go to no place, anyplace where the boss might steal somebody's job for you and then let them go cause he can have you for nuthin'. So you better off with a small place, just two or three, where they got more than they can do and can't hire anyone.

Well, I guess I'm kind of young to be giving out advice. And I'm still on Welfare. But I've got plans and hopes. I'm learnin' to read, to put in insulation and paint, learnin' to talk in front of folks, learnin somethin new about housekeeping, and keeping a yard, and I'm gettin more confidence all the time. And I'm going to pass my GED if it takes five years.

So I ain't just working for no pay. I'm just gettin' another kind of pay. You can laugh at me. But, you watch. I'm gonna make something of myself. God willin' and the creek don't rise.

I Done Wrong - Kathy Jackson
(To audience)
(I need to talk to somebody awful bad. Can't talk to anybody I know.)

People have been saying to me "what's wrong with you?" You got dark circles under your eyes. You look sick. Are you into dope?

I wish I was. When I get a chance--maybe that's just what I'll do. It's like this: I'm tearin' myself up. I done a bad thing. I wanted a certain fella--oh from first time I seen him standin' up in the weeds lookin' surprised when I come down the road. I found out he had a girlfriend--someone I kinda knew.

They was gonna get married. So, I got to be her friend. Oh I'd call 'er and talk and we'd go places together. We got real chummy. I'd tell 'er my secrets--some of 'em.

And she'd tell me hers.

Meanwhile, she was seein' him. And the children'll grow up. They'll fight each other at school--we'll all see to that. Might even be a killing. That's the way life is. If it could just be alright to tell somebody--you was wrong. But you don't ever admit it here. It's almost like a law. I'll tell you this sits on my shoulders like it was pressin' the life outa me. I see the cemetery risin' up in front of me. And I wonder if there is any peace.

Are you listenin'? Do you hear me? You're just strangers. You don't know anything. Maybe if you could forgive me. I could make it up, could be free to give somethin' good to him, and maybe go to her, tell her. And maybe, someday, tell him.

Stranger--I hope that's all you are--I put on you a robe. Now don't you feel embarrassed if I just kneel here a minute. I'll just try it out. Now, don't worry.

(Kneels)

--For- Forgive me.

Do you?

(Depending on the audience)

You do?

(Gets up. Starts to exit slowly, relaxes but then turns. Solemnly:)

OR

You don't.

(Gets up)

I just don't know how I let myself do it. Like she had been his for months. And sometimes they'd have little riffles, you know? She says, Oh you know what he said? He told her she was crazy--or dumb.

He makes her mad. He won't wash after he's worked. And is all smelly. Such little things, you know? Oh, if I could be close enough to smell him. And I'd say to her--well, he sure thinks a lot of himself. Why you wanna marry that ole thing? Why, everybody knows he's do-less. Just lookin' for a wife to do for 'im. You're better'n that.

She paid no attention. She'd just shrug. "Well, I love 'im. And that's all I care."

And I'd just curl up inside. Wishin' I could be the one to say that.

But, it went on, he'd do this or that. And I'd always put in a little seed, you know. And she'd sometimes listen and think about it, and grow real still. Until one day, well--they broke up.

I got what I wanted. Only--now when he takes me out and puts his arms around me and breathes, and says he's so lucky he found out about her--oh, I told him things about her too, worse things, and when he says I'm what he wants, I feel funny--sick. And afraid.

So, yesterday, what I was dreadin' happened. We was down at the post office and run into her. She was kinda sick lookin' when she saw me. Looked at him, and then at me. And I saw a click in her eyes. She knew. It was right there in her eyes. And he saw her and frowned, and then he followed her eyes and he looked at me. Four eyes, two brown and two blue, quiet, looking through me.

Oh God, what could I do? I haven't been able to eat since then. I hate myself, and if I could I'd go and drag 'em both behind a bush and where no one could see I'd say I done you wrong. WRONG. Can you forgive me?

But. No one ever does that here. On the TV stories and at church they talk about forgiving but no one ever forgives here--and I don't know to ask. We all live our whole lives without it. Our children, his and mine, they'll learn that the woman is bad--and she ain't bad. And her children, she'll tell 'em that I once upon a time robbed her in broad daylight.

Dora's Story by Judith Walker

(Judy reports that she rearranged some of the information for this piece. Otherwise it is very close to the interview she taped with "Dora," a name made up because the person interviewed did not wish to reveal her identity. This piece shows how a tape-recorded interview can be made into a very effective scene, even one about a person who did not wish her identity exposed. Judy performs the piece herself though, again, anyone could do it.)

Dora sits in a chair with her leg propped up, crocheting. She is surrounded by things like books, yarn, plants. A small inked sign reads "IT MAY BE A DUMP BUT WE'RE FRIENDLY."

Dora: My goodness. If I'd known you were going to be such a distinguished-looking bunch, I'd have tidied the place a bit. Well, no. I probably wouldn't have. It looks good enough for me, it'll have to do.

Now they tell me I have only 10 minutes to tell you the story of my life. That's going to be a major undertaking. But I've always liked a challenge, so I'll get right to the point.

When I die, I want my gravestone to read: "DORA LEWIS-MOTHER-TEACHER-NATURALIST."

Oh, you're probably wondering about my leg. It's not a pretty story, but I'll tell you what happened. One day back in May, I had just gotten up from a little nap and immediately headed for the bathroom to relieve myself. I had on my shorty gown. The phone rang. It was one of my sons wanting me to babysit for his two children. I wasn't too excited about the prospect because I was going camping with my 92-year old mother, so I tried to excuse myself. Anyhow, by the time I hung up, my need for the bathroom was urgent. I again headed for the bathroom. I didn't make it. And what happened next was that I learned to do the split faster than any Dallas Cowboy cheerleader ever did. My right foot stoved into the tub, breaking my leg, and a couple of toes.

There I was on the floor of my bathroom, in pain, in my shorty gown, wet. I wasn't about to call a neighbor. So I called my son, the doctor, who works in Welch. He said for me to just hold on, he'd be there as fast as he could with an ambulance. I hung up. Then my sister from California, the one who is married to Huckleberry Hound, called. She said, "What are you doing, Dora?" I said, "Well, I'm sitting here on the floor with a broken leg, what are you doing?

You want to know what one of my biggest worries was? That my son with the two children would think I was just making an excuse not to babysit.

I was born on Resurrection Sunday, April 20, 1919. Don't try to figure it out. I'll tell you. I'm 75.

My father was a veterinarian. My mother had gone to finishing school, where she learned to play the piano, sing in the choir, paint a picture, and have a tea party. That was all my grandfather thought a girl needed to be an efficient wife. Of course, he didn't figure in the five children she eventually had and the suicide that left her widowed while the children were still young.

But my childhood was happy before my father died. I have fond memories of my siblings, especially my brother who was always a challenge to me. He was only seventeen months younger. I remember once we fought over who got to lick the cake pan. I ended up pinning him down to the floor, sitting on him, and I licked the pan. Even then I was a sturdy thing.

By the way, my doctors have told me to lose sixty-five pounds.

I'm trying.

I've never kissed but one man in my life. My husband. I met him when I was working my way through the University of North Carolina. He was impressed with me because I refused to go for a ride with him because we didn't have a chaperone.

> I thought, *this is the way life is supposed to be*, and I did the best I could with it.

Our courtship wasn't what you would call romantic. He had left home when he was fourteen, and was a pitiful person. I felt sorry for him. My mother said he aroused my maternal instincts. She said, "You feel so sorry for him now, but one day you'll feel sorry for yourself."

After we married and the children started coming on, I realized I had married a child in man's body. I had three children, then a nine-year break, then three more. He never felt responsible for them, leaving us alone months at a time.

Of course, he was home sometimes or I wouldn't have had six children.

But the longest we lived together straight in the nineteen years we were married was eighteen months.

But I'm not complaining. I was raised on the novels of Grace Livingston Hill and Jean Stratton Porter. I was and am an idealist. I thought, *this is the way life is supposed to be*, and I did the best I could with it.

Although Jesse never provided for us as he should--I hate to say this, but he was a gambler--we got along, the kids and I. The years I had spent roaming the woods as a child, examining every plant and tree, and studying in a science lab in college, paid off. When food was scarce the children and I would gather mushrooms, freshwater crabs, wild asparagus. I could stir up a delicious, nutritious meal for them anytime I wanted.

All this happened while we were living in Virginia. My husband had gotten a job in the arsenal there for awhile. I remember the night we arrived from North Carolina on a bus. I was carrying one child, leading one, pregnant with one. We got off in the middle of the night and walked a mile and a half up a hill to our little house. Well, skunks lived under that house. And they mated there.

You've never heard a noise like skunks made when mating.

Those were the really lean years. I remember once we ran up a grocery bill for $88.92. It was way past-due. I told Jesse we'd better borrow money from the bank to pay it. He said for me to do it, my credit was better than his. Well, when I went in to talk to the bank president, he asked me what I had for collateral. And I said this: "If my face isn't good enough for $88.92, then forget it." Then I walked away.

Well, he called me back and said, "I'm sorry, Dora. I shouldn't have asked that. If $88.92 was all I owed, I'd be a lucky man. How do you want the money?"

I said, "Eighty-eight dollar bills and ninety-two pennies." That's how I paid my bill. I don't know what made me say that. I guess I just wanted to see how that much money looked like.

You know, when you're having a hard time making it, it seems like everything that could possibly go wrong does. During our years in Virginia, I did substitute teaching, eventually getting my degree at Radford. But stretching my small salary--and it was the only money I could count on--to feed and clothe three children was difficult.

I remember when my little girl joined the church. I wanted her dressed in a white dress and patent leather shoes. You know how we mothers are about such occasions. Well, I scraped together the money somehow and bought the clothes at Leggett's. Then, as we were leaving the store, I saw some three-for-a-dollar jewelry, and put my bag down to look at it. Well, when I reached for the bag, it was gone. Never did find it. My daughter had to join the church in her old dress.

Then there was the Christmas tree incident.

I had made the children's gifts--clothes, rag dolls of Mickey Mouse, Donald Duck-- all of fabric remnants. I wrapped them in bright red tissue paper. On Christmas Eve--I was alone, as usual--I arranged them all under the tree. The tree was standing in a bucket of water. During the night, the tree fell over, the water spilled out, and all of the gifts were stained red!

Our last move was to Mullens. I got a job teaching.

The final straw with Jesse was when he failed to pay the rent for three months. I had been giving him the money each month thinking it was being paid. I thought if a man thinks no more of his children than to risk the roof over their heads, then he needs to go. I also found out about that time that he was seeing another woman.

In the eighteen years following our divorce, he contributed $45 to the support of our children. He never involved himself in their lives, wouldn't even speak to them on the street. I encouraged them to respect him, but he never responded.

I thoroughly enjoyed raising the children. They're all doing well. I provided them with as much culture as I could. We always had good, classical music in the house and good books. I never allowed cheap literature around. And I took them to church. I've always been a devout Methodist.

I've led a straight-laced life. I can look anyone in the face and not be embarrassed. I can see the point in being a moral person. I sometimes feel cheated, robbed of a marriage. But, remember, I'm an idealist. This is the way it's supposed to be. And I was born on Resurrection Sunday. I always felt that that made me special, spiritually speaking.

Well, I've enjoyed talking to you. There's a lot more. But I just guess you'll have to wait til I write my book.

The Neighbors By Judith Walker

(Walker performs this piece herself modifying her voice for each character. It may also he performed by two actors. It has always been one of Judy's most successful pieces, and it demonstrates how an EcoTheater person can turn some everyday experience into a very moving scene that reveals much about how differently any two people may privately view the same experience and what keeps people separated from each other.)

MRS J: Now, I don't want you to get me wrong. I don't think I'm any better than my neighbors. It's just that, well, we have different priorities. Look over at what they've done to the property next door and you'll see what I mean. When Mrs. Anderson died two years ago--now, that was another case of misplaced priorities, let me tell you. The windows in that house hadn't been washed in years. But we were hoping that the new neighbors would have a little pride, like we do.

I've lived here for twenty-five years. It's a good neighborhood. People keep their dogs tied up and the kids play in their own yards. And there's absolutely no gossip.

Once a year we even get together and have a neighborhood picnic. People paint their houses regularly, and keep their lawns mowed. It was a nice neighborhood--until recently, anyhow.

BETH: I love this neighborhood. Never thought I'd live in such a pretty house. Never really expected to. You know where I grew up. Houses didn't look like these. I guess my mom and dad did the best they could, but I was always ashamed of the way we lived. I wouldn't even invite friends home with me. When I first met Jeff, I wouldn't let him come to the house either. I'd make arrangements to meet him in town or somewhere.

The front porch sagged as long as I could remember. And, Mom, well, she wasn't much of a housekeeper. And she'd get mad when I'd try to fix things up. She'd say, "Who do you think you are, anyhow? If this house looks good enough for me, it's good enough for you."

I remember once when I was a little thing, probably in first grade, I told her that when I grew up, I'd marry a man with a lot of money, that he'd buy me a big house and pretty things, and that I would have white lace curtains on all my windows. She snarled up her nose and straightened me out real fast. She said, "You'll probably fly all over the clover patch and then land on a pile of manure." Only she didn't say manure.

But she was wrong. Oh, we don't have any money, yet. We kind of got started off wrong. The baby, you know. Came along early. But at least we got married. I have my self-respect. Jeff was my first boyfriend. And we had to live with his parents for almost a year. That didn't work out at all. His daddy drank too much and his mom didn't like me. Guess she thought I'd taken her baby away from her. My school bus used to pass along this road. I'd dream that someday I'd have a house like this, with a neat yard and green shutters on the windows. I love this neighborhood.

MRS. J: When they moved in, I treated them like any other neighbor. Fixed them a coconut pound cake and took it over. Welcomed them to the neighborhood. Couldn't help noticing weeks passed, and those cardboard cartons on the porch were never unpacked. And they never hung any curtains, much less wash the windows. Now, that would have been the first thing I would have done.

Then he pulled in that old junk car. It started looking like "Hillbilly Heaven" over there. All hours of the day and night he would work on that car, hammering and banging. And she came knocking at my door one morning about 9:00. I hadn't even finished reading the paper. Wanted to borrow some milk for the little girl. You know, that child is three years old and still in diapers. She left fingerprints all over my clean storm door.

BETH: The lady next door, Mrs. J, is so beautiful, and she dresses so nice. I'd like to be like her. She doesn't know, but I watch her. I like to see what she's wearing, how her hair's fixed. She looks clean and neat even when she's working in her yard.

I've only been next door once. We hadn't lived here long, and I was in one of those black moods I get in sometimes. I don't know what causes them. I know it's not good for Annie to see me like that. Annie's my little girl. I named her for Annie Sullivan, Helen Keller's teacher in *The Miracle Worker*. I read that in the tenth grade. That's when I got pregnant. I pretended I wanted to borrow some milk, but I really wanted to see inside her house. I don't know how she keeps house so good. Everything matches. Her kitchen is green and white and pink. Everything. Even the dish towels and dish strainer match.

And I wish you could have seen her house at Christmas. I didn't go in, but I walked by every evening. She had blue candles in each window. And the tree was lit up in blue lights. And there was a big wreath with a blue velvet bow on the door. Next year, if Jeff is able to work by then and we have some extra money, I'm going to fix up my house like that.

MRS. J: I don't know how they live. They must be on welfare or something. He's supposed to have back trouble, but it sure doesn't look like it to me. He's inside that car hood or under it all day. Gets covered with grease. Last week he came over to use the phone. What could I do? I had to let him. Got black stuff all over the receiver. I had to scrub it with Ajax.

BETH: Something's wrong with me. I get so depressed. And I shouldn't. I'm only nineteen. I have a beautiful little girl and a husband I love. I know times are hard for us right now. Jeff's dad pays our rent. Some day when Annie gets older I'll finish school and get a job to help out. Maybe I'll get over these moods. Maybe it's that PMS they tell about on all the talk shows or something. I wish there was a pill I could take to make me feel better. I don't want to cook or clean or anything. And even if I wanted to, I don't think I'd have the energy. Sometimes, I know this is awful and I shouldn't even think it, but sometimes, I wish--I could die.

MRS. J: You know what I've decided? That girl's just plain lazy. I never see any activity over there. Sometimes she sits on her porch in that swing for hours. When does she get her house cleaning done? And she's pretty ignorant, too. You won't believe this, but right before Christmas, I was taking some cakes to the car for the church bazaar. She came over and looked at them, complimented me on them. I do make excellent fruitcakes. She said she'd like to bake cakes, but she couldn't understand the recipes. She said one recipe she looked at called for separated eggs. Asked if I knew how to do that-- sep-a-rate eggs!

BETH: Once in a while I think I'll invite Mrs. J over. I get real excited and fantasize fixing iced tea and cookies-of course, the cookies would have to be store-bought, but I'd get a name brand like Nabisco so they'd be fresh, and I'd dress Annie up in her prettiest dress, and the house would be clean. And I'll even start straightening things up. But then something always happens. Jeff'll bring home one of his buddies to play cards, or Annie'll cry to be held, and the feeling will pass. Besides, I could never have things nice enough for Mrs. J.

MRS. J: About three months ago--it was in the spring--they brought in these strange-looking ruffled-tailed chickens. Built a pen in the back yard. But it didn't hold them. Those chickens scratched their way out and started roosting on my front porch. I chased them off with a broom, but they came right back. Chicken droppings everywhere.

> "If you can't live like the rest of us, with a little pride, you don't need to be here."

I told them as nicely as I could that they needed to pen those dastardly critters up. They tried. Spread wire over the top of the pen. But those chickens were too smart. They dug their way out! They tried to make amends by bringing me fresh eggs. Those chickens were so foreign-looking, though, I wasn't about to eat those eggs. Threw them in the trash. Now, you can't tell anyone this. But I got to the point where I had to take matters in my own hands. I got some chicken feed and rat poison, mixed them together. And when no one was home next door, I went out, called, "Here chick, chick, chick!" And those little pests came running. Within two weeks, they'd lost all their feathers. Then I got scared. Beth was still bringing me eggs, and I began to wonder if the poison might get from the chickens' system into the eggs. And if they were eating them, especially that little girl-well, you see what I mean?

But I didn't have to worry long. After about three weeks, all the chickens died. It was disgusting, but what else could I do?

BETH: Nothing seems to go right for us. I can't understand it. Jeff took that mechanic's course through the mail, brought that old car into our driveway to practice on.

Maryat Lee

But he lost interest after awhile, said the instruction manual was too hard to read. Now the car's sitting out there on cinder blocks, rusting.

Then he got the idea to raise Black-tailed Japanese chickens. They're supposed to have eggs with less cholesterol.

He said with everyone being on a health kick these days, we could breed the chickens and sell the eggs. But they all died within a few weeks. I don't know what we did wrong. We followed all the directions. And I'm so lonely. There's Mrs. J over there on her porch reading the paper. If I had the nerve, you know what I'd like to say to her? I'd walk over and I'd say, "Mrs. J, I really admire you. You're the kind of person I'd like to be, always clean and beautiful, and doing things just right. Would you be my friend? I need a friend. I wouldn't bother you much. But when you have time, if you could, teach me how to clean house like you do, and plant flowers, and fix my hair. I know I don't have anything to offer you, but maybe someday I will, and I could be the best friend. Could I talk to you when I'm feeling blue?"

> Who would I tell it to--this thing I woke up thinkin' about? And you know, there's nobody, not a single person I could think to tell it to.

BETH: MRS. J.

MRS. J: There she is doing nothing again. Wonder where her trifling husband is. Probably off to buy some more chickens. I'm so upset. If I had a little backbone, I'd give her a piece of my mind. I'd go straight over there and say, "Why don't you go back to wherever you came from! This was a lovely neighborhood til you two moved in. Why don't you move into one of those low-income housing apartments. They're plenty good enough for people like you."

Good morning, Mrs. J. Nice day, isn't it?

Good morning, Beth. It certainly is.

Funny You Said That – originated by Lucinda Ayres

WOMAN (any age upwards of forty) (She jumps up from her seat)

Now, that's funny you said that--about playing your part. Took the words right out of my mouth. *(Now notices and includes the audience without surprise.)* Why I woke up one night last week, I always wake up once or twice anymore, and it all came to me. I knew something I never dreamt of hardly. Just took my breath, even before I had my eyes open. And that's it. Just what you were talking about. And you know? You can go through a whole life and miss it!

Well, I rolled outa my bed, put on my slippers and a wrap and went over to the window, pulled up the shade and looked out at the river crawlin' between the mountain on one side and Hinton on the other--all dark except the pin points of the street lights like the stars up there marking the towns through the heavens. Ever thing was still. Not a tiptoe. Everybody was asleep but me, and the river. Everybody asleep but me, and I was wide,

wide awake.

There was a cutdown moon, real bright and lopsided and the river picked up a glint or two from it. Just think about those men who can walk around on it way up there. But that isn't what I was thinkin' about. But that night, all alone, in my little old bedroom, I was thinkin' about something just as far--fetched (and anymore, it's not so far-fetched anyhow, is it? Why shoot, I betcha their footprints are still up there. And their little flag without any breeze to blow it. And not enough gravity to let it drape real nice, just sticking straight out like some pasteboard thing.)

Well I was pacin' here and yon, shivering and sort of excited, and begun to snap my fingers. I got it. Now what do I do with it? Can't get a patent on it? Who would I tell it to--this thing I woke up thinkin' about? And you know, there's nobody, not a single person I could think to tell it to. Why they'd think well I don't care to tell you what they would think. But, that's just it. I've played my part. I've played my part. All my life. This is, in a nutshell, the thing I woke up with. And it made me weak in the knees.

Now you'd think when I close my door and in my own house and all by myself, now with the husband and children gone, you'd think I could take off what I've been hiding--well that's the only word for it--hiding behind, and just be whoever I am. I'd just like to know how many of you can do that! Can you do that? I can't. Cause I don't know who I am besides mother and now grandmother. Well, I'm proud of that.

> I've respected people all my life No, not respect. I've *feared* people, and what they might say.

I just love those kids. But. Well, I tell ya, that just couldn't be all there is to it. Who in peanut butter fudge are you when they're gone--and your husband too? Who? God must have some reason for you to stay on here after raisin' the kids. Otherwise when they're gone, we'd just be collected when we're finished, just be collected up and taken off up there in a chariot or the Senior Citizen bus and have a goodbye party to send us off in style. Seriously. That would be the nice way to do it. IF that's all there is to it. We'd just go on down to the old river when it's runnin' high and swift, and take a first and last swim and go whish through the white water (Maybe that's why they never let us swim in it! Savin' it up till the end!) But, that's a sin. See, it don't make sense.

But a worse sin is to set home and feel blue. Now, what really woke me up the other night was: I've been playing a part--like my life, our life, was one great big play, and I was given my little part at the beginning, and I never *never* took it off? See? But you know what?

(*Asks narrator and audience, but with gentleness rather than belligerence*)

I don't care if it sounds crazy. Ever since the other night when I woke and knew this thing, I really don't care. I've respected people all my life No, not respect. I've *feared* people, and what they might say. I've held my tongue--well, most of the time. I just stayed inside my safe little pigeonhole. And now since the other night, it's time. It's time to not believe everything I hear or read. It's time to use the things I've saved away for somebody else to enjoy. It's time to be foolish and fun when it can bring a little light into the pigeonholes where somebody else might be trapped. Time to whisper--say, it's alright to step out. Try it. Try it before it's too late. In fact, it's time to speak, not squeak. And you know, since the other night, I don't give one dagum doodly squat what anyone thinks. So. *There.*

(Optional ending: The triumph suddenly turns into mousiness.)

Say, you don't think I'm being foolish do you? (Catches herself.) There I go!

Ethel Hinton – Originated by Lucinda Ayres and Maryat Lee

NARRATOR: Hinton, the county seat that lies along the banks where the two rivers join, was a robust railroad town, and now since the '50's a sleepy little town, alongside the silent railroad yard which for so long was the chugging, sooty heartbeat of our life. Mountains rise up on one side, like a cupped hand around it. On the other side recline vast ladies of stone under the foliage, who sometimes whisper to each other as the skies lower into deep blue. A few harmless ghosts walk and mumble through the nights on one way streets.

ETHEL HINTON: The name I'll go by for the next few minutes is Ethel Hinton. Born 1883. Died 1965.

I left few papers telling about my family and the town. These papers lay moldering in that old house in Avis, the one they just recently tore down overnight in a big rush. The oldest dwelling in Hinton. Jimmy Costa, who loves old things, rescued some things out of a pile of trash when it was being hauled off to the city dump. Then he passed these papers to Fred Long who printed them. I'm glad of that. Maybe they will help clear up some things that folks argue about. There's always been a lot of talk about the Hintons, and how Hinton, the town, got its name, and Avis, right next to it, close as skin and bone.

Now there's a difference between founding a town and having one named after you. As you will see. Some say this town vas named after Evan, my uncle, and some say after my grandfather, Jack Hinton, buried in that marble box behind the House of Hair (a beauty shop) right next to the road (you can't miss it) as you drive into town from the mall. Except for the name of the town, that's just about the last trace of the Hintons. But the town wasn't named after either one of these men.

Jack Hinton had a lawyer's shingle; he was a big outdoorsman, came here when the place was a howling wilderness, as old Judge Miller used to say, because he dearly loved to fish and hunt. Why, he could jump over a large wagon wheel from a stationary position on the ground with both feet together. Now who would want to practice law, when they could jump that high.

But nobody would've thought to name a town after him if it hadn't been for his wife, Avis Gwinn Hinton, my grandmother, who I can remember from when I was a girl.

She was a widow a long, long time. Jack died before the Wan between the States. After that, she ran the big farm which covered all along where Hinton is today. A good farm too. Why, the wheat was as high as a man's head. When he was alive, they lived in a house where the C & O tracks are today, then built a big store where Sears is. Later she built a small house across the road where we moved and lived--the one they just tore down overnight to everyone's shock. It happened 4 days after a committee was appointed to preserve landmarks in the town.

> In the old days, people just went ahead and died. They didn't fool around. They just died, or lived. That's all there was to it. Today they just can't make up their minds.

Anyway, with Jack Hinton dying in the 1850's, 25 years before the town came to be, you can plainly see that he did not in the remotest way, found the town. It was Avis Gwinn Hinton who donated the right of way for the. C & O. It was Avis Gwinn Hinton who donated the 40 acres of land to be the streets, lots and alleyways of the town. It was Avis Gwinn Hinton who did not receive one penny, nor very little thanks, and not so much as a railroad pass for what she did. How and why she did this? Well, that's another story. I just wanted to set the record straight.

Ole Miz Dacey (and Niece or Grandchild)

Note: The character of Dacey was originally created and written entirely by Maryat Lee based on her recorded interviews with old mountain women, but the character was so popular it was used in numerous other scenes, especially in scenarios originated by Lucinda Ayres, such as this one, and later by Martha Asbury Faulkner.

CHILD: Grandma, how come you're washing clothes with a washing board? You don't have to do that, how come you won't use a washin' machine and a stove, why do you do all this work, when we can get 'em for ya, when we give you these things you give' em away, or put' em out in the grainery? What is it with you?
Grandma: Well, a squirrel can have babies in the oven, but that don't make biscuits,
CHILD: Huh?
Grandma: Hand me that bucket.
CHILD: I'll get your water.
Grandma: Well, what are ya standin' around for, flappin' your jaws?
CHILD: We was talkin'.
Grandma: Can't you work and talk too?
CHILD: Well, I guess so.
Grandma: Humph, he learned to do it, or there wouldn't be no talk at all.
CHILD: Grandma, tell me somethin, are you happy?
Grandma: What's that?
CHILD: Are you happy?

Maryat Lee

Grandma: Law, nobody ever asked me that before. But I seen' em ask that on ever television story--"Are ya happy? "Are you happy? And so on with that kinda flap-happy talk, I never seen or heard of anyone yet on them stories that was happy, I'll tell ye that.

CHILD: Well, are ya?

DACEY: You always was the kind that never give up. Well, now, I'll tell ya something'.

(She stops work, dries her hands, sets down with youngster.)

I ain't never seen the world out there, except once. An I never been sick. An I'm happy about that. Cause more people is sick today than ever they was when I was growin' up. Why it's a plumb miracle if you're well today, and people come around to ask. what your secrets is. (And then, they try to get you to change your ways--so you'll be sick with the rest of 'em.)

There are lots of half-dead folks just hoverin' on the fence--yes sir--for years. And their kin folks feel real bad when they wish to heaven when they'd make up their minds to go or come or like we used to say, pass or get off the pot.

Youngster: Yeh yeh, we say that too.

DACEY: Ya do. Well, it's a good sayin. An I'm tellin' ya right now, when my time comes, don't try to hold me back.

Youngster: But Grandma--

DACEY: I don't wanna hear about it. It ain't love or anything like it to hold a person here when they give up doin' for themselves. It's just like bringin' up a young'un, and holdin on to 'em to stay home when they're ready to fly out of the nest. Don't hang on to me. Promise. Doctors don't know everything. All they need to do is to save lives Don't worry their heads about right and wrong. You got to decide about that. (She touches the young'un, and waits for an answer.) Now, to some folks to live out your life here--far from everything ain't livin'. They think you need to travel and see the world. But I've got all the world I want--right here. The bird twitters, the seasons comin' and goin', The one makes you love the other more each time. You can fish, hunt, plant, gather, eat, sleep, sing--dance! Now, I what do I need them blame machines for that save yer time? Ever last person I seen that's got 'em don't never have the time. The machines was 'sposed to save 'em.

Now that's the funny part of it. Even when they come and visit, they can't just set there, they're so worried about time. They squirm and tap and wriggle, and honey--they're everwhere. else but here. No time just to set and be. Now does that answer your question? I'll tell ya something, I ain't never seen the world, but I've got my health, and that's a lot of it, and I never been sick--and you know, more people is sick today than ever they was when I was growin' up, why it is such a miracle if ya ain't sick, that people come 'round to ask ya what your secrets is, it's got so that it's normal if you're sick and it's like you're weird if you're well. Does that answer it? Well--when are ya gonna get my bucket filled?

Young'un: Grandma, you remember how you used to love to dance?

DACEY: A little bit, I reckon.

Young'un: I guess you're too old to do it anymore.
DACEY: (Snaps) Old. Now let me tell you somethin. You're never too old to love--and most times, do--what you done when you was young. Don't forget that. Even if your joints is arthritic, why the love of it, oils em up. See?
(She gets up and dances)
Now--when are ya gonna get my infernal bucket filled, or am I gonna have to do it?
Young'un: (Jumps up, kisses her and runs off with bucket)
DACEY:--You might just turn out to be somethin 'yet. And if ya don't--I'll hain't ya.
(Smiles)

The Waiting Woman – Maryat Lee
(A woman waits for her railroad-engineer husband to come home to a cold dinner and thinks about her loneliness, his betrayal, their desolate marriage. She enters in housecoat and curlers. The Narrator hands her her mail. She looks through it and mutters about bills, contests, various common mail items. Stops short at one letter. Slow burn)

Flossie Freeman. *Miz* Flossie Freeman. As if she was single. Why does her mail keep coming here. It really gets to me the way these women want it both ways. Burns me up. Not a lick of pride, not a smidgen of respect for their men. And old Sam Lotawill just lets her do it. And loves her. He loves her. Brings her store flowers or candy at least once a month. Why as far as he knows, she could be getting love notes from men she meets on her job. How would they know she's married?

(Looks at envelope with light behind it.)
All she need do is slip her ring off. He's gettin' the runaround and it don't bother him, he's just dumb. And he don't even take comfort in a little innocent flirtation on the side. I know. I tried him out gave him a little squeeze when I handed him the wrench that day T had the leak.

> I wanted at least to gather all the unhappy children I could into my home, give 'em room to grown and learn and play.

And here I am waiting! All my life, piddling around doin' the wash, the dishes while I wait. I waited to get married--well, no, I had a few ideas then. Then I waited till the children came, then waited till they grew up, then waited until they got married...
Once in a while I talk to myself. Well...
What are you waiting for? (Whispers)
I wait to hear the train whistle. When he hits the East Yard or C&O Cabin he starts blowin' a certain way and I know he's comin in. He's been an engineer for eleven years. Always blows when he comes home, and I can have a nice hot meal ready when he comes slammin' through the door, his arms all open. Oh, the kids listen for it too. They'll be playin out in the yard, quiet, and then we heard two longs, a short, and a long (whistle blows) and they jump up and run down the street. Well, (pause) most of the time they do. (pause) If

they could hear me now they'd say, oh Mom, we ain't done that for years.

Wonder when he's getting' in. I never know now when to get supper on. He just arrives and nothin's cooked and he'll get all cross. Or if I do cook and have it ready he runs late and it just curls up in the oven and he says "What's this. Who wants a dried up old shoe, hardtack, and a senile potato?"

(Talks to him as if he is there.)

"Listen, buddy. If you want to come in here just anytime it suits you, you just have to take your chances. I don't know what you do. I hear your train come in, and I guess you're on it, and I listen and there's nothing, or some other man's whistle. And then you walk in later hours and say, Just stopped off for a beer with the boys.

"Miz Flossie Freeman don't have *any* dinner waiting for her husband. He treats her like a queen. She goes where she wants. She has her own car, her own bank account, HER OWN NAME.

(Pause. To herself.)

She's nothing but a two-bit-- A floozy dressed up respectable with a ring.

(Studies envelope. Flatly:)

She's free--and I've turned into a-- I'm an (whisper) awful person. I wasn't always like this. One time when I was a little girl, my dream was to be a missionary in a strange country. And if I wasn't worthy I'd have lots of books and I'd talk and listen to them. I'd let ambition come alive, to take care of themselves, make decisions, find out what they could do. Then you came along. "Honey, baby, I need you. You don't need to take care of other people's children. I'll give you some of your own. You'll be my sweetheart. On honey, you said, I can't live without you. And I was hooked like any little old 6-inch fish. Oh, you young girls, don't ever marry someone who says I can't live without you, because once they get you, and they put you in their house and they give you the children and have you all occupied they'll go and find someone else they can't live without.

(Shock)

That's what he's done...

You've found someone else. You can't live without...

You've found someone else...

"For a long while..."

...I can leave?

You want me to leave--my house, my things...

That's what he's done.

You've found someone else you can't live without.

(Gives him time to answer, repeating some of his words.)

  "for a long while!"

I knew it, knew it.

I leave? My house, my things that we saved for, that

I helped save for?

You'll--split it with me. Oh.
You're through.
"Through."
SEE! It's disgusting.
> (Rumples up the letter and throws it down furiously. Then, horrified, picks it up, and flattens it out on her leg and looks at it, stunned.)

What's happened to me. This is awful. I wasn't like this.
> (Folds hands almost as if in prayer. Closes her eyes)
> (Shock)

I don't like it. I can leave? This--?
My house--my things? Uh! Ah! Oh! (Little outraged grunts, as if being struck)(then rage)
Oh Buster, I don't have to leave. I already left.
(Turns to march off. Stops suddenly.
I--left?
(Pause)
I left?
I--left.
(Pause--near tears)
I left you--when we were very very young. I left.
I left you the day that you put your ring on my finger and they called me Mrs.
I left. I left! (Exit)
I left.

Miz Dacey and the Roofer

Narrator: There is always, always, change. And how we fight it. And never never know till later if we should have fought or welcomed it. We are so wise. We suffer to see our children grow up. And wonder who they really are or will be.

Our children who don't know what we went through and don't know what work is, and--how will they manage? I don't know what my parents went through. I wish I did. I really wish I did. I used to make fun, God forgive me, of my grandmother. She didn't play her part. She didn't go along with the crowd. She just was herself.

OLE MIZ DACEY: (Optional: Now some of you have met Miz Dacey how many of ya? Well, you've seen a man play her and a young woman, and now me. (Puts on apron, bonnet, etc.)
> (Sweeping porch vigorously.)

Well dog take it, if it ain't the pollen, its the leaves, and if it ain't the leaves, it's the dust, and if it ain't the dust, it's the (Stops suddenly as she sees audience apologetically sweeps dust daintily back toward her.)

Oh, I didn't realize I had company!

(Straightens her apron.)

Now, some of ya may remember, I had this--well, it's funny now, but at the time it bothered me a lot--a little trouble with my television set. And they finally sent out a repair man to fix it. They was little green men that come out when I turned on the set, well, all kinda things began to happen. First it was little green men, then a real estate man wanted to buy me out all 25 acres and the house at $2500! Then a nutrition woman came along to tell me how I should eat, and she was havin' stomach pains ever minute she sat here. I even had to help the poor thing to get her pills out, and then it was, well, it was Orfin Furlow, the man, the boy I guess. He was who come to fix the tv. Well, he come back after a few days, not to see the set or the green men (he never did see them), but to see and he kept comin'. Well, I begun to cook again--ya don't cook good for yourself alone--and he brought a spring to my step, I can tell ya that. He was a pretty thing, I'll tell ya. When I set here on the porch and he took my hand, why I had all kinda feelings I thought I was almost too old to have anymore.

Why, I started hummin' and whistlin' and everything I looked at--even that old dog--was just aglow, like some light was on it. Why, everybody--even that ornery old niece of mine that comes by to see if I'm all right all the time and tries to talk me into me into using these appliances. She don't have any sense. Why as soon as I didn't have to light my fire in the stove and could set back and let a machine wash my bloomers, I'd wither up and blow away. I even had a kind word to say to her, though she doesn't have the sense to know it, and got me as aggravated as ever.

[optional: And then those college girls she brings. Soon's they hit the porch they're ravin' "Oh Miz Dacey what a bee-utiful view." And, what they're thinkin' is: "How much would it cost me to buy this little old front porch. They even look at them rose bushes the govment put in here that's takin' the place over. The Federal roses? Multiflora? You know the ones that's takin t over the farms so bad a cow e an' t even find a place to drop a pie in. And they go all googly eyed about them "purty" roses. Even the dog can't stand 'em around much, barks just like he's abarkin' now.]

(Pause. She looks out, sees Mr. Termins at her gate, afraid to come in because of her dog.)

Now who's that. Ain't seen him before.

(Pause.)

Oh, I know him. He's the roofin' man. Well, I been callin' him for months to come and put me on a new roof. This'n Zeke and I put on 33 year ago, and buddy, there's hardly a place anymore I can put my bed and stay dry for a night when it rains. Oh.' Come 'ere dawg! Dawg! (Calls to him.)

Don't pay him any mind.

Termins: Howdy, Miz Dacey.

Dacey: Howdy, Mr. Termins.

Termins: Your dog won't bite?

Dacey: Well, if he did, it wouldn't hurt ya. He's lost his teeth now for years. All I can give 'im to eat is soft cornbread and eggs.

Termins: Well, so he done give up huntin, have ya boy?

Dacey: He done give up ever thing. What's that? (pointing)

Termins: Well that's my tool box. What a pretty view you got, Miz Dacey.

Dacey: You plannin' to do some work today?

Termins: Well, I thought so.

Dacey: Oh. Today? (troubled) Can ya just wait a minute? I think I got some water on. (exits)

Termins: I'll just go pull my truck closer. (exits through audience)

Dacey: Uh, Mr Termins, afore you get your ladder and the shingles--

Termins: Yes ma'am?

Dacey: I--I don't really want it put on today, I thank ya for coming out here, but--

Termins: The shingles?

Dacey: Yes sir, I don't want 'em on Monday, I'd like ya to come back Wednesday or after Wednesday.

Termins: Oh, you're goin' out somewhere. That's alright. You don't need to be here. You can go ahead an lock up.

Dacey: No, I ain't goin' nowhere. I just don't want it put on today. It's not a good time to roof a house.   (Facing front)

Termins: Well, it looks like a good time to me.

Dacey: Could you do it next week?

Termins: Now Miz Dacey, you been callin' me up for six months now about puttin' on a roof.

Dacey: Five. Five months. But now see, the signs is wrong. It's in the light moon. You can't roof in the light moon.

Termins: What's the moon have to do with it? I put it on durin' the daytime.

Dacey: If you put it on now, the shingles'll turn up on me. They won't stay down.

Termins: Well, I've been puttin em on now for a long time and that's the first time I ever heard of that.

Dacey: Cause most folks won't tell ya. Cause you're so smart. They're 'fraid you'll think they're foolish.

Termins: Well, Miz Dacey... (As if to a child, which aggravates her.)

I don't think you're foolish. Now don't you worry. It'll be just fine. I'll just back my truck in a little closer now. (Starts off right)

Dacey: (Wielding her broom after him) Listen, Mister Termins: Answer me something, if ya don't mind. Do you always have 100 per cent results with your roofs?

Termins: Why--I've got the best record for roofin' in this county. (Stage R)

Dacey: That don't answer my question. I know you're good. But tell me who was it who roofed that Meadows house?

Termins: Oh--you mean that old house on the ridge? Yes ma'am. I roofed it. One of my best jobs.

Dacey: That ain't the one I mean. That other Meadows house up on the other side.

Termins: Oh...

Dacey: Somebody told me you roofed that house.

Termins: Well--that house was so old it wouldn't hold 'em on.

Dacey: If the sheeting was rotten, why didn't you tear it off first?

Termins: Well, it didn't look rotten.

Dacey: You mean to tell me you was climbin' all over it, and you didn't see it was rotten? (She begins to smile.)

Termins: No ma'am, It just didn't show.

Dacey: Then maybe it wasn't rotten, Mr. Termins.

Termins: It had to be, for them shingles to curl up and fly off the way they did. The nails pulled out and they was good twisted nails. I never seen anything like it.

Dacey: (Gloating.) Umhum. So you don't always get 100 per cent good results.

Termins: Well, nobody's perfect Miz Dacey.

Dacey: Well, let me tell you somethin. If you have the dates on your calendar that you shingled that house, I'd set down with ya and I just about bet ya you roofed it in the light moon.

Termins: (Pause.) When is the dark moon, and the light?

Dacey: (She sits down, relaxes, fans, etc.) The dark moon starts on the night off the full moon.

Termins: But that don't make sense. That's when it's lightest.

Dacey: That's when it starts toward going to dark.

Termins: Oh. Then the light moon begins--

Dacey: With the new moon.

Termins: Oh. (Switches.) Listen. If I started to put tin roof on by the moon why I'd be outta business half the month. More' n half the month, cause I can't work on rainy days anyway.

Dacey: I see what ya mean. But you could start a business that was good in the light of the moon.

Termins: Like?

Dacey: Well, you've got a little garden, or some land?

Termins: It don't do me no good.

Dacey: You don't plant in the right signs.

Termins: I plant in the ground.

Dacey: And it don't do much good? How like today--I was gonna plant me some corn, and it'll do awful good, cause it's the light of the moon, and in the arms.

Termins: Arms.

Dacey: Arms and the light moon is best, come on, if you wanta help me some, and I'll show you my taters. And beans. Why, I was plantin' my beans and ole Mr Lilly come by and said "Miz Dacey, ain't you looked at your calendar, what day you think it is?" And Lord, honey, I planted two rows in the wrong sign. So I thought, well, I won't dig 'em up. I'll just plant more in the morning. I can show you the difference. You can tell it already, and they wasn't planted more'n twelve hours different. (On exit:) Oh, you can do lots of things by the signs. You'll see a difference. Lord honey, I planted two rows in the wrong sign, so I thought well I won't dig 'em up, I'll just plant more in the mornin', I'll show you the difference. You can tell it already, and they wasn't planted more'n 2 hours and... (Exits still talking)

Termins: I'll be right with ya--(to audience)

Y'know, I useta hear my granddad talkin this way, an I didn't pay attention. We used to laugh at 'im and--ever since he died,

I sorta wished I'd learnt more. I hate to do roofin' alla time.

(Exits)

Excerpt from *John Henry* (adapted by Maryat Lee and performed by Kathy Jackson)

John Henry: A machine--three times fast as me. Well now, I ain't sure, Cap'n. Like I said before, a man ain't nuthin' but a man. That machine could beat me. Sure it could. But if it do--it'll beat all us, Ya'll too. Right? (To audience. Waits for response.) Now, I hear ya. You say we got a year more on a job here. More'n a year. But we're like a family. The onliest I got. Now, what we gonna do? Where we goin' a machine takes over? We gonna lie down an pray?

(Smiles. Then sudden strength)

Or we gonna stand up and pray? Tell me. Talk to me.

(Listens to the nonverbal response)

Is that right. Well, they always said, hammer'll be the death of me. Umhum. I hear ya. But lemme say this. We can die, any time, any minute the Lawd wants, right? Whenever I go in 'er I might die, Cap'n. Whenever I drive the steel, my shaker could die. Whenever I come out to the sweet light of day to my friends, I just might die that night. So I'm thinkin'--brothers and sisters--cause that's what we is--we live while we live, as lovin' as we can. We play while we play as playful as we can. Ain't that right? And mostest of all, we work while we work as good, hard, as proud as we can.

> I'd like to ask, Lord, why do you let me have this anger that makes the hair on my neck--stiffen in anger with my people who are so lost?

(Building to climax)

An fore I let that steam drill beat me down, I'll die with my hammer in my hand! I'll do it. Brothers and sisters, AMEN.

(Quiets, waits.)

Maryat Lee

Hey now, c'mon now, yawl. Don't everbody look like I done got beat already. This here gonna be a BIG day, maybe proudest day in this man's life.
>(About to exit)

AN DON'T YA'LL FORGET--IT ALL MEANS SOMETHIN'--EVEN WHEN YOU DON'T WIN. (EXITS)

Trail

I am sometimes a ridiculous spectacle: think of it, a patch in a whole quilt describing the whole quilt, a leaf of a tree trying to tell what the whole tree is like to the very depths of its roots, a leaf that is destined to fall to earth within one season, there to decay, slowly buried (by a new season's leaves) and add to the food which enriches this tree and the new leaves of each succeeding generation.

In my brief life, my passion is to describe those leaves, the ones sprouted here in this country, this *county* in a corner of southern Appalachia, leaves that lie buried deep in the ground now, and nourishing all the leaves of this generation. It is a journey we all live whether we know it or not, through time and space, coming to life and then death with no awareness of its meaning, or with a sense of participating through a thousand generations who are still on the ground nourishing us, or those thousands yet to come who are to join us in nourishing the great tree that lives on and on--to learn that it is to learn our own peril, if the tree of our history is forgotten, cut down, and none were to be allowed to grow again.

The Local Historian

Part of the soul of that which is a human being. The study of the history is the seed, roots, trunk, branches and little twigs on which we all find ourselves as leaves for a brief season.

And this history comes to us in rays on remnants, like the pieces that patches which a historian, like a quilt maker, assembles into a pattern that makes sense and beauty of the patches, and who then makes the careful loops of stitches that hold it altogether. The quilt both warms us, and gives us pride at its beauty. As with quilts, each of our histories is different from the next quilter. The patches that I find--in an Indian mound, or in dirt, blackened by fires long ago where a brave fort stood facing the dark fear of night.

Or in the names written small in musty volumes of history referring to places and people who lived where we live, who had to cope with the same kinds of floods, landslides, strokes of lightning that still strike alarm deep inside us--these are fleeting glimpses of where we came from as seen through the window of a railroad passenger car. The scenery passes abruptly, and while dwelling on one valley, we almost miss the bridge next to it.

Businessman Maryat Lee
Man: We are a religious people here. This is the Bible Belt. People go churches--

Baptist, Methodist, Presbyterian, Episcopalian, Catholic. Many still have prayer meetings on Wednesday nights. A Christian town you could say--that's lost its way.

Sometimes with all my heart I long to stand on top of a mountain, shave off the trees and (for a moment) shave off "ambition," so I can be close to heaven so I can look around and see my town nestled down there, spread along the river bank, a little strip of houses, homes, that look as if caught in a story book dream, so I could ask, Where shall we go? Which way, and more important how can we get ourselves together to move in one direction without the next fellow undoing it. Anyway, even, nothing can be done about that. In their daily battles they can't see anything of your vast plan, so they can't work together, can't agree on something that might help bring us out of our stagnation, to have better schools, for instance. Lord, I'm a simple man. You know that. I try to do my job the best I can to raise my family to have respect for your creation we are so hellbent to destroy. And Lord. please don't let us do that.

I had a dream recently. A dream that won't let me go.

I was in a woods, and I wandered all by myself for hours, this way and that, and I was filled with joy, and then a surprised terror. There were no hours of the day. The sun was slightly tipped to the south, but it would not move. It was still; the sounds of insects and birds were very distinct and in my ears I heard a brilliant, deep horn.

I sat down in shock on a fallen log. The air was without motion. The warm air was coolin'. And then I heard the word in a distant voice that was strong and serene. I jumped up and looked around me. There was nothing that could speak in these woods--except myself. YES, I answered, I'm here. You, the voice said slowly. You! YES, I said hungrily, I'm here. I'm right here. You are called, It said In a quiet, bemused way. YES. I said. Where, when, how. I asked in a frenzy wanting to run in all directions at once. And as I was prancing to be off, It spoke: For heaven's sake, be still and shut up.

My heart about to burst from my chest, I put my hand over my mouth to stop my foolish words. And then It was gone. Come back, I cried. I knew who It was. Lord I cried, please come back.

I'm called--called what? Forgive my agitation. But I'm filled with such elation I can't stand still. I'm answering the only way I know how to. Don't abandon me now after I've waited so long.

I was in tears. Then I woke. I had fallen off my bed and was shivering in the cold. My poor wife was trying to comfort me. I got back in bed and lay awake in the dark long after she went back to sleep And my anger grew. My chest swelled, I stiffened. No one listens anymore. Everyone is babbling to each other, reciting a tape inside them. No one using their marvelous brains and these miraculous eyes. Then the grey light of dawn quietly broke, and I suddenly had nothing to say. Nothing.

I got up and looked out of my window. Over the roofs of homes, I saw the mountain ridges as always, and as I looked at them, I realized I never saw them before. How could I dare stand on top to preach at everybody down here? Then I watched, and very slowly and gently the mist moved up silently, magically curling around their shoulders, removing the summit from my eyes. The breath went out of me.

Mountaineer
NARRATOR: The mountaineer is wily, stalks his prey, finds where its weakness is, pretends to be naive, friendly. It's all protective years of practice. In surviving.

JIM ALGOOD: Say now, we are awful glad you came to live here. I'm Jim Allgood, from the Welcomers, and we send somebody out to make the new people feel at home and to see if you wanna ask any questions about this county and town.

NEW: Why that's real nice. It's a beautiful place, why I chose this place. It's real neighborly of you to visit.

JIM: Well, it's not easy to get to know folks here. I can help ya with that a little. We've been isolated a long time here, and we're kinda cautious people. But it's important to us to have more people, more of the right kinda people, you know?

NEW: Oh, yes I know. It's natural to feel that way. Every place feels a little concerned about that. Uh, what, how you all gauge the right kinda people here?

Jim: Oh, It's no different. People are all the same. You know, responsible, church-goin', maybe, pay their bills, taxes. Not that we're all alike here. Don't mean to give you that idea. Well, I work on the railroad and know what it's like to be in a new place. get to travel a little bit. On the tracks. I guess you've lived a lot of different places?

NEW: Well, no, not many.

JIM: People wonder why people wanta come and live here--oh It is beautiful alright. A lot of us, if we had a chance we'd go somewhere else. But then, somewhere else ain't as good as here. And we're tryin to keep up with the world, best way we can. It's not easy. But we're doin it. We don't have problems here--like race problems, or stealing, or drugs. Why, for instance, if you had some Black friend, I'd even try to help and get them a job on the railroad.

NEW: Why that's real kind. I'll pass along the word.

JIM: Now don't tell anybody I told ya, but I'll give you a ring when they're about to hire. They don't publish it. You can pass along the information. Tell 'em to give me a call and I'll show them the ropes. Well, It sure was nice meetin' ya, and just let us know if we can help. (SHAKE HANDS.)

    (Both seem pleased. Ad lib exit)

NEW: Hmm. How nice. I'm really impressed.

(Thinks about it a minute, puzzled, then it dawns.)

So--that's how it's done.

Miz Dacey has a weak moment – originated by Lucinda Ayres
Chars: Miz Dacey and Mr. Tapper

MIZ DACEY: (Mending a dress. Carrying a pistol has worn its pocket thin.)

Sometimes--oh well, it's been a long time--when you live alone, you get a cravin'. Oh, I admit it. Now I think some folks get carried away with their cravin's. But sometimes, like I say, your nature I think gets away from ya a little. Why, I'm embarrassed when I think about it, but about a month ago, this poor man comes down come the path. Lord, I don't know what he must think. But he just come down at the wrong time! It just goes to show ya, that none of us is perfect, and the Lord uses this our natures--to keep--us from gettin to proud Oh--ya wanta hear about it? No--it's somethin I'm not proud about. You think it would do me good to tell about it? Well I'll tell ya one thing--they always talk about the man bein' the pushy one but I'll tell ya, that ain't always so. I just don't know what came over me! Psst, of course I know what came over me. It was like this.

I was just sewin' up my frock here which I have to do ever so often cause this little gun I always carry since Zeke died. See it wears a hole in the pocket. I was settin' here sewin' up my pocket on an evenin', not much past dinner time, and I heared a smallish car come to stop out on the road. A door slam--some quick pit pat steps end here he comes--pore thing. Whenever I'm sewin up this pocket. I keep my gun in, I think about Zeke--and there I was and there was these little pit pat Steps I heard coming dawn the walk.

> Why you'd you just be a stone or a stick if you didn't have a cravin' ever so often.

TAPPER: (From the gate) Hello? Excuse me? Anybody home?

DACEY: Lord, I thought to myself--what am I gonna do?

TAPPER: Oh I thought I saw someone sittin on the porch as I drove by.

DACEY: Oh, I'm settin on the porch alright. I'm settin' tight.

TAPPER: Well I heard you lived up here, and your neighbor has just bought some insurance from me and thought you might be interested. I'm from Old Life Guarantee.

DACEY: Insurance. Well, I need a kind that you can't buy.

TAPPER: Oh I represent a big company, I bet we could find exactly what you need. I bet we could fit the bill.

DACEY: (with a side glance) You probably could.

TAPPER: Don't you want to tell me what you're lookin for?

DACEY: Mr. Tanner

TAPPER: Tapper. Ted. Tapper

DACEY: Mr. Tapper--I don't know what you've got on your mind--

TAPPER: Insurance!

DACEY: Oh that's right. I almost forgot about that.

TAPPER: Now about this insurance--for only ten dollars a month, you can get this wonderful package that'll no give matter you how $100 a day, every day you're in the hospital long. And then for an extra dollar, your beneficiary will get $10,000 dollars. Why it's almost like it's worth dying for. And then if you'll just read through this real quick, and sign up today, you can get your house painted.

DACEY:--Uh, what time is it I gotta pull a cake out of the oven--

TAPPER: A cake!

DACEY: Well, it's just a little old cornbread.

TAPPER: Cornbread!

DACEY: An then I gotta do a big warsh.

TAPPER: Well, how about this insurance you said you needed? It's a little late to do a wash.

DACEY: Mr.--

TAPPER: Tapper.

DACEY: Mr. Tapper, I think you better go--it looks like a storm is headin' our way

TAPPER: Oh I'm not afraid of storms. Don't bother me at all. In fact, I like a good storm. Don't you-- (Dacey is getting bumfuzzled.) Say-- (Looking at her more closely) you look mighty familiar Don't I know you. Oh I remember you. Let's see you name was-- weren't you a majorette in the band? Well it was pretty long time ago.

DACEY: (slightly defrosting) You mean...we know each other?

TAPPER: Well, I think so. (in some doubt.)

(They look at each other carefully.)

DACEY: I don't know. You look just like a lot of people--men I know.

TAPPER: You've always lived here?

DACEY: Born and bred.

TAPPER: You musta gone to school.

DACEY: You might call it that.

TAPPER: Don't you think we mighta been in school together?

DACEY: Mr. Tanner--I mean, Tapper--

TAPPER: Ted.

DACEY: Ted? Ted Tapper?--Ted Tanner. No. Ted Tapper? Ted...

TAPPER? My Goodness.

TAPPER: Yes!

DACEY: You were on the team--oh I remember sneaking off to the ball games just to watch you play.

TAPPER: Well, I wasn't on the team. I was on the bench.

DACEY: Oh. (awkward pause) Well--I musta sneaked off to watch you warm the bench. (Share a little laugh, then awkward pause) Well, a long time's passed. You got married.

TAPPER: Oh yes, was married about twelve years.

DACEY: Was?

TAPPER: Yeh, she's been gone a long time. You married?

DACEY: Was.

TAPPER: Oh, your husband left you. I'm sorry.

DACEY: Died. Been a long time. A long time. (She fans.) You remarried.

TAPPER: Umhum...I bet it seems like a long time. Do you get lonely?

DACEY: Lonely! Why I never get lonely. I got my cow and my dog and chickens and garden, and once in a while my niece and grandson. Lonely. Why what would ever give you that idea!

TAPPER: Livin' alone, up here, I don't know what I'd do.

DACEY: Well, to tell the truth, once in a long while, I do need some recreation with someone my own age.

TAPPER: What do you do for recreation? There much to do for recreation in town?

DACEY: Same thing.

TAPPER: Oh. That's the way it goes. (getting her message) Now, what about that insurance? You need life, or fire or?

DACEY: I remember you. I remember you. You remember that dance recital you were in? That's right you was never on the ball team. It was dancin. Ain't that right?

TAPPER: Oh yeah, I was in lot of those.

DACEY: I remember you had on these black pants that had a stripe down the side with a little ole waistcoat thing and the big tall hat?

TAPPER: Oh that was the time I danced in dinner plates.

DACEY: Dinner plates! That was the prettiest thing. I betcha don't remember any of that. I guess you're too old to do it anymore.

TAPPER: Aw, sure I can do it, some of it. We aren't that old. That was mostly time steps.

DACEY: I'd most give anything to see you do that. But I don't reckon you could creak off a number.

TAPPER: (remembering) Oh you were in it too?

DACEY: No--well, I was there.

TAPPER: You were in it.

DACEY: How bout doin' a couple of those steps?

TAPPER: Come on, I'll show ya. you can do it, it's easy.

DACEY: Can I hold on?

TAPPER: Sure. Now, here you go. Just stomp your foot. STOMP on one, hop on the other. Step. Stomp, step, stomp. (He works with her a bit, and then she steps back to admire his footwork.) There. Now you do it. (Steps back)

DACEY: (She starts) Mr. Tapper, I don't have breath. Whoops!

TAPPER: Now, let's turn on your little radio and see if we can get us some music? You don't have a radio? Well, I've got one that I wear on my rounds--only it has ear phones. Let's see, I'll put it on me, and you'll pick it up from me. Or do you want to wear it. Or-- (He pulls out a portable radio)

I'll tell you--you hold one side to your ear, and I'll hold the other side to mine and we'll make out somehow.

> (They maneuver so that each is holding part of the ear piece. He is dialing to find the right music. Finds it and they begin to have fun swinging and swaying around the porch, and there tap dancing, now and then tap dancing, now and then ballroom kind of dance, and once some old fashioned boogie. These are two aging people having a ball.) STOMP on one, hop on the others Step. Stomp, step, stomps. (He works with her a bit, then she steps back to admire his footwork.)

TAPPER: There, now you do it. (Steps back)

DACEY: (She starts) Mr. Tapper, I don't have the breath. Whoops! Catch me now. (She falls into his arms. He drags out of his pocket the papers for her to sign up for his insurance. Just at this point, she remembers the cake is probably burnt.)

DACEY: Oh Lordy, Ted, I forgot my cake, and--

TAPPER: That's alright I'll come in with you, and we'll mix up another one.

DACEY: (Gives him a long look) Ted, you can come in, I'm not interested in insurance.

TAPPER: (Gets her message. Starts to follow her across the threshold. Stops. Thinks. Turns back. Shakes his head and slowly walks off through the gate.)

Two women parting after work

CLOY: Well see you Monday. Now don't get into poison ivy.

FAITH: Oh, I won't be anywhere near it.

CLOY: Planning something fun?

FAITH: I'm goin to see--well, I'm gonna see a friend, and see how Bunny is doin'.

CLOY: Oh--

FAITH: Well you have a good weekend.

CLOY: Faith? I didn't know you were--good friends.

FAITH: I should've told ya.

CLOY: You gonna tell her what I said?

FAITH: If it's about her, she has a right to know.

CLOY: Well what did you let me blab on and on about her?

> (They freeze, then FAITH moves around to the other side of CLOY and talks directly to the audience.)

FAITH: Seems like this happens to me a lot. I'm up here with Don't tell this one, and don't tell that one, and I always say, Oh, of course I won't tell. Why do I say that? There's this curiosity to hear something secret or bad. And yet I know when I'm with that person, I'll be thinking about what I heard. Why, it's like I owe everything to just anybody that comes along that says, Don't tell...I shouldn't listen in the first place. I should say: I--

> (She returns to exact position she was in when they froze. CLOY now breaks out of freeze and goes behind FAITH'S back and talks to audience:)

You know, I don't want to hear about Bunny. I'm sorry I listened. See, now it'll be in my mind, and I'll ask Bunny--I'll have to ask Bunny--if it's true. If I don't ask, then it's like I'm thinking it is true. And Bunny don't have a chance. Just because I listened to some dirt, somebody told me not to tell. Cloy, if she's my friend--if you were my friend and she said some dirt about you--how would you feel if I didn't say anything, and just kept it to myself and wondered if it was true. And I was trying not to betray the son of a gun that told me, and at the same time I was betraying you? See what I mean?

(FREEZE)

CLOY: 'Bye Faith, don't get into any poison ivy this weekend.

FAITH: Oh, I won't be anywhere near that stuff.

CLOY: What are ya doin' tomorrow?

FAITH: I'm goin' to see a friend.

CLOY: (Pause)--Bunny. (Faith nods.)

(This information does a number on CLOY; it affects her movement, her intention, her ease.) (clears her throat)

Oh.

(THEY FREEZE. CLOY then goes behind Faith and talks to audience.)

I didn't know she was still close to Bunny.

FAITH: (goes around and also talks to audience)

How do you avoid situations like this?

CLOY: (Back to Faith. Starts to speak, then notices Faith is not attending. Then FAITH TURNS and faces her) Faith, you promised you wouldn't tell her what I said.

FAITH: (FREEZES)

CLOY: (Moves to another part of the stage. Now it's later.) You know, I'm glad she's gone. She had such bad manners, never did fit in. She told me once that now you mustn't tell this, don't ever tell her I said this, she told me that she and the director had broken up.

FAITH: Well, he didn't make any bones about it. Everybody knew.

CLOY: You knew? how come I didn't catch on. Here, give me that box. I've got this pile done. It doesn't pay to mix fun and work. Usually it doesn't pay. (Laughs) But I can think of some times when it did pay!

FAITH: I thought you were real close to her.

CLOY: I guess we were.

FAITH: What happened?

CLOY: You know what happened. I started working here on this job before she ever came along. And then after six months, here she's put supervisor over us. Just came in and the Director fell all over himself.

CLOY: Well, she was awful good and efficient.

FAITH: And I'm not. Is that what you're saying (Laughs) Well, if you want to call that efficient. She took some of my reports and put her own name on them. Pretty darn efficient.

CLOY: Did you tell the Director?

Maryat Lee

FAITH: No! Of course not.
CLOY: Did you face her with it.
FAITH: Why are you going up there to see her?
CLOY: (stumbling around) Well, I liked her, and I still like her.
CLOY: (smirks contemptuously)
FAITH: Can't a person like two people?
CLOY: (airily) No reason not to.
FAITH: (aside) She's not leveling with me. She's lying.
CLOY: (aside) She acts like your friend, and then just smacks you in the face. I should've known.
FAITH: Cloy.
CLOY: Faith. (CLOY exits. NOTE: Following section can stand on its own.)
FAITH: If I listen to one friend tell me dirt about another friend--who do I owe my loyalty to? If it begins to get into my brain, and spread little doubts about that person, and then I can always find some little tatter of truth or half truth and say, oh yeah, I remember she did that, or yes, now I see what was going on and so on then the next time I see that friend, something is changed something so subtle that neither she nor I recognize it at first.

> There comes that moment of silence--oh it's not a bad moment, but a cool moment and you both know though you can't speak, you both know that something has just died.

But when she starts talking to me, I begin to look at her and part of me is saying--not that she's lying exactly, but I'm wondering if she is telling me the whale truth. I move away from her, though I'm still standing right there. But I've moved way over here and I'm looking at her as if she's all of a sudden, someone else, a stranger, or an IT.

And then, she begins to feel a little chill in the air, and begins to cover herself up a little and she backs off a little, and she almost acts "guilty"--and...and you can't even let on that you sad about it. She looks as though she smells something bad. That makes you think, it must be true. Then you go away she goes away, and you feel like you got to DO something--get busy at something, call someone, tear the house up to get it clean, or have a little drink. Then what do you do? You call the friend that told you the inside story--the dirt and you report what happened. And now, you're in it deeper. You've decided--because you betrayed that friend, to--betray her some more. You say: I saw her, and I agree with you. She knew I'm on to her. She got huffy and distant. It was clear. She's got the guilts.

Not realizing that what I was looking at was a wound. Looking at a wounded animal that backed away from me. I wasn't seeing her guilt--but my own.

She didn't do me harm. What makes me take sides like that. It's almost like the two of us just got together to lay on her our own troubles, and then kill her. And, the funny thing is that I've been in her shoes. I know how she felt. Betrayed.

Now I've got to get myself together. You know, we're all taught a lot of useful things. But weren't taught how to handle this. Why any old gossiping somebody can came up to you and tell you some delicious stuff about somebody, and then they say: "don't tell 'em I told you." Honor bound to not to betray this person even if you have to betray someone who was really a friend. Next time someone starts in, if I can just have my wits about me, I say I don't want to hear this stuff secondhand. Or, if I get off guard and let them tell me some dirt, when they tell me not to tell, if I could just say, well I can't promise that. This is about a friend, and she ought to know what you're saying.

I can guarantee that you'll lose one friend, but you'll feel like you haven't sold your other friend down the river.

Proctor Kirk

Folks my family and I run a little restaurant down the road. I'm not 'sposed to tell you the name of it. As anyone knows who's in the food business, that kind of work can-- pardon the expression eat you up, Especially in a small town in an outatheway place where you can't get a volume of people to eat regularly. And sometimes I do a lot of thinking-- about people--and about consuming. And you can tell a lot about people in a restaurant. Any restaurant.

And I admit, I'm fascinated with people, always have been. And what you can learn just by sitting around with different folks around the table when they're eating--and not even in their own kitchens. You can learn first of all about what they really don't like. In the way of food, in the way you prepare it. (*fill in example*)

But there's a lot more than that.

You can find out a lot--if you care to know it--about what else they don't like--and what they're thinkin' about. Why I could take a pretty good poll on almost any subject you could think of in a week's time--from the weather to the sex life of a gnat, and it'd be pretty darn accurate--accurate for a place like this: I doubt if anyone has ever composed a poll-- opinion poll--sophisticated enough to reflect what the small town and country mountain people think.

Not only that, you can hear quite a few stories. Now they say that we are well known for our shining ability as storytellers. Well I can tell ya, I wouldn't mind betting that our little restaurant has more stories being told, being created, shaped, formed, stretched, whispered, sometimes broadcast per square inch of any other restaurant in the whole world But you know my real interest--even more than people has always been nature. Really at heart, I'm a naturalist. You can't make a living out of loving nature.

So I have my restaurant not just close to the river, but right on the top of the river banks. I can spit over the railing and watch my momentary fleeting spit hit and disappear into the fast flowing currents, become one with one of the oldest rivers in the world. Of course I don't spit that often. Especially since I'm an outspoken, ornery opponent of pollution. I must really love water--and it's all around us in Summers County, two rivers, a big lake and so many little natural tributaries falling off the mountains.

I must really love water a lot--'cause I get myself into so much hot water besides all that wonderful cold water. You know? You remember what happened to the Roman Empire? I've come to understand that bit of history, through seeing what we do. The toleration for pain and the sweetness of delayed satisfaction is almost disappeared on the earth--at least in our "developed" countries. Heaven help the undeveloped countries to have more sense. What in the world have we done to ourselves?

Used to be here that sewage emptied into the river. You'd have to wade in your boots out through it to catch fish--but they were out there. Now with our high powdered detergents, all the caustic materials, chlorine and people washing a lot more than they used to--it's built to a level that lower levels of life are not surviving. Well, I have a lot of respect for the lower levels--if they go, it won't be long till we go too. We're built on them.

I think we've forgotten Mother Nature's most humbling rule: To survive, each of us has to adapt. And I think the folks of the Roman Empire got to wanting everything to adapt to them. And that's why it fell.

Well, I've got to get back to ordering next week's food.

Hard to change – Originated by Lucinda Ayres

It's so hard.

To change.

Oh, I don't mean your mind, that's the easiest thing in the world to change, I've done that for years.

And I don't mean your name or your address.

Or your telephone number, or the party you vote for.

Or the church you go to, or a job, or a school your kid goes to, or even your lifestyle. Any one of these can be mighty difficult, but--they're possible. I mean, you can do it. You can go down and change your name--or get married. You can change the job you're in--even when you haven't been fired. Or you can get yourself fired. You can do any one of these things when you have to, or want to.

But there's another kind of change--inside--changing a habit, a way of thinking that you realize is keeping you tied up in knots, or in a prison, just because you were taught it years ago.

I told you last year, and the year before, oh yes, I'm going to change. I'm going to start wearing my hats, and writing some poetry. And I was going to do a lot of these little changes.

Well. But it's not so simple. Well, it *is* difficult to do a lot of these changes. Moving! When you've been a collector all your life. A job! When they're aren't any jobs around, and you're hanging on with all your might because the next one might be worse. This is not simple or easy. Don't get me wrong. But--and I'll tell you the truth when you make that fatal decision that you want really deep inside to change that your habits--either you'll give up like any

> One night I even entertained the idea that since there was such a scarcity, that the Lord wouldn't mind if a man had two women.

The Appalachian Plays

sensible person would as she smacks her head against the walls the tenth time, or--you're in for trouble.

So you wake up one morning and decide that you've missed something big--you've read a book or two and it starts you thinking--oh, not what you're thinking, living in a little town hidden away in the mountains has made you miss seeing the world. We all think that once in a while, and then if we've saved any money at all that doesn't have to go to the plumber or doctor, you might take your trip off to one of the worldly places, and see the sights no, it starts you thinking. You start wandering inside. You don't begin to plan to take a little trip--you start a trip right while you're reading. I love my television, but I never have had that kind of thinking when I'm watching it. It's reading that does it--because you can drift off away from the words for a minute, or a half hour, and then you can come back to the words and read 'em again if you want to. You can be the boss. With a book, or a magazine or newspaper. You can go off on a side trip and then come back, and it don't matter. You haven't lost the next wrinkle, it's not over, the commercial doesn't come in on you.

But that's not what I was talking about. What I'm talking about is--you know, I'm not even sure what you could call it. I know that I have touched on it once in a while in my life and realized I had my hand on something--and then it would disappear. For a long time it did this. Well, I didn't have time to do anything for myself. I had children to raise, all their things to go through with them, my husband well he needed all the rest of my attention, and then he went died.

So, all of a sudden I had time. And I was just settin' around feeling blue, and then I started doing things--helpin' at the senior center, joining and givin' more time to the church, servin' on the committees, making a few crafts for the bazaar, knitting, crocheting, quilting. Oh yes, I made a grand quilt or two. But something was missing. A man! And I looked around--oh yes I did. That might have meant everything.

I could have gone right on and had a good time at fixin' and fussin' over a man. I enjoy that. I really do. Once I got over missing Ted. But--when I really looked around, all the good men were--of course--married. So, it was a choice, and I'll swan, one night I even entertained the idea that since there was such a scarcity the Lord wouldn't mind if a man had two women, as long as he's honest--and didn't use the women to hurt each other. Well, I didn't think about that too long. I was too much in the habit of having a man to myself. And I could just see the look on their wives' faces--women I knew--at even the thought of such a thing.

And I knew in my heart, that I wouldn't be able to be a good Christian and share with the wives. In spite of myself, I'd be trying to put a wedge in between them so I could have him for myself. So I gave that idea up, right now.

And now--well, I'm confused. I say things that come out of the old life, and I don't have a new life yet, and once in a while a big bubble of it will blurt out and the astonishment on the faces of my friends and children--well, it's hard to describe. Why, I told the old friend of mine the other night--he was pushing me to come see him--another time I would have just given in--but I said, knock it off, buddy. I never said that in my whole life. I don't even know where it came from. Well, when I said lay off buddy, you'd a thought I let out a string of the ugliest cuss words in the world. He started ravin' over the phone, started cussin' and carryin' on something awful I couldn't help feelin guilty causin' such a commotion. But you know something, all I did was just hold my ground instead of bein' the silly little piece of putty I've always been. That's all. And you'da thought I had up and shot his old dog Spot.

You'll say--well, you been doin' too much of that readin'. It's beginning to be a bad influence. Well, is it a bad influence? So I started readin' the great books. Yeah, they have 'em at the library. Oh, I'm so glad we have a library. Why, there are whole worlds in there if you need to be in touch with 'em. You can travel, you can be on a ship, you can go the city, you can learn how to fix a faucet, how to paint a wall so it won't peel.

It's hard to change though. I guess I'm glad, or I wouldn't be doin' it. In fact, I can't imagine stopping it and going back--I really can't. And I don't want to go back. Not to just my friends. I really don't know who I am any more. It's confusing, mixed up, and I know my friends are talking about it. Well--let 'em talk. I guess that's the only thing I can say. Someday, maybe I can set down and explain what I'm goin' through, because it'll be in the past. But now--it's happening right now, and I just guess everybody will have to be patient--or upset. That's just the price of tryin' to grow up, I reckon.

Grandma Parker – Susie Boone Keffer

For eleven years, she retreated from men when her intended gave her up because his family felt she wasn't good enough. She was engaged and the boy loved her, but her grammar wasn't perfect and her education was meager. She wouldn't make the proper wife, his family decided and the engagement was broken. She shied away from men--till she met and married Newton Parker when she was twenty-nine.

Newton Parker was a drinker. He'd stop off on paydays--he worked for the C&O--for just one drink, and come with empty pockets. She sent the youngest son to the train station on payday so he could bring Parker, and the paycheck, back home.

She could never accept help from anyone. At fifty-eight, when she was a widow, she supported herself by looking after old people. She owned her own home. That was important in her thinking. She had already lost two homes they had owned by "gain on" bank notes for people who didn't pay them back.

A pact with a snake

I'm a modern mountain woman. Some would say a mean modern mountain woman. Oh I was taught to be hospitable, gentle, loving. Oh yes, it comes natural, being kind. It comes natural, being kind and neighborly. But there's those other times. A nice man comes to the door and says, Lady, I'm sorry to bother you, but my Boss needs a way to get up to his mine. Now we don't want to put you out, but you wouldn't mind if we just made little road on you, way over yonder, we'd pay for the use of it. See, here's a paper. Soon's you sign it, you get $50 a month--whether we use the road or not. Yes ma'am. Sounds good, doesn't it?

What'd be the harm? No harm--'less your well and your neighbor's well starts spewing up tobacco juice-lookin' water and comin' out the taps. Oh, honey, don't sign your name on those contracts 'til you find what that language really means.

> "Mister Snake"--I didn't know if it was Miss or Mister--"If you don't hurt me, I promise on my word I'll not hurt you."

So we learned to cover up the kindness with meanness. No other way we knew to fight 'em.

This has always fascinated me--the contracts people get into. In these mountains we don't put them in writing as a rule. A woman—and sometimes a man too--they are as good as their word. Even the wildlife here, it's almost like they took on some of our way. I like to tell this story about a contract with a snake. Over in Boone County where I grew up, out in the outhouse one day, and while sitting there a bit, my eyes wandered. Up over the door, no more'n four feet away, was stretched this long heavy rope that was movin' just a little bit, and at the end of it two beady eyes and a little forked tongue that sent out its finger to test the wind.

Oh me, here I am and no way to go but where he could drop on me. Out loud I said: "Cross my heart."

Well, I got up and walked on out and he let me pass. People come in with snake stories, getting bit while out the garden, findin' one in the kitchen potato bin. But I never had one to bother me.

Oh yes, I ran in the house and told all about it, and my brother stopped what he was doin and started for the grainery and came out- with a hole and started to the outhouse. I had a feelin I shoulda kept quiet about to it. I ran out and stopped him. Said: " I made a promise to that snake. And when I make a promise, I keep it."

He says, "Well, none of the rest of us wants to go in with him there. *Your* snake!"

I said, "That snake is not gonna give you or anyone else any harm." But my heart skipped a beat, and I felt sick for minute: I realized that I was in water over my head. That pact with Mister Snake was just between it and me. But I said:

"Now, just take that hoe right back to the grainery. Nobody's gonna get bit, and nobody's gonna kill that snake." Then he puffs up like a turkey cock: "Who says?"

I didn't know it then, but that was one of my first lessons in politics (or public life) First: when you think only about yourself getting special privileges, you might be paving the way for some innocent to enter the outhouse and get snakebit. Second: Maybe we should've put the agreement in writing. I went on in the kitchen, but kept my eye on the outhouse.

Then after a minute or two, I saw my brother again, coming out of the grainery--

with that hoe--and heading for the outhouse. I went out and hollered at him. He went quick to the outhouse and stepped inside. I held my breath. It was real quiet. I couldn't move. I was prayin' hard as I could. Few minutes later--though it seemed a long time--he comes out sort of hangdog, says nothing, just went over and hung up the hoe.

The snake was gone. And never did come back, that or any other, as long as we lived there.

This was also the first taste of time I ever had. Some might say, "Oh, there wasn't a snake in there in the first place--just her imagination." But others said, "Why, she made a pact to a snake, and buddy, she kept her end of it."

Miz Dacey and the Nurse

(Miz Dacey comes out with a chair, sits down and fans herself, and exclaims about the heat. Note NURSE's up-ending sentences.)

NURSE: (Off) Miz Dacey?
DACEY: (Looks around.)
NURSE: Miz Dacey? Is this where Miz Dacey lives? (Looking at her papers)
DACEY: Now I wonder who that is. (Aloud) Well, that's my name. Are you the new woman down the road?
NURSE: No, I'm Miz Smith, health nurse? (What about your dog?)
DACEY: (Fans) Well--come on up, honey. Come on up on the porch. Dog won't hurt ya.
NURSE: How are you Miz Dacey? I was just drivin' by and thought I might check up on ya, see how you're feelin'.
DACEY: Oh, I'm feelin' pretty peart. Set down, honey.
NURSE: Nothin botherin' ya? Sugar or high blood?
Dacey: well, I don't think so.
NURSE: Well it's good to meet someone in good health. Sleepin' good? Eatin' good? Got a good garden this year?
DACEY: Oh yes, I got me a good garden. Tomatoes, onions, corn garlic. Don't need a thing.
NURSE: Well--
DACEY: I don't mean to be buttin' in, but what is that paper you're studyin'?
NURSE: This is my lines from the Health Department? They asked me to check on some of the folks out in the country?
DACEY: Unhun. Well, sometimes I have me a little stitch right here--and my knees sometimes gives me a fit, this 'un. And my ears--I get this roarin' in my ears most times.
NURSE: Oh. Well, maybe we'll just take your blood pressure.
DACEY: Oh, my electrolytes is fine. Put'em in 6 years ago.
NURSE: And a pap smear--

DACEY: (Drawing back) A what? (Arms covering her bosom)

NURSE: This is preventive medicine Miz Dacey--to see you stay hale and feelin' good.

DACEY: Oh honey, I don't go to doctors. Thank ya, but I'm just fine.

NURSE: I'll have someone come and pick you up--you don't have to pay for it, ya know.

DACEY: Now, maybe you don't understand--I just don't go to be doctored. I thank ya, but I just get along fine, I take my garlic for my high blood, an onion is good for it too, don't have visitors no how and garden violet--that's good too. And for the arthritis, comfrey, that's the thing, poke weed's good too. and sometimes juniper. And for my gout, why there's nuthin' better than a dozen cherries--everyday fresh or canned, either. I never get it unless I run out of 'em. And speakin' of toes why I read about a man that cured his colds by puttin his big toe in ice water for a minute. Well, that foot bathin' is nice, helps the circulation and the very-close veins, it's real good for them.

NURSE: Umhmm.

DACEY: Oh honey, I forgot my apples. Dad drat it, I burn that kettle ever time. Why don'tcha stay awhile, and I'll rustle up some railroad soup?

NURSE: Oh, I got to be goin' Miz Dacey. You're fine. I got to be on my way. But say now, I wish I could send some of my patients to you!

(They say goodbye. Dacey rushes in the house)

(On exit) Well, we sure don't have many like her anymore. I wish we did.

POTSY

(in railroad clothing of the 50's. To audience:)

You ever been the bearer of good news and then find out it's bad news?

You ever been on a special job, a job created to put your friends outta work? Put your friends, your kin, your town, into a tailspin?

Well, I'm the ghost of one of them people. I designed and installed all the places along the C & O tracks between Newport News and Cincinnati. These were places where the diesel engine would stop. It was in the late 40's and 50's.

(ENTER PEANUT BUTTER, CROSSING STAGE, MID-FIFTIES)

Hey Peanut, where you goin?

PEANUT: Fishin' don't look too good, but that's where I'm goin'.

(Enter JIM)

POTSY: Jim--? Hey Jim. What's the matter? Can't talk to me?

(Jim turns and listens coldly)

I didn't need to tell you yesterday about that, in fact I shouldn't have told you the changes that are coming down. But I thought I owed you and Lisabeth a tip--just for your own good.

(PAUSE)

Maryat Lee

Now you don't need to be short with me. I don't mean no harm. If you know what's ahead, you can be ahead too. I know you are about to put a down payment for a new house. I don't want a boss your business, but if it was me, I'd wait. Wait to see what's gonna happen.

JIM: Potsy, you and all the yard knows them dinky engines can't make the grade. Not between here and Clifton Forge. And I know you wouldn't be doin this, if you believed it wouldn't work. Least I don't think you would. So--I've worked since I was 15, and I've heard lotsa stories, they're gonna move the terminal away from Hinton, gonna be a ghost town.

POTSY: Jim--I think it's gonna work. I'm sure, as a matter of fact. This time it's true. They're gonna move lots of terminals and shops.

JIM: We're friends, Potsy. You gotta do your job, that's all. Didn't hurt my feelings one little bit. I don't mind tellin' ya, some of the men are a little put out. But it didn't hurt me, like I said. You gotta do your job. That's what I tell 'em.

POTSY: It ain't just my job. I've seen 'em work. I've seen the figures. I'm in a place over in Richmond where I know what's going on, and you're ridin' for a fall. All of ya. There won't be hardly one percent of the force left to run things.

JIM: Pss. One percent. Then tell me who's gonna supply the train, inspect them, repair them, who's gonna lubricate them, who's gonna stoke them.

POTSY: They don't need anyone to do it. They don't need 'em. They don't need 600 men in the roundhouse. They need just a handful.

Yard Master (Sims Wicker) and Train Master

Train Master (on phone): Say, just got a call from Baltimore.

Yard master (on phone): I'm listenin' in.

TM: OK, now they want us to reclassify all the coal that goes by Potomac Yards together. Got that?

YM: I got it.

TM: And, we're to make three classifications of Tidewater coal.

YM: Three?!

TM: Yep. And they're expectin' us to get our first train out of here by 10 this mornin.' And then another about every two hours.

YM: Ten? (Looks at watch.) Ten!

TM: That's right, and then another every two hours.

YM (thinking): I'm gonna have to have another yard engine to do what they lined up.

TM: I don't know about that. (getting angrier)

YM: Why couldn't we use one of the engines from the other yard--at least part of the time?

TM: Well, I'll see about that.

YM: Well, if you can get one over here for me to use from the East End--even then we probably won't get it out by ten.

TM: Why don't you think you can do it?

YM: Well, you know, I've got about the pokiest engineer that ever sit up on the seat box of an engine. And the crew--you know who I got workin' for me, don't you? They move so slow, like they got the seven-year itch.

TM: Well, time's a' wastin'. Better get going.

(LATER)

TM (on phone): What's the matter down there? You haven't ordered that train yet.

YM: We just can't get that train ready for 10.

TM: Well, I know you can do it.

YM: You can call it what you want, but if you want this train ready by then, you'd better get another yard engine over here.

TM: Well, I can't get you another yard engine.

YM: Well, if you can't get me a yard engine, then call a man in my place. I can't do what you want done. And I don't have time to talk about it.

TM: Well, we'll just see.

(LATER)

TM (on stage, waiting for yardmaster. YM comes in): How you getting' along with that train we got ordered for ten o'clock?

YM: Well, we're workin' on it, but we still got to go to the head ends.

TM (looking at watch): How long is it gonna take?

YM: Listen, I told you I can't do what you want done with this crew. Now if you want this work done you either call another crew or call a man in my place. (Exits.)

Railroaders (The Romance of a Lifetime)
Originated by Sims Wicker

CAST: Mr. YOUNG (Or Ms. YOUNG), Mr. WICKER

(YOUNG is rushing to work. Looks at watch. Sees older man. They nod.)

YOUNG (Walking to WICKER.)

YOUNG: What time have ya got?

WICKER: (Takes out watch) It's 2:33.

YOUNG: (Compares with own watch) Are you right? (Begins to set watch.)

WICKER: Oh yes, I check it every mornin'. I guess I got the habit years ago and never stopped. You workin' for the railroad?

YOUNG: Yessir, I'm a brakeman. In the yard. I'm a little early.

WICKER: (If talking to woman.) Well, I heard they were doin' this kinda thing.

YOUNG:?

WICKER: Hiring, girls, I mean.

YOUNG: Well, a lot of us--women--are doin these things now.

WICKER: Umhmm.

YOUNG: I guess you're retired for a long while now?

WICKER: Well, it'll be 15 years next November when I climbed down from the cab of a diesel engine for the last time.

YOUNG: Do ya ever miss it?

WICKER: Well, sometimes. Sometimes.

YOUNG: When did you start with the railroad?

WICKER: (joins YOUNG) I can remember to the day. It was September 10, nineteen and eighteen.

YOUNG: That musta been after the war?

WICKER: That's right.

YOUNG: I guess you were pretty young? how did ya start in those days?

WICKER: Well, I started out when I was 14. Carried water on the section. And I was wipin' engine jackets and. Supplying engines at the Roundhouse. Coal was shoveled by hand to keep the engines hot, in those days. Yep, I was fireman, and in those days of course that was work. I was promoted to engineer in 1923 and from then till I retired. I pulled just about ever class train that ran between Russell, Kentucky and Clifton Forge, Virginia. And most of the branch lines in between,

YOUNG: So you've operated both steam and diesel engines?

Well, yes. If you want to call the diesel an engine.

YOUNG: You make it sound like the diesels are toys or something.

WICKER: Well, let's put it this way: When they replaced the steam engine with a diesel, you could say that's the day romance died on the railroad.

YOUNG: All the old railroaders talk that way about their love for it. What's so different? They was dirty, noisy, hard work.

MEADOR: (interrupting) Now wait.

YOUNG: Yet if you loved it so much, a fellow would think you'd come down the station once in a while.

MEADOR: Well, it's hard to put into words. I just can't go down there. It's--if you really want to know it's like vistin' an unburied corpse. For us-- it's kinda indecent to walk down there. Take the roundhouse where you had stalls and could shunt seven engines in there or repair. Why, I've see the roundhouse full of engines and some still waitin' out in the yard to go in for overhaul. A full-time operator was turning them engines all day, takin' 'em down to put coal and sand and water on 'em. You had men working to wipe the engine jackets, shine 'em up, clean and polish the number plates. Pipe welders, machinists. You had over 600 men workin' there in the roundhouse every day.

> It's like takin' a walk through a ghost town, and feelin' like a ghost yourself.

YOUNG: 600?

MEADOR: And you want us to go down there and look at an old diesel today sittin' there with its motor runnin'--and visit the roundhouse with not a soul in sight. Why, son, it's like takin' a walk through a ghost town, and feelin' like a ghost yourself.

YOUNG: (Shakes his head) It's hard to understand. But sometimes--even to me--it feels funny down there. Sometimes while I'm waitin' I walk into the roundhouse--the little piece of it that's left--and I can almost hear echoes of a whole lot of men and machinery, and smell the smoke.

MEADOR: The diesel is just another piece of machinery. But when you climb up into the cab of a steam engine for the first time and hear the hissing steam, and see the water pulsating in the water gauge and feel the rhythmic surge of he air pumps, it's not hard to think of it as something alive. As you work the steam engines, you get to be aware of the strength and weaknesses of each one, and hope each time you are called that you'll get that engine. That's right, it's not too long before you find yourself falling in love with one particular engine, and when you get that engine, you catch yourself giving it a little extra attention, a little more loving care. Well--it's just like that sweetheart you fell for--a romance is born. And it can last a lifetime.

YOUNG: (Looking at his watch) Well, it's time to go to work. Thanks. (Turns back.) You fellers loved that work. We don't know much about that.

MEADOR: Yep. Be careful. Don't get hurt. We all told ourselves it would be better for you all. Easier work. Better pay. But--sometimes a feller wonders. 'Bye son.

The day Hinton died

Narrator: Well, evenin' is here again. Fallin' quiet and peaceful. And there's the lady. Always there.

> (He has been carving a piece of wood and gets up to show his handiwork to her.) She takes his chair, as he exits:) Watch over me.

LUCY: (Looks at Narrator as he leaves.) Come here, Charlie. Come here Jean (or Bill or Scott or--) The nights are cool now. The river running clear again.

JEAN: The New River has some good walleyes this year.

LUCY: But the gnats are aggravatin' as ever.

CHARLIE: But one good thing about 'em. They never bite outsiders.

JEAN: And if you get bit you just know you've been accepted as one of the family.

CHARLIE: Greenbrier is that strange blue-green,

LUCY: The color of beautiful eyes.

JEAN: You can count two people every 100 yards in hip boots out in the middle.

LUCY: Did you hear the passenger train come through last night?

JEAN: Nobody awake in the train enough to know they passed right through the gorge, spewing up mist to the stars.

CHARLIE: Cutting deeper and deeper through that huge crack. Passed right through Hinton and heading for Big Bend Tunnel.

LUCY: I remember the day the last steam train came through.

CHARLIE: That was a big celebration. Why I was a little boy and all the people in town stood by the tracks up and down river, and the ol' 614 came 1hrough.

JEAN: That was quite a day. Everybody bowing their heads like a dead Queen was passin' through, blowing her skirts in front of her.

LUCY: They were all so quiet.

JEAN: The train sweepin' like a long bustle behind her, around the corners and corridors, and the long passage ways and tunnels. Something happened that day.

CHARLIE: People looked at each other, went to the store, got cans of paint and started painting their houses white.

JEAN: Something happened that day.

LUCY: (Thinking.) Yes. They joked--joked about missing the soot. They act like--

CHARLIE: (Catching an undertone.) That's right. They act. They act.

JEAN: Something happened that day.

CHARLIE: I'll tell ya. I'm not afraid to say it. Life bit the dust.

JEAN: You mean--

CHARLIE: I mean Hinton *died*. (Pause.)

LUCY: Hinton didn't die.

CHARLIE: The heck it didn't.

LUCY: Hinton didn't die. (Cross in front of Jean to stage right.)

CHARLIE: Died dead as a doorknob.

LUCY: Well, what happens when you turn a doorknob?

JEAN: A door opens.

CHARLIE: They've tried that. They've tried all kinda things.

JEAN: A door opens.

CHARLIE: They act. They act--maybe like a possum. By gosh. Lying there on its back, its eyes shut tight, its little paws wilted.

JEAN: A door opens.

CHARLIE: Naw--a possum'll get up soon's you leave it alone.

LUCY: There's a story about a bird that every 500 years jumps up on a bonfire and lets itself burn to death.

JEAN: A door opens.

CHARLIE: And a new bird flies up out of the cinders?

LUCY: (Cross toward Charlie.) It'll happen. It's already happening. Why they'll be a funny looking little thing coming up out of the ashes.

CHARLIE: Out of the cinders.

LUCY: Cinders.

JEAN: And it'll have feathers.

LUCY: Bright curling feathers.

CHARLIE: Wings.

JEAN: Wings.
LUCY: Wings.
CHARLIE: And big feet.
JEAN: Big feet.
LUCY: Big feet?
CHARLIE: It'll have to be a big bird.
JEAN: (Pause.) A door opens.
LUCY: (Pause. Puts arm around Jean.) Maybe it will open.
CHARLIE: Open.
LUCY: Open.
JEAN: A door opens...

Maryat Lee

Audience Response and Discussions

Post-performance discussions were an important part of the feedback loop for Maryat. Performers and later guest humanists would stay after performances and discuss the play(s), often leading to changes or clarifications in subsequent performances and a deeper understanding of what the performance meant to its viewers. The following comments were recorded after various performances of A Double-Threaded Life in 1983 and include audience members as well as guest humanists (those named here) as discussion leaders. All humanist guests were invited to stay for awhile on Maryat's farm and become familiar with EcoTheater, its philosophy and purpose, and the company, in preparation for their role of discussion leaders.

Dr. Sophia Blaydes: There are just a couple of things that I'd like to add, and one comes from Margaret Mead and I think it has happened here tonight. She said a society can be defined as a group that knows the same story. They are from Hinton and clearly they know the same stories. And for a moment this evening, all of us, I'm not from Hinton, we have become a society. It is a most extraordinary moment. I like going back and having that kind of affirmation. But it seems to me that out of what Maryat has been doing with what we call indigenous theater, that is, the drama that arises out of stories in a particular area and told from the mouths of the people of that area, it is something that is unique to an area, a place, at a particular time. But it also speaks to anyone anywhere and that seems like a contradiction. I found myself cheerful and I found myself moved by people I've never met before and by a performance that I feel was as professional as any I would want to see on television. I don't know if any of you would like to comment on any of this from Margaret Mead on down to the indigenous but I would welcome any comment from any of you.

> "The negativity is that extension of where we all are in terms of the life here and in terms of life anywhere else on this continent. The hope is very real in this play."

Woman's Voice: I just have one thing about John Henry that was very, very moving, very dramatic and I thought that with this age of computers and robots where will we be with jobs in a few years? All of us are faced with that so I thought not only of the past but of the future too. What are we? What are we doing?

Sophia: So that the death of Hinton is everywhere....I saw affirmation here though, I saw that there was an affirmation for love. I found it communicated through the story repeatedly even where Kathy was asking forgiveness, to me that's an affirmation, where there was love and beauty. I remember the word beauty coming through repeatedly, even though there was some pain. The theme of morality kept coming through and on occasion I thought it was funny, you know? Miz Dacey is funny and yet it seemed that over and over again there were those little moments of triumph as well as misery....

Al Cone: If there is negativity here it is because the play is a microcosm of life itself. As she was saying (lady from Detroit), The hope is the love, the forgiveness, the hope is the beauty. And the hope is perhaps, taking off the mask. Those are all parts of it.

Sophia: So much of the play seemed to be in the realm of identity and I think since the series "Roots" we have been looking with care at where we have come from and I think that this sequence of scenes has offered us what any where Hinton came from, how it got its name, why it's important. I think you put it - "To set the record straight." (referring to Lucinda\Ethel Hinton) So. Who are we? I think of that as being the essence of our identity....

Male Voice: The kind of thing that I was thinking about was that my grandmother used to preach across these West Virginia Hills. You know there was a time when a pastor would get up and preach and if the audience agreed with it they would say Hallelujah...And if they sorta agreed with it they would say Amen. But you had a dialogue going along there of course. And occasionally you sorta get it in our more Pentecostal churches. And I was thinking back when we were living in Massachusetts, as I am now, we had a centennial celebration a few years ago and our pastor dressed up in a powdered wig and we were going to do an old fashioned service and I was the only one who was sitting there saying Amen, and everyone thought I was strange. I thought everyone was to play their parts too and I was the only one, and they just could not come out of their role as modern sophisticated people and let themselves go back although the person up on the stage was playing the role of the deacon or whatever and with their suit on and all and it is very hard sometimes for the audience to get out of the role, unless you think of some way to get this started because we are playing the role of the audience.

Maryat: What about the other idea of getting to know who we are apart from the roles we play. Is that striking anybody?

Vaughn Zopp: This is the third time I've seen this play and I was real thrilled tonight as I heard some of the changes in this play. You know I was sitting here wondering all the while do I really know myself or not. But I really don't think I have been playing a role. I've always thought you know, that I've really been and talked and said and felt just what I am and I feel like when I hear this I want to say no, that's not happened to me. Are you trying to tell me that that's happened to everybody? But I appreciate this in the play that I. can see growing that depth of appreciation for the real person, what the person is and I don't see any negative feeling at all and last year I remember hearing something from the audience about the negative feeling in it and I don't feel that way because of this thread of the real you and the role playing idea being brought out. As long as there is one person that is real in a place, that place isn't dead....

> "As long as there is one person that is real in a place, that place isn't dead."

Male Voice: I enjoyed it. I thought there was a lot of depth in the play and I think we ·play different roles in life and I think it captured some of the beauty of West Virginia and the little town of Hinton.

Dr. Judith Stitzel: Hi, we are going to speak briefly if at all as friends of Maryat and friends of the players and people deeply committed to West Virginia and the people who are interested in what is going on down here. There is one thing that I very much would like to know from the audience, that part of the thing that fascinated me about this kind of theater is that the audience here is also playing a role. I mean you're here on vacation, right, and there's nothing to do on Wednesday night. It's a wonderful place here and you've finished playing golf and you had a number of choices and needn't have come here and you came here rather than X,Y,Z, for a reason that you may or may not have thought through completely. Expecting something like this or maybe something not like this and then as soon as you were here and they were here (referring to the stage) what happened was in some ways very unexpected, but not totally unexpected because you have some expectation of what theater is. Some of which this fulfilled and some of which it didn't. But I would be very curious about where you felt your expectations and roles as audience fall away and where they were confirmed. Maybe there is a better way of asking that. What do you think you're going to remember when you leave from what you saw? I ask you just very quickly now, are there some scenes that are going to stick and do those scenes that are going to stick give you some hint about which of your roles were touched and which dropped away and which ones perhaps you want to reinvite into yourself in a new way? That's what I'd like to know about.

Male Voice II: Well, I think it is the identification. I think we came here to be entertained and with an open mind about the entertainment and you really don't know what to expect and then as the script unravels there is a lot that you can identify with in terms of a small town hidden away, human characters, people that you have known, like people in Hinton. I think you carry away with you a reinforcement of you as a human being. This is basically what happens in a theater such as this and in a script such as this. It's a matter of identity.

Female Voice: Even if we each felt there was some negativism…even if we felt there was some of that in the play I think it was the kind of negativism that is in life. It's not trying to be brought out in this play, it is part of life, it's part of everybody's life and we see by the characters and their skits how negativism is handled in this part of the country and these particular people and in this region and we can take that home with us and maybe some time down the road when something negative touches us, we might draw out a comparison from this play....

Dr. Elaine Ginsberg: I want to say that one of the things I like about this is that I like this kind of theater. I mean the play is one thing and the stories in the play another, but the kind of theater it is is what strikes me as important too. Just by coincidence last Wednesday I saw a matinee on Broadway of a dramatic play and I was very moved by it and I remember the empty feeling of being moved emotionally and applauding the actresses--there were three women in the play--and the light came on and I stood up and everybody else stood up around me and I didn't know any of them and we didn't talk to each other, we just all walked outside into the bright sunlight and into the traffic on 48th street and got on the subways or got into our cars and went home and you really thought you wanted to share the experience of that play with the actors and with the people and you couldn't do that because that's not the way they do it in that kind of theater and they couldn't afford to spend that extra hour, I mean you're paying enough for it, why not (laughter) and that's what I like, the kind of theater like this, the kind of theater that Maryat is suggesting that is a better kind of theater. It would mean a tremendous amount to the people of a community to be able to develop such a theater...

> "I think many of you would agree with me that, after being here tonight, we leave just a little different, we're a little different person when we leave. We take with us these personages, and Hinton ceases to be simply a ring on the map and becomes a community of human beings."

Dr. Frank Scafella: Once I found myself remembering my grandmother and grandfather and myself as related to them. And that for me it was story-making--it is what story-making is about. So my roles are all gone. And I don't teach literature in the sense we think of it most often as an artifact to please us for a bit and then to wash off like dust. It is story-making: things that make us feel and think differently than we commonly do. And *Maryat:* I'm glad you bring that up because one of the things that interests me are MOMENTS. You know, we've all had MOMENTS to remember....we call them MOMENTS--we will never forget them and sometimes they are good and sometimes they are rotten--and they stay with you. Those are the times when your life takes a slightly different direction than it had before. So I began to wonder if the whole idea is, taking a risk to be yourself for even a minute...

Dr. Bill French: I've seen this maybe a couple of times before last summer, and each time it's a little bit different, because the cast is a bit different, the scenes are a bit different, and Maryat keeps tinkering with it. But I would like to say that I certainly did enjoy it this evening, and that I want to thank the actors because they do take a risk... When you step up on the stage in front of the audience, you shed something of yourself. And I was thinking as I watched you tonight how powerful some of your performances were. Each of you gave very direct powerful performances that were very moving and very impressive. And I was thinking, Well, you're not professional actors, you haven't been trained to do this, you've stepped into it. And I think that's a wonderful thing. You can't judge the kind of acting you do by the sane standards that are used to judge professional actors. It's a completely different kind of acting, and that doesn't mean it is any the less valuable. In fact, in a way, it makes it all the more valuable and more precious.

Nancy Lee-Riffe: I'm not from West Virginia--I'm from Eastern Kentucky University. Last week I drove 400 miles to Chicago to see a play--this week I drove 300 miles to see EcoTheater. I teach Shakespeare and drama of different sorts, from the Greeks through today--and I'm fascinated with what Maryat is doing. Three of us were having a conversation before I had had a chance to see the play, and talking about definitions, and what to call this kind of theater, and what is the nature...That's the kind of question that would be ruined if you found an answer for then there wouldn't be anything to talk about. You have given us in the play so much to think about: not just roles in our personal lives, a very important, enormous thing to ponder; but for those of us who love the theater, what are roles in the theater? Where is the play? What the writer puts on paper or is it something more? But that is what made it such fun. And I appreciate tremendously the difference.

Maryat Lee

Female Voice: How we place roles on people. I was thinking that the people who have really made an impact on me--the people who have stepped out of the roles people expected them to play. Like my grandmother who was from West Virginia--and I thought, Gee this isn't how a grandmother should be. And then when I got away from that I thought Well, maybe that's how a grandmother should be And I--when she (Lucinda) was playing that role of the grandmother, I thought Gee, that is just how she used to be, she was herself. She was what grandmothers should be.

Male Voice: That was beautiful. But in answer to your question: one of the reasons we don't go to the theater more than we do is simply because I can't stand generally the themes of the plays and so forth coming out. It is mostly garbage, as far as I am concerned. And this is about life--about wholesome family living, it's not just problems and all that. And yet we're talking about people we can identify with in some way or another. I don't have--I hope I don't have too much in common with some of the things that you see on Broadway which is always either sadistic or lustful or some manner of homosexuality or some garbage such as that....

Frank Scafella: I'm wondering how each of you received the play, as to whether you thought it was negative or affirmative, whether you thought it was pessimistic or optimistic. What did you get from the play? Was it hopeful or not?

Male Voice: I think it goes back to--as far as play-acting--"to be yourself." Be what you are and not try to play a higher ego role in life. When things are down and out, you don't go to the things you want to be or dream to be--you go back to basics.... A psychology teacher asked me in high school--he was preparing us to get a job and he went through the want ads and said, here's a good one, ditch-digger. And he asked the class what pride could you take out of being a ditch-digger. Well, the kids just sat there, and I put my hand up. He said, "Well, what?" And I said, "Dig it straight. "He thought for a minute and said, "Well, you're right". No matter what you do--sweep, sweep it good, clean up, or whatever, take pride in what you do and not be ashamed....

The Appalachian Plays

Male Voice: I'd like to ask you one question. Since this is such a liberating thing for Hinton, is anything like this being done in other communities. Can something like this be done in other communities?

Maryat: It can be done in other communities.

Male Voice: I'd like to make a comment. I'm from a big city and up to a couple weeks ago I never even heard of Pipestem let alone Hinton and I'm not afraid to tell you that I was a little bit concerned about coming over to see the show and am delighted I did come and I would say this a comment as to whether this is or is not the future of Hinton but of the people who are standing in front of us today are even moderately reflective of the spirit of that then I have no fear about Hinton, I think I'm more concerned about Pittsburgh than I am about Hinton....

Nanine Bilski:... A lot of this has been kept kind of a secret by the people in Hollywood and New York who want you to believe that only they can do it and that you have to buy it from them thereby they corner the market. Now people think they can sing in the bathtub or the shower and they're willing to do that and they go out to dances sometimes and they're willing to do that, and they like writing mushy poetry when in love so they might do that, but very few people will get up and act unless someone like Maryat is in the community and encourages them to do that. Now this is where you can see you're missing a great deal. You could be adding a great deal to your life and

> If you want to have a good time at the next party you go to ask the people there "Why are you an American? How did you get here?" And you will have enough stories whether it's two people or twenty people to write twenty plays and thirty operas and twenty-four books of poetry, because everybody's story is fascinating.

community and you wouldn't have to bring these people to Pittsburgh because there are a million people in Pittsburgh who would like to be doing this too. And one of the ways to do it is the secret of the local history. And not only that but in a country like this that's the glory of the country I mean that's why we are what we are because everyone has done this and if you just accept the canned versions of American life they put on television and movies, people are eventually going to forget who they are. This play is about who you are and stripping away these roles that you play... So if you take back anything from tonight it shouldn't just be "oh gee aren't those people lucky because of Hinton they have EcoTheater and they can do things and I wish we could bring them to our town." Go home and make your own....

Jim Thomas: The thing that is interesting about this is the play, it's like a real good preacher who preaches a sermon which comes from his experience and from people's experiences and that of his community and that's what the play is about and it seems to me that is an interesting thing and it seems to me, I think every community ought to have a good church at least one, if not many others, and as well, a good community theater. They are not the same thing but they treat the human conditions from a different perspective. It seems to me that what Eco is trying to do is treat the human conditions, in this case talk about the history of Hinton and this region in the words of people who live here and the actors who live here and it seems to me that's another kind of theater. The fact that you came in the first place, and in the second that you stayed, I think that proves to a degree the validity of this theory, that we're interested in both theaters which are valid... That is the most exciting thing about EcoTheater and my cap is off to you....

Billie Jean Young: This is my third return I think and I've seen the theater evolve from kids and children to now seemingly perfectly middle class people up on stage, it just is really refreshing and you do it so naturally. Sometimes tonight I felt like an intruder out here. I wonder how it feels for you because you're not putting on a whole lot of other attitudes. I wonder how that feels--the feeling of being yourself?

Barbara Smith: I was trying to say that each time I see this play with Maryat and the troupe and so on that I have this same reaction to it and I haven't even mentioned this to Maryat before, I have this--it gives me a new renewed faith in mankind and it gives me a faith that in a way I very much admire people who can be honest and as forthright and courageous as you individual people are when they do the playwrighting and the acting and so on. It really does give me renewed energy and renewed strength to be a better person myself.

George Allen: As you know I'm in Television and I deal with a couple of networks and write television scripts and all and you might call me a communicator. Tonight, I was watching the audience from down here and this is in the age when all the special effects that television can produce, magnificent things they do, this is the most minimal kind of theater with people, even reading their scripts, and the audience responded. And What was going out there (referring to audience) was very well received in a way that the formality of the big screen and small screen could never gather. I'm not quite sure why it works. But, it works....

Male Voice: That's amazing. I mean, this is a nonprofessional theater and that's what's so amazing. I'm sorry. Excuse me. My apologies. This is embarrassing. I mean he's a furniture man and he stands there laughing and I mean a house wife, and an insurance man and I mean they acted, they moved me far more than I've been moved by anything I've seen on Broadway and certainly the movies the cinema you can forget about it. You have moved me.

> "I concluded what was going on was communication of the most genuine kind that television and films could never really reach."

Sims Wicker: That's what makes EcoTheater worthwhile. Remarks like that.

Maryat Lee

A Double-Threaded Life: The Hinton Play: Scenes/Number of Players:

Funny you said that – one
Board of Inquiry – four
Potsy and Jim – two
ABC The woman caller three
Sims Wicker scene – two
Ethyl Hinton – one
Yardmaster/Trainmaster – two

The Appalachian Plays

Miz Dacey and grandson or granddaughter
Woman waiting – one
Woman waiting (with husband) – two
Miz Dacey and roofer – two
Hal – one
Man who came home – one
Father and son – two
Miz Dacey and Mary Matthews
Drunk Marine – one
Man trapped – one
John Henry – one
Your honor – one
The local historian – one
Bigfoot – Haywood/Scaggs
I done wrong – one
Miz Dacey and nurse – two
Miz Dacey has a weak moment – Mr Tapper – two
Faith and Cloy – two
Susie's grandmother – one
It's so hard to change – one
The restaurant owner - one
Kathy's scene – one

Maryat Lee

Acknowledgments

This book would not have been possible without the kind assistance of many, among them: Mary Dean Lee and Robert Lee, on behalf of the estate of Maryat Lee; Mary Dean also for her evocative dedication; Maryat's brother, Robert "Buzz" Lee, who before his death readily answered my questions by telephone and in letters; John Cuthbert and Lori Hostuttler of the West Virginia and Regional History Center at West Virginia University, which provided access to much of the material excerpted here for *A Double-Threaded Life* as well as photographs and play notes; the Samuel French Company for permission to reprint *Four Men*; Professor Carole Harris, a Flannery O'Connor scholar who provided helpful insight into Maryat's life and friendship with O'Connor; the late Dr. William (Bill) French, who became a close friend to Maryat and to me, for his thoughtful introduction and notes on to these plays--Bill, I'm sorry you didn't get to see this collection, but thank you this and for many absorbing conversations; Martha (Marty) French, for providing access to Bill's previously unpublished materials; Rev. Dr. Georgia A. Newman-Powell for her Foreword and discussions about Maryat and Flannery's relationship through Georgia's privileged look at their many letters and Maryat's journals; Chris McClary for use of an article about Maryat and EcoTheater by Jane McClary and photos by Nelson McClary; Terry Stoller for talking to me about her research on oral history as theater; Jean W. Cash for her knowledge of Maryat and Flannery's relationship; Beth Morgan of Centre College Special Collections and Archives; and to the innumerable people, young and old, city and country, whose lives Maryat touched.

I know that were Maryat still alive she would especially want me to acknowledge essential contributions to her work by the late Fran Belin, a talented photographer and musician, and Lee's one-time partner and co-producer of early versions of *John Henry*; Kathy Jackson, Maryat's protégé, who went on to perform and teach workshops after Maryat's death; Lucinda Ayres, who started as her office manager before blooming into

The Appalachian Plays

writing and performing her own scenes as well as "becoming" Miz Dacey for many performances; and many others who assisted Maryat at one time or another, including: John Soleau, Dixie Mowen, Jimmy Costa, Karen MacKay, Martha Asbury Faulkner, Mary Ann Caverly, Judy Walker, Jennie Mayes, Roger Paige, Jan Barrett, Ina Rudd, Federica Tecchiati, Kathy Jackson, Rita Cominolli, Theresa McDaniel, Charlie Haywood, "Sarge" McGee, Nanine Bilski, Ossie Davis, Frank Collins, Billie Jean Young, Mike Buckland, Addie Davis, Dr. Ancella Bickley, Sims Wicker, Jackie Robinson, Mamie Carte, Tammy Jackson, Eileen Kramer, Terri Yates, Susie Boone Keffer, Carol Hall, Joyce and Gene Marshall, Nancy Lee-Riffe, Jerilee Cain-Tyson, Lou Erdman, Ed Warfield, Anita Meador, Jinx Johnson, Myrtle Hosey, Michael W. Harding, Emily Keaton Briers, Rebecca Browning, Frank Scafella, Sophia Blaydes, Maureen Shea, Jim Thomas, Helen Lewis, Marion Love, Joan Brooks, Barbara Wyant, Benny Allen, Judith Stitzel, Jerry Peterson, Don Corothers, Cheryl Linkous Ormsby, Lisa Wynes, Joe Bigony, Jewell Bigony, Janet Banks, Scott Briers, Mamie Carte, Mitch Scott, Eileen Cramer, Mary Mathews, Carolyn Cobb, Katrina Davis, Kay Hardesty, Lucy Bell, and Vicki McPherson.

David T. Miller
Editor

Maryat Lee

A Note on the Sources

Given the nature of Maryat Lee's approach to theater--indigenous, organic, participatory, "rough"--it's unsurprising that they haven't been collected before. She continually reworked them even after they had long been in production. This was, in part, based on the performers she had at any given time, with their personal histories, quirks, and talents, and the location where they were performed--which might have been a theater stage or just as easily a truck bed or prison auditorium. Thus, her working copies of scripts are covered with notes to herself and to the actors, mark-throughs and additions, all in service to getting somewhere closer to the truth of a scene, then and there. She was very careful in her dialogue and staging, but if she found a better idea she'd try it. (She wasn't averse to creating what she thought was a better ending for *Four Men and a Monster* even after that play had been performed and published commercially, and the copyright renewal for her play *Dope!* notes that it was revised almost twenty years after its initial ground-breaking premiere.) After *Four Men* the most settled of the scripts is *John Henry*, which was sharpened by many performances across a decade, though still remained flexible enough to vary the performances for length and available actors and musicians. *Ole Miz Dacey* is similar but even more modular, in that individual slices of it were moved in and out as needed for a particular performance, and new material for this unique character was generated as *A Double-Threaded Life* came together from many different voices. In this volume I have tried to settle on a reasonably consistent version of the plays from the marked-up scripts Maryat left behind, incorporating her notes and strike-throughs where her intent could be determined. I have let stand most of the variant spellings and dropped gerunds and occasional malapropisms where they seemed to fit with the character's natural speech.

Both Dr. French's introduction and play notes and Maryat's scripts and author notes were prepared in rough draft form prior to their deaths, and I have worked from those to prepare this book. Thus Dr. French and Maryat herself are often speaking in the present and future tense, and I have left those as-is; neither were looking back. *A Double-Threaded Life* exists (as far as I can tell) only as loose pages in a three-ring binder among Maryat's literary effects now housed at the West Virginia and Regional History Center. For that play--really just a series of sometimes-connected scenes--I worked with text extracted from scans of those pages, conforming them as closely as possible to Maryat's (sometimes illegible or contradictory) notes. I have included a few that obviously never got past the maybe stage, and left out a few that Maryat obviously thought weren't working.

--Editor

Maryat Lee

About the Authors

Maryat Lee (1923-1989) was born in Covington, Kentucky and studied drama at Northwestern University briefly before transferring to Wellesley College. She graduated with a degree in religious studies and did post-graduate work at Columbia before receiving a Master's Degree from Union Theological Seminary, under the direction of Paul Tillich. Her first play, *Dope!*, was a "street play," drawing on the lives of Harlem residents who also performed in it. The play attracted a great deal of media attention (including in *Variety* and The New York *Times*) and she continued to draw on urban life for a series through the Soul and Latin Theater (SALT) which she founded in 1965, taking on then-uncommon themes of gay life, drug use, racism and poverty. In 1971 she moved to rural Summers County, West Virginia and established EcoTheater, creating plays from oral histories and involving as performers many of the local residents, her goal being to create a "people's theater." She wrote that "The words 'acting' and 'actor' have an association with pretension for most people outside the theater. I want something different. I just want people simply, and not so simply, to be themselves."[48]

Lee died of heart disease in 1989, leaving a total of sixteen plays and numerous published short articles. At the time of her death she had created a formal structure for learning the EcoTheater process, leading would-be directors through a series of workshops in West Virginia, Kentucky (both in her native Covington area and in Eastern Kentucky), Illinois and elsewhere. EcoTheater itself, which was setup as a nonprofit, continued operations after her death. The workshop series she developed was eventually abandoned, with the nonprofit being dissolved formally in 2001 for lack of state legal filings.

Despite losing Maryat as its guiding force EcoTheater as a concept continued to spread, chiefly through the efforts of Maryat's protégé Kathy Jackson (who portrayed John Henry in many productions and after Maryat's death led many performances and

---

[48] *Coevolution Quarterly*, No. 43 (Fall 1984).

workshops); Joyce Marshall (through a nonprofit called Realistic Living), who had completed the multi-level training workshops created by Lee in the last years of her life; and the performers from the original Hinton troupe and other West Virginia seed companies. Workshops also continued in Texas, Massachusetts, Kentucky, and Minnesota, as well as several groups (some of them independent from EcoTheater proper) in southern West Virginia.

Dr. William W. French (1932-2012) was an Associate Professor in English at West Virginia University and a much-admired classroom instructor focusing on modern drama and Shakespeare. In addition to numerous journal articles he wrote only previous book on Maryat's work, *Maryat Lee's EcoTheater: A Theater for the Twenty-First Century*.[49]

David T. Miller is a writer and editor based in Lexington, Kentucky and grew up in southern West Virginia. He worked as a summer intern with Maryat Lee in an early incarnation of EcoTheater's summer youth program as musical director and actor as well as overseeing teens recruited to work at the theater through a state grant. After leaving the state to obtain his juris doctorate he later served on EcoTheater's board of directors. He can be reached at *david@davidtmillereditorial.com*

---

[49] 2d ed. (2020), Bacchante Books, Lexington Kentucky.

Maryat Lee

Appendix
Maryat Lee

Toward a definition of EcoTheater

> EcoTheater is a theater created with people and presented to people who are not theater going. It serves a sliver of the total non-theater going public which is estimated at more than 90% of the population in this country. EcoTheater approaches acting as *being* rather than *pretending* or putting the self away to be someone else. The action of the plays is usually the re-creation of a local event or a mirror of local society. The actors from the local society, however, infuse the mirror image of the script with the dimension of authority through taking off their normal roles and being who they really are. (1983)

I have always had a fascination for the plight of human beings who through some unevenness, omission or quirk on brain development, have such anguish in identifying who they really are--or even needing to do so--beyond such self-evident criteria as gender. Indeed our "sex" is the only thing that one can be sure of, and there is often horrendous doubt even about that. There are many for whom it is no longer play, many who successfully bury the "inner" other person in themselves and become the roles they adopt. Or so it seems. But I am amazed that so many people are aware that these expeditious roles are "non-themselves." Hence the quotation, "All the world's a stage" seems to have universal meaning, whether or not it is what Shakespeare meant it to mean. At all levels of Summers County society, people know and understand meaning in this metaphor.

> As interim solutions to the uneasiness we all call into adulthood the childhood gift of mimicry to play--in everyday life--at being one or more identities with which we gain a degree of needed protection.

In *A Double-Threaded Life: The Hinton Play* I have as a writer attempted to deal up front with the ubiquity of role-playing in life. And, as director of the play, I have had to remove myself from normal theater practice particularly with reference to the intriguing problem of role-playing on a stage. In 1983, the play and the directing both focused on the human being as a role-player in search of a moment of being "real", a moment of non-role life that I believe more and more to be possible in the safety of the stage. "If all the world's a stage, who then are we, when we go home and go to bed?" The question is posed by the narrator. The scenes and the acting are variations on the theme.

> "A performer of the ritual is handling the things that can kill us--which the actor is only playing at."

While role-playing is something that happens in all societies and seems to be demanded of people in our culture as well, yet at the same time, we cherish and harbor, indeed, insist upon, an ideal of truth, and being "real" as evidence of truth. How we bring these dissonant priorities into harmony, is somehow our task in life--and very importantly, our chosen task in theater where the act of roleplaying itself is a deliberate, studied, and central process. Once one begins to think about roles and masks, one risks getting lost in a room of mirrors mirroring themselves. For instance, it is presumed by most people that role-playing on stage is somehow different from role-playing in the street. If, in both cases, skill and practice, deliberation and setting the scene are at work, there may not be such great differences. What is happening when a role-playing person plays a role in a play? Is the play role substituted for the everyday role and therefore equally unrelated to the inner person, or is the play role glued on top of the existing role coverings? Does the role as written into most plays mirror the roles that we all experience in normal life? And is an audience of role-players really content to witness role-playing actors playing roles? That is, are we looking at automatons being observed in a formal setting by automatons? Or do audiences at tend in the hopes that the role may slip off for a moment so we can glimpse "another" reality? Quite honestly, I have often felt, as a sometime theatergoer, that I witnessed on both sides of the curtain, a bizarre spectacle of sleepwalkers' fulfilling their duties. At these times, a breakdown of any kind--someone forgetting the lines, or a piece of scenery coming loose, is a relief, a revealing crack in the carefully contrived perfectly ordered surface. The fleeting appearance of something betrayed by the merciful accident, however, is met with a suppressed belly laugh of recognition and relief--mixed with embarrassment, since such breakdowns in production are held to be the ultimate sin by serious theater practitioners.

What happens if the play itself is about a person hiding behind roles? The classics of theater that are most cherished, are, ironically, just such plays, and they deal in depth with the question of who we are--Oedipus and Hamlet heading the list. And yet no one gives a fig about whether the actor playing the part is really concerned with the question, except to give a believable rendition as if he/she were. In fact, the actor is encouraged to *become* the role and also keep a distance from the role as if it were tabu. One must not merge, in the sense of disappearing into the role. Theater people like to cite examples of those times when this "artistic" distance was breached and what dreadful results ensued from it. I listen to such testimony and ask myself if the dread were ever due to an actor's slipping into non- role playing, being real, which could be like a gold piece slipped into brass play money: At any rate, as presently practiced, the actor keeps distance from the play role, and can be as insensible of the personal meaning of the words being spoken as a priest who is the mouthpiece of sacred literature, but out of touch with it on any conscious level--except for being its mouthpiece. In both religious and histrionic schools there are those who have justified this alienation with theory that is almost inarguable. This practice has a legitimate place. The question is whether the practice should monopolize the stage (or altar or pulpit). My interest is to make a place for another practice in theater, a practice closer to what I surmise religion and theater were in primitive years when they were together in the sense that at their center, was being in an action of non-worldly import, where, as Paul Lehman used to say, history is bisected by the eternal, or in a flash one is enabled to glimpse God through the dark glass of the image.

> The perfectly replicated performance (not often realized) designed for my pleasure or benefit in fact leaves me out of the event except as spectator or as voyeur engaged by the performance only if I were one of the actors.

My own question continues to be why we have theater at all today. Why should people go? What's there that can't be gotten from television or movies or a good book at home. I prefer in fact, to stay home with a book. Unless I sense that the performance itself will not just "affect" me, but that in some small way it will be changed or affected by my presence as anonymous but very real audience. Although theater people talk a lot about the audience, their aim is a perfect performance for the ideal-- not the actual--audience. Yet, in theater, the highest goal in theatrical production is always - Truth. If the theater is based on necessary deception for which we must suspend disbelief,

> "There's anthropology, religion and theater, and I'm sort of muddling around in the middle of all three, where they're all involved...From all we know about early days there wasn't a theater and there wasn't religion, and there wasn't healing-- sometimes the same person was doing all those things. Specialization began to separate them, and in so doing some very important things were lost." Lee in conversation with Mary Clare Powell

does this compromise its goal? Or is it conceivable to go in reverse, provide a place where theater actor and audience can, within the safety of form, remove the weight of roles and risk a glimpse of what hides behind the masks and roles. I suspect that religion and theater once were joined at precisely this nexus. Victor Turner's work in theater and anthropology at the University of Virginia came to my attention this year, particularly his idea of ritual: "A performer of the ritual is handling the things that can kill us--which the actor is only playing at."[50] Am I, I wondered, a ritualist in requiring the actor to be

> "While I was in scenes I could feel they were spellbound--but that's not the word either; it was as if something was being released in them, like a memory bank."

"really there", handling things that can destroy us--the energies that seem to leap out just when they take off their protective masks, or stick their necks out ? The experience our actors report when the hatchet of the audience does not fall, has an extraordinary effect. They report that a feeling of love and trust with the audience, in whose laps (mercies) they

---

[50] Victor Turner, "Performing Ethnography," The Drama Review, T 94.

Maryat Lee

put themselves in a defenseless state, is in some way overwhelming and mystifying:

August 31, 1983 (A man in the audience): That's amazing. I mean, this is a non-professional theater and that's what is so amazing. I'm sorry. Excuse me. My apologies. This is embarrassing (he is near tears). I mean he's a furniture man and he stands there laughing and I mean, a housewife, and an insurance man and I mean they acted! They moved me far more than I've been moved by anything I've seen on Broadway and certainly the movies, the cinema you can forget about it. You have moved me.

The following is a paraphrase of what one of the very brave actors, Lucinda Ayres, had to say, December 6, 1983:

> From these audiences, we know we were doing something right, but--then--what the heck are we doing right? People don't accept you off the stage, and here they are strangers--accepting you in all kinds or deep ways, bringing us gifts. They keep asking who trained us--but we aren't trained--well, we are disciplined, and there's a standard of quality. You don't let us "act." That's all. It's insane--yet it works. While I was in scenes I could feel they were spellbound--but that's not the word either; it was as if something was being released in them, like a memory bank. I could see it and l talked to it even in my scenes. I needed it. And this summer, none of us changed afterward--after we performed and we talked with the audience. Before this summer it was easy to fall back into what we're like off stage, but this summer except for one or two times, none of us changed, we continued. I used to worry about after the performance, who I was--and I'd be different, but now I don't change until we all pack up and go home. So far, no one describing EcoTheater understands this part of it, and so I'm going to sit down sometime and write about it.

EcoTheater Standards and Patterns

STANDARDS:

1. We are a theater created by people and directed to people we believe that people want a place where their sometimes invisible communities can be seen, be in touch with, and

nourished by the truths and riches hidden in the corners and under the surface of everyday life.

2. EcoTheater accepts as true that unless these rich everyday local realities are looked at, celebrated and owned, the community withers or erodes away without distinction

> As experts in their own surroundings, ordinary people, if given confidence--in the safety of the stage and within the security of a script that is rooted in their lives--can transcend the limiting roles they play in everyday life.

and purpose. The means by which the community and the individual can be profoundly seen, is removal, not adoption, of roles on stage. EcoTheater requires an actor who does not want to act, a playwright-director who helps people not to act, and who likes to tailor roles to fit the performers, and an audience that might welcome part or all of the above.

3. In EcoTheater, the people of the community have the first right to perform words that come out of their community. And when they are

> An eloquent ardent artist sleeps inside everyone.

released to give utterance in their own accents to their own inner stories, their own vision, their own concerns, and their own wisdom, they are electrifying.

4. EcoTheater is not a religious or political arm or tool. EcoTheater is not for grinding axes, not to be "used," not even "for people's own good." The cost of "using" art and authority in the service of ideas and intentional change is the hardening of barriers which art was intended to breach. It is often hard work to keep it focused on the task which it is equipped best to do. Art is any purposeful concentrated communication that, in fact, successfully bridges or dissolves human barriers. Nothing else we know can reach across time, language, race, education, class, geography, politics, religion, gender and age. In this respect, if it is doing its risky work of lowering barriers (removing restricting roles in the safety of the stage and story) it is not about anything else but the mystery of our connectedness. And all people are equipped to understand it and (not generally known) all people are equipped to express it directly. We see it revealed in moments of disaster. We

can see it emerge for a moment in the safety of the stage.

5. Theater, Francis Fergusson suggests, comes before all the arts or sciences or philosophies because it is more primitive, more subtle, and more direct than either word or thought or sound. Therefore, we look to theater as a window on the ever-shifting realities of the human being caught in time prior to any restrictive rational or irrational thought. And it is through that amazing gift that is everybody's art form, the story, that we find--in the safety of the public stage--the past is present, the future is present and this confluence melts away the divisiveness, through the story of this individual or community, into a moment of being. And the moment of being, in the safety of the stage, always heralds unexpected, surprising possibilities for all people.

> The actors truly have shared authority on stage from the beginning. A seasoned company, to the untutored eye, will flip authority back and forth so rapidly that it cannot be seen. At performance, the authority is finally flipped to the spectator.

PATTERN

1. The playwright-director (PD) has authority by virtue of being the author. But because of theater's primacy, in early days, it was possibly characterized by a lack of specialization that later developed in the arts and sciences. The playwright-director co-creates with the performers (and the culture). This is accomplished not through sharing authority, but through keeping the authority in tact as a whole, and "flipping" it. Because the authority of the PD is balanced by the fact that the company of performers is expert in its community, the authority therefore passes back and forth as a whole. Authority is not cut up. The script (the selection and order of the words) is always clearly that of the PD. But at the same time, they seek to fit the script to the performers. In time, as the PD gains confidence in the process, the proprietary sense of playwright ownership often mysteriously dissolves. But it is a vital part PD's growth to claim the script fully, copyright it, etc. EcoTheater play has a playwright who, because she/he is also the director, can work freely and collaboratively with the performers to make the script fit them, rather than the other way

around.

2. An EcoTheater company is made up of non-professionals. EcoTheater plays and scenes are performed by local untrained EcoTheater is not to be confused with or merged with community Theater or professional theater. While both EcoTheater and traditional theater have a legitimate place, together they cancel each other's strengths.

3. From the beginning, the company must generally be made up of diverse people. People of different ages, education, races, work backgrounds and different politics. A few outsiders may be helpful, but the company must be predominantly local, and leadership (which should rotate) must always be theirs.

> EcoTheater plays are in scripted form, and are never "finished." Since EcoTheater encourages people to get in touch with forgotten or neglected aspects of their minds or feelings, the plays reveal the various facets constantly evolving of the ultimately mysterious self, in the safety of the stage.

4. The company members are undisputed experts in their own lives and in the ways, history, mores, weaknesses and strengths of the community.

5. Material in the plays comes from local history and stories: personal experience, oral history, gathered by any means, e.g., newspapers, letters, stories.

6. Each member on becoming part of the company must agree that all personal matter revealed in creating the performance is strictly confidential--and out of respect, not even discussed within the company.

7. From one year to another a scene may be revised to fit the new growth of a performer, or the new performer of a scene written for another person. (Scenes or plays may be published at a certain point in their development, but they nevertheless may go on evolving.)

8. Because EcoTheater stems from a primal form of community and personal expression, it. does not impose styles, ideas, formats, or structure on a company; or community. In fact, the task of discovering these things over a period of time belongs to the company. And the

discovery usually happens from within. There is an ever-present tendency to imitate. In particular, television styles unchecked can repress natural development of the company's own "fingerprint," and simply needs reminders and exercises to correct.

9. EcoTheater is a network, and gains strength from learning of the successes, experiments, failures of other members of the network at periodic get-togethers.

10. No one owns the concept of indigenous or grassroots theater. The name *EcoTheater* and the idea is older than written history. The combination of characteristics described are, however, peculiar to EcoTheater. We therefore claim ownership of the name and concept in order to enable it to continue without being assimilated, watered down, or crushed. Any local group which agrees to follow these standards and pattern, and take the playwright-director training, and work under periodic review, can request approval from the EcoTheater Council to become an EcoTheater "seed company." After three years with a playwright-director-in-training, the group may apply to the Board of Directors or the Council to use the name EcoTheater in conjunction with the name of their community. Any group using the EcoTheater name without approval and supervision will be subject to suit.

Notes for an EcoTheater Mission Statement

To access the genius of ordinary people.

To build the methodology that can be a key to fit the lock of that dungeon where so much exceptional personal resource and brilliance is confined for life.

To develop a fresh look at the oldest art form.

To establish a new standard of excellence in performance by non-professionals that is different from professional standards.

To nourish small new audiences through "non-cultural" performances.

To recruit and train non-professionals to be playwright-directors and develop their own seed companies.

To encourage and support a networking relationship between the seed companies for their continuing training and inspiration.

To strengthen communities by becoming a true voice of a community; to express the community's history, dreams, mistakes, hopes and its hidden strengths, through the mouths of its own people.

To provide the stage on which its youth can reveal their dreams and gifts and gain their confidence.

To provide, through writings, a theoretical base, a clearly defined concept and process of creating this new theater.

To offer advice, counsel, and information to fledgling seed companies; to put them in touch with each other for support.

> Theater is reality, not illusion.

To do all that is necessary to provide leadership to the EcoTheater movement, and continue its quiet expansion and its continuing exploration of concepts and practice for the good of humankind around the world, toward opening up all people's innate gifts and intelligence from which follows awareness of connectedness and the lowering of barriers of distrust

Unifying Principles of a New Theater

1. Authority that is indivisible. Authority starts with the author, the playwright-director. This theater restores authority to the playwright to both write and direct.

2. The playwright-director (PD), having full authority, can vest this authority In the performer. But the performer does not keep the authority. It is vested and returned to the PD during the course of preparation. During performance, performers hold the stage with authority, and vest it, during performance, in the audience.

3. Before learning the skills of this new theater, there must be a willingness and commitment to let go other processes of the old theater, for actors and PDs.

4. It is an occasion when people can remove the roles normally played in life, and be themselves in the safety of the stage.

5. Belief that ordinary people have extraordinary reserves: bravery, genius, brilliance, and that it is accessible.

6. Theater is a function of community. Theater *is* community--its story, its voice, its identity, its honesty.

7. Theater is a safe place to remove roles. It is a laboratory as well as an occasion to risk being seen. The laboratory helps break old habits as they are happening and start the process of understanding the exact instant that we grab back the roles and reject the opportunity to be visible, bold and brave.

8. A set of standards and patterns are necessary for developing theaters to protect them in their growth from being annexed by established theaters or being used for other purposes.

9. The purpose of art is not to communicate superior ideas or causes. Art itself is the only communication that can transcend barriers through its emptying itself of parochial, limited, self-interested power. To the degree that it speaks to and from the heart, is it doing what only art does. That which transcends barriers *is* art.

The Role of the Scholar of the Humanities at EcoTheater

In the past few years, we have experimented with our scholars of the Humanities (with their full cooperation) in various formats to find the best way for them to be presented to the audiences--to the point of their actually taking small roles in the plays with interesting and sometimes quite able results. But it was never quite right. And it still isn't. But this summer, we learned some fascinating things that may eventually make a breakthrough possible between scholars and people. As our philosophy comes to be a little clearer, and our audiences have become strikingly more articulate and comfortable in talking from their own feelings and experience, in ways that are illuminating and profound and simple, we encouraged the "Humanists" to be part of the audience and to wait until the dialogue started between audience and actors. "Audience discussion" is almost a misnomer now. As one listens or reads through the transcriptions (which are available) one feels that immediately after we finish, make our bows, come back to sit on stage to talk, that the end of the play is really an intermission. The play, in fact, continues since the audience is talking in a similar or parallel way to what the actors were saying. More than one audience person has commented, for instance, on the roles that they for the first time became aware of in being part of the audience. The constraint felt to them like a straitjacket during the play; they found it hard to express their immediate reactions even though they wanted to--especially when Kathy confesses to them a bad thing she did and needs to be forgiven. The audiences in fact have extended or amplified what I, as chief playwright, had in mind in writing this play on the ubiquity and meaning of roles, and confirmed the possibility that theater could be redefined as the place one is permitted to dispense with role-playing and pretense in the interest of "being our real-selves-for-a-moment." One of our actors responding (almost as an audience might) to the remarkably candid expressions from the audience (who seemed to be the actors) confessed that being in the play was the only time she didn't feel fat and shy. Not so much a confessional remark whose aim is titillation or amusement, but a simple admission that she was continuing as she was in the play, to feel free of her usual awareness that she did not fit into the usual visual standards of ones role in society. This suggested that our mystification over the audience this summer may be because there was a reversal of actors and audience. My actors were informally given the chance to be the understanding audience of the audience-now-become-momentarily-very-real-actors.

The scholars as part of the audience, and yet as apart from the audience were in a strange position: they had expectations to contend with as appointed guest scholars of the evening: their normal roles as scholars/teachers could not be put aside. Had they been actors, or anonymous as others in the audience were, they would have had a different set of conditions altogether.

That is, the scholars had neither the protection that the actors have that enables the actor to lay aside the normal roles and become in fact more themselves, and they did not have the protection of the actual audience which also--given the premise of the play--could continue the play and identify who they were solely by their ideas and feelings that they felt called upon to express--and yet remain nameless. An immensely fascinating thing was going on that we are still trying to decipher. And it happened even when our performance was flawed and we forgot lines momentarily or goof, committing the most grievous sins known to the theater. It didn't seem to matter. Incidentally this did not tempt us to take any less care in trying to be flaw-free. If anything the intrepid actors for whom I have profound gratitude and respect, doubled their efforts to be honest, disciplined and well prepared.

It gives me joy to identify these daring people: Lucinda of course, Kathy Jackson, Sims Wicker, Scott Briers, Joe and Jewell Bigony and Mitch Scott. They all seemed to know what was happening, but quite baffled as to why. It was almost as if they took the risk of being just themselves AND the audience had such deep respect for them, obvious from the questions they asked, that the actors didn't know what to make of it.

Up to this time my own search has concentrated on re-establishing in this country a theater that comes up from its own roots, as over against being modeled after European theater. And while we have proven that a viable theater can be created with people not trained in "theater," the scope this year, has clearly broadened. We have pushed further and further back to explore theater, only to find it is not a separate entity, but in exploring its roots we stumble on what may be that ancient meeting ground in a cleared place in the bush where the concerns of religion, anthropology and theater overlap.

> The audience seemed, in a sense, to see them as if they were a special little priesthood for the moment. A presence.

I am personally grateful beyond words for the dedication and insights of the actors and the perspectives and support of the guest scholars. The scholars have benefitted me enormously through continued contact with them, as well as benefitting my company and our audiences. They have sustained us as we continue to press beyond the accepted boundaries of our misunderstood vocation.

Starting a Seed Company

Try. Start with one person, not a group. Not a buddy. You have to take the risk of crossing through that barrier to a stranger. If the first doesn't work, try a second. (We're all connected.) Pick out someone that you are drawn to, or curious about, about, tell them you're going to write a scene. (Remember, don't ask, you just do it. If they really object, you'll find out quick.) Then you talk, make an appointment, listen, and then write the scene. Then they might want to do it, but you can ask someone else, also a stranger, to perform it. Sometimes it's okay for them to do it themselves--give them another name and sometimes they can do it fine.

Second, *set a date of performance.* Before you're ready? Yes. You prepare that scene for the performance, and then you realize, "Oh, I can't do just one scene. I'd better do one, two, three more." You set a date of performance anywhere you can. At a club, church, or in the middle of a mall. And if it's a mall, you take whatever you need to clear a small space for your stage. Three boards on six cinderblocks will raise the stage a bit. It's hard, but it's part of the training period to find that you can do it anywhere. You adapt the writing to this kind of milieu. If your person washes out on you the day before the performance, you spend a couple of hours learning script and do it yourself. If you have problems take time to work on them. But you need to try it first.

Maryat Lee

Copyright Notes

As Dr. French notes, Maryat credits some of the scenes in *A Double-Threaded Life* to "the people of Hinton, West Virginia." As is true for many scenes presented in performance by EcoTheater, these had their roots in stories rising from the community's memory and experience (or gossip), then polished by Lee or written in toto by Lee after someone told her the story. Whatever the informal attribution, the material was copyright to Maryat herself. I am certain she meant no slight to those who lived the material; but it would be unwieldy and untrue in an artistic sense to say anyone other than Maryat *created* the scenes so I have not made an attempt to sort out the true "authorship" of them. If your work, but not your name, is included here, I apologize; let me know and I will correct this in a future edition.

Unless otherwise noted, all material is copyrighted by the estate of Maryat Lee and used by permission of her estate and her archive at the West Virginia and Regional History Center; the Introduction and other material by William French are copyright his estate, and used by permission of Martha French. A later version of his introduction to *A Double-Threaded Life* appeared in the Summer 1982 edition of *The Drama Review*. Preface copyright David T. Miller. *Four Men and a Monster* is copyright 1969 by Maryat Lee and reprinted courtesy of Samuel French, Inc., A Concord Theatricals Company. The dedication poem "To Maryat" is copyright Mary Dean Lee and used courtesy of The Write Launch. Material in *A Double-Threaded Life* originated in scenes sometimes created by a large, rotating cast and then rewritten by Maryat, so that it's not possible to determine the "author" of a particular scene, other than EcoTheater as an entity and Maryat as the final word on a piece (and pieces were never "final"). Where available, the originators of the scenes have been identified in the excerpts here. The name *EcoTheater* was trademarked in 1991, two years after Maryat Lee's, death, and according to trademark office records was cancelled in 1998 for failure to provide timely filings and a record of its continual use. Other "ecotheaters," some that trace their lineage to Maryat and some not, continue to use the name, however. The official nonprofit EcoTheater corporation Maryat created was dissolved in 1991.

-Editor

Maryat Lee

Bacchante Books
Lexington, Kentucky

www.ingramcontent.com/pod-product-compliance
Lightning Source LLC
Chambersburg PA
CBHW081831170426
43199CB00017B/2696